The Gentle Radical

The Gentle Radical

A BIOGRAPHY OF

Roger Williams

BY

CYCLONE COVEY

And be not conformed to this world. . . .
—*Romans* 12:2

NEW YORK · THE MACMILLAN COMPANY
LONDON · COLLIER-MACMILLAN LIMITED

F
82
.W727

The Macmillan Company, New York
Collier-Macmillan Canada Ltd., Toronto, Ontario

Printed in the United States of America

TO

BONES

Acknowledgments

THIS book is especially indebted to Max Savelle, who inspired it a quarter of a century ago; the astute and magnanimous editors Richard P. Cecil, Jerome S. Ozer, and Cecil Scott; Marvin T. Edmison and the Oklahoma State University Research Foundation; the Fund for the Advancement of Education; George Rogers Taylor and the Carnegie Corporation; University Counsel E. Moses Frye; Dean (now President) Robert B. Kamm and the department heads Max A. Mitchell, Richard E. Bailey, and Harry M. Campbell, who have graciously concurred in arrangements which have enabled this and other productions to proceed.

I am further grateful to E. Porter Dickinson, reference librarian of Amherst College; Carolyn E. Jakeman, director of Houghton Library, together with her assistants Mary K. Daehler and Julie Johnson; Alice Reynolds, in charge of interlibrary loans, Harvard College Library; Clarkson A. Collins, III, librarian of the Rhode Island Historical Society; John B. Stratton, assistant librarian, Oklahoma State University Library; Alton P. Juhlin, head, Special Services Department, Oklahoma State University Library; his emergency co-successors, Mary Helen Jaime and Esta Lee Albright; Esta Wolfram, master proofreader; Dorothy W. Bridgwater, assistant reference librarian, Yale University Library; Clifford K. Shipton, director of the American Antiquarian Society and of the Harvard Archives; Jeannette D. Black, assistant, John Carter Brown Library; Beatrice Godwin, John Dustin, and Katherine Daniel, successively librarian of McKendree College Library; Frances King and Anne Hyder of the Huntington Library staff; and innumerable other librarians and libraries coast to coast, particularly the St. Louis Public Library, the Portland, Oregon, Public, West Newton Public, Massachusetts Historical Society, Reed College, Amherst College, Stanford University, Fresno State College, University of Chicago, University of Michigan, Newberry, Forbes, Widener, Lamont, Essex Institute, Library of Congress, and the University of Oklahoma and Oklahoma State University libraries.

NOTE: Dates are given as the colonists knew them by the old Julian calendar. (Add eleven days to make them correspond to the Gregorian New Style.) Years, however, are dated from January 1 instead of March 25.

Quotations as a rule appear in the earliest form that survives. The fact that our oldest source is often a modernized version in some degree accounts for discrepancies in style other than those that prevailed in colonial times.

CYCLONE COVEY

Contents

New English Voyages, have taught most of our *Old English spirits*, how to put due prices upon the most *common* and ordinary *undervalued mercies*; how precious with some hath been a little *water?* how dainty with others a piece of *bread:* How welcome to some the poorest *howsing?* Yea the very *Land* and *Earth*, after long and tedious passages?

There is one *commoditie* for the sake of which most of *Gods children* in *N. England* have run their mighty *hazards*; a *commoditie* marvellously *scarce* in former times (though in some late years by *Gods* most gracious and mighty hand more *plentifull*) in our *native Countrey:* It is a *Libertie* of searching after Gods most holy *mind* and *pleasure*.

. . . Having bought Truth deare, we must not sell it cheape, not the least graine of it for the whole World, no not for the saving of Soules, though our owne most precious; least of all for the bitter sweetning of a little vanishing pleasure.

For a little puffe of credit and reputation from the changeable breath of uncertaine sons of men.

For the broken bagges of Riches on Eagles wings: For a dreame of these, any or all of these which on our death-bed vanish and leave tormenting stings behinde them: Oh how much better is it from the love of Truth, from the love of the Father of lights, from whence it comes, from the love of the Sonne of God, who is the way and the Truth, to say as he, *John* 18. 37. For this end was I borne, and for this end came I into the World that I might beare witnesse to the Truth.

—ROGER WILLIAMS, Second Preface to *The Bloody Tenent Yet More Bloody* and the Preface to Parliament of *The Blovdy Tenent, of Persecution*

The Gentle Radical

1 : *"And I Was Weary with Forbearing"*

(From Birth to Marriage and Migration)

ROGER WILLIAMS is an appealing and historically significant personality who also presents an ideal touchstone or integrative
thread for relating most of the major developments during the time
of the first and second generations in New England, and not only in
New England. Although the results of his career remain equivocal,
he was the first person to advocate and bring into actual practice
complete freedom of conscience, complete dissociation of church
and state, and genuine political democracy—all three together—on
either side of the Atlantic. Besides much else that attracts us to Williams, there is the unique adventure of his long life, providing a
worthy epic in itself.

He has gained a more general acceptance today than at any previous time as a symbol of a critical turning point in American thought
and institutions, notwithstanding that many of the commonly expressed notions about him continue confused. The confusion ex-
tends equally to the Massachusetts system he dissented from. The
volume in hand undertakes to clear up this double confusion by a
sharper focus on not only Williams himself but the men he inter-
acted with and the power struggle in both England and New
England which took place in a moment of intense change—cultural,
economic, political, social, and ideological. This drastic change
occurred earlier in American history than has been assumed. It is
Williams in relation to the crucial few years of this revolutionary
experience which will primarily concern us. Williams stood sometimes at the center of it, sometimes on the periphery, but throughout as an indestructible present fact to be reckoned with, he and
his role changing and circumstances continually revising others'
view of him.

The son of a London shopkeeper, Williams was the only important Puritan leader in America who did not grow up on a farm or in
a small town. Many American Puritan leaders, to be sure, lived
some of their lives in London but, with very few exceptions, only
after reaching adolescence or manhood. Williams's urban orientation helps explain his rapid, vehement manner of speech (the
"fierceness" of his talking in public, as Cotton Mather said) coupled
with a nonviolent, nonbitter, nonmalcontented nature—implacably
dissenting yet peaceful. The peace of his "calme midnight thoughts"
was not merely a professed objective but a characteristic state of his.
He constantly urged arbitration and restraint and, contrary to common supposition, acted more as a peacemaker than as a troublemaker
in the sum total of his career. If he appeared inflexible, inflammatory, and quixotic, he more usually showed a quality of elasticity and
conciliation, rising above turbulence and composing his differences
with the world and within himself. If he sounded narrowly self-
righteous in many of the opinions he set against the prevailing ones,
his mature Seekerism brought him to a magnanimous suspended
judgment. He turned from the metropolis to pioneering in the wilderness with no perceptible qualms and most of the time went
serenely about his daily work, content with his lot. The most fasci-
nating figure of America's formative seventeenth century was a
gentle radical.

WILLIAMS leaves us in some doubt concerning the year of his birth,
which cannot be verified because too many records have perished.
He told Governor John Winthrop in an undated letter which can
be placed from internal evidence between midsummer and midfall
1632 that he was "neerer vpwards of 30 then 25"; he stated on February 7, 1678, that he was "about seventie five years" and on July
21, 1679, that he was "neere to Fower Score Years of age"; but in a
deposition of November 15, 1662, he testified that he was "aged
about 56 yeares." The outright contradictions would be resolved if
we assumed he meant fifty-nine when he said fifty-six in 1662. If
fifty-six happened to be right, he was born in 1606; but his other
three statements make it more likely he was born late in 1603, which
in Old Style dating included up to March 25, which would be April
5, 1604, New Style.

Williams's mother, Alice Pemberton, who did not marry until she
was about twenty-three—quite late for those times—would have

been about forty when Roger was born, and she had another son after him. She came of a well-connected lesser-gentry family. Her three sons showed more than usual enterprise and thereby social ascension: Roger, in becoming a clergyman and colonist; his younger brother, Robert, who migrated after reverses as a merchant tailor (which had led him to defraud Roger of his inheritance) to become a schoolmaster in Newport; and an entrepreneur older brother, Sydrach, whom Roger identifies as "a Turkey merchant." There was also an older sister, Katherine. Alice named Roger after her brother, Roger Pemberton, a country squire who in 1618 became a county sheriff.

Young Roger's father, James Williams, was a merchant tailor (i.e. textile retailer). Although he managed to spare his children grinding poverty, the family circumstances seem to have been mainly hard. He sent Roger to a nearby free grammar school (meaning Latin grammar) and possibly also tutored him at home. He grounded all his sons in the trade of merchandising cloth, which Roger pursued in America as naturally as preaching. The name "Williams" is Welsh, although that tells us little more than the probability that Roger inherited a Celtic strain in some degree, which could have had a bearing on his ardent and eloquent predilection.

Roger was born probably while his family still lived on Long Lane, which led to the vast open area on London's northwest side known as Smithfield. Along with the cresting population the Williamses later moved out to Cow Lane, near the sheep-pen section on the western edge of Smithfield. The Separatist Bartholomew Legate went up in flames March 18, 1611, at Smithfield, practically in the Williamses' front yard, when Roger would have been around seven years old. Williams later espoused some of the heretical tenets held by this martyr and by the draper Edward Wightman, who burned for his religious beliefs at Lichfield in April 1612. Williams told Winthrop in a letter of 1632 that he had been "persecuted even in and out of my father's house these 20 years," which apparently means that he had taken to Dissent from the age of eight or so and suffered for his choice both at home and after leaving home for work and school. He did not divulge who "persecuted" him at home, one or both parents or the older children or all the family.

The Cow Lane home stood just a few hundred yards from St. Paul's churchyard, where Williams witnessed public celebrations as a boy, as at Smithfield, where St. Bartholomew's Fair still flourished during his childhood. The neighborhood was one of respectable tradesmen whose lives largely centered in their guilds and the parish church, St. Sepulchre's. James's closest friends, according to his will, were a coachmaker, a clothworker, a currier, and an innholder. Other neighbors and family friends included a scrivener, John May, Roger's most probable teacher of shorthand. The Williams home lay just across Smithfield from an ancient Carthusian monastery which a philanthropist, Thomas Sutton, had recently converted to a preparatory school for indigent boys and which had come to be known as Sutton's Hospital or Charterhouse School. How Roger became enrolled in that school involves a famous member of its board of governors and Roger's demonstration of shorthand skill in the court of equity known as Star Chamber (from the gold stars painted on the courtroom ceiling).

A daughter of Sir Edward Coke, Anne Sadleir, said decades later that Williams would "present" his work to her father, who, "seeing so hopeful a youth, took such a liking to him" that he sent him to Charterhouse. She added: "Full little did he [her father] think that he [Williams] would have proved such a rebel to God, the king, and his country." The likeliest reason Williams would "present" his work to Coke is that Coke had hired him as a "diarist" to take down a private record of the court proceedings. The custom of official court reporting had not yet come into being, and Coke had made himself the greatest legal authority of the seventeenth century by having, since 1572, his first year as a student in the Inner Temple, assumed the task of reporting as many cases as possible, along with commentary on the law and courts they illustrated. Therefore, Williams's work in the Star Chamber, if done for Coke, would not necessarily have involved cases in which Coke participated, either as prosecutor, plaintiff, defendant, or judge.

Being a court of equity, Star Chamber was inquisitorial in procedure, although a far cry from the instrument of bigotry it became under Charles I. It had no jurisdiction in capital cases; it in fact usually amounted to a supreme justice-of-the-peace court, with an array of privy councilors as judges. It sat on Wednesdays and Fridays during its terms, in a long building of the Westminster palace complex at the edge of the Thames back of Westminster Abbey, always playing to a full house of spectators.

Coke's sensational career as attorney general, which frequently took him to Star Chamber, ended when Williams was only about ten; but it is conceivable that Williams had been taking shorthand in that court as early as November 2, 1617, at the sealing and delivery of the deed which settled the marriage portion of Coke's beautiful daughter Frances, whose hand Coke gave to Sir John Villiers, brother of the king's favorite, the Duke of Buckingham. One of the witnesses, evidently signing in behalf of Coke, surprisingly was John Endecott, future governor of Massachusetts Bay, whose activity in London remains a major mystery of the movement which brought the Bay into being. Endecott and Williams give the appearance in the early 1630's in Salem of having been friends before in England, although it is sheer speculation to say they came together on this day in 1617, as it is that Coke met Williams on this occasion, perhaps through Endecott. Coke's haughty second wife, Lady Hatton, brought suit against Coke in Star Chamber about 1620, and Coke retaliated with a suit of his own there. But it is most probable that the call for Williams's services came with the convening of the historic Parliament of 1621, which opened January 30 and sat four months. It could be that some other dignitary, like Sir William Martin, had engaged Williams in January, either for a case in which he was concerned in Star Chamber or for his personal information as a member of Parliament. We do not know how Coke's follower and Winthrop's acquaintance, Sir William, came to befriend Williams; but a letter of Martin's to Winthrop some fourteen years later proves a long-standing closeness. Williams plausibly started his private court reporting during a suit the tailors' guild brought in Star Chamber. Puritan connections, both at home and across the Channel, crisscrossed the merchant tailors' guild, in any case. When Coke took up residence at his wife's palace, Hatton House, the Williams family lived hardly half a dozen odd-shaped blocks from him, although this cannot quite account for their acquaintance, which, however, did come to pass—possibly through Uncle Roger Pemberton.

In time, in any event, Coke was pleased, says Williams, to call him his son. Williams adored the old man, as his mid-century correspondence to Dame Sadleir verifies. Williams says that it was Coke who inspired him to industriousness and patience. Coke must also have set the boy a permanent example of bluntness, forthrightness, eloquence, and indomitability.

On February 1, 1621, the incorruptible Coke turned sixty-nine. His distinguishing mustache and goatee, now nearly white; his big, spare frame, skull-capped high dome, and ringingly resonant voice had become familiar to many thousands of spectators at the various courts where he sat (and stood) in one capacity or another. He had gained universal recognition as the leading theorist and organizer in England against unlimited authority. Back in 1593 he had bested the cunning little courtier (and complex genius) Francis Bacon for the attorney generalship and had gone on to prosecute successfully such defendants as the Earl of Essex (Bacon's patron, on whom Bacon was humiliatingly obliged to turn at the trial), Sir Walter Raleigh, and the Gunpowder Plotters. In the summer of 1614 he had risen to the King's Council (which Buckingham dominated). But about this time Bacon contrived his own elevation to the attorney generalship, and Coke was booted upstairs from chief justice of the Court of Common Pleas to chief justice of the King's Bench. Bacon shortly managed to make the Privy Council himself, and to bring about Coke's dismissal from it in November 1616 because of Coke's effective interposition of the common law to check the church hierarchy and the king's divine-right prerogative. Bacon's fall, after an incredibly high rise—to Lord Chancellor—ironically began when he sided with Coke's wife, Lady Hatton (for whose hand Bacon had again been an unsuccessful rival of Coke's), in the lawsuit for guardianship of Coke's daughter, Frances. The king, James I, found justice on Coke's side and restored him to the Council the Sunday after Michaelmas in 1617.

In the Parliament of 1621 Coke played a stellar part as chairman of the Committee for Grievances and became the driving force behind the impeachment of Lord Chancellor Bacon. Williams must have milled in the crowd day after day in the corridors of Westminster virtually adjoining the Star Chamber. If he did not see Bacon early in this session going to or coming from the House of Lords, Williams would certainly have observed him on other occasions. We know from a later allusion that he read Bacon's essay on unity of religion; he probably read the rest of Bacon's popular *Essays* as well, also *The Advancement of Learning*, published in 1605 and widely owned among Dissenters, including William Brewster. Bacon, broken and contrite, heard his sentence on May 3, 1621. James adjourned Parliament on June 7. It reconvened November 20, and James readjourned it December 18, although that very evening it completed a *Protestation* of Parliament's right to its privileges by ancient British birthright rather than by the king's grace. James put Coke in the Tower for his leading role in contesting royal divinity and kept him there for seven months. Coke nevertheless won election to the Parliament of 1628 and, at the age of seventy-seven, rose to his highest stature as a public servant in driving the milestone Petition of Right into law. He was not a Puritan, although he had the implacable, fearless manner of many Puritans of his time, and his natural allies and disciples tended to be Puritans, like the great Sir John Eliot, the great nemesis of Charles I, John Pym, and young Williams's friend, Sir William Martin. Coke established, in theory and practice, a constitutional position which came to be identified as Puritan and largely over which the civil war between the king and the Puritan-dominated Parliament eventually erupted.

Williams was the second boy Coke placed in Charterhouse School; he matriculated in 1621, presumably in the fall. Whether late spring or fall, it happened to be soon after his father's death. Roger excelled, which made it possible for him to proceed to Cambridge, formally matriculating at Pembroke Hall on June 7, 1624, when he was about twenty, some six years older than most of his classmates. He attended as a pensioner, i.e. a student who paid his way; he did not enjoy the privileges of the aristocratic fellow-commoners, who had to pay double, but neither did he have to work his way through as a sizar. His "exhibition" from Charterhouse carried with it a £16 stipend (the "pension") that met the bare minimum of expenses. Coke may have helped out beyond this; interested Puritan gentlemen like Martin may have also; and Williams must have received a small inheritance from his father.

Pembroke Hall presented an intimate group of 140 students and faculty in the throes of being forced to reverse their Puritan bent. The college had a reputation for high standards, which it seems to have maintained, in the face of tightening strictures, at least until a few years later. In January 1627 Williams signed the oath required for graduation, acknowledging the king's supremacy in spiritual affairs and accepting the Prayer Book and the Thirty-Nine Articles of the Anglican faith. The following October he returned for graduate study, intent on becoming a clergyman. He said in 1671 that it had been in his childhood that the Father of Mercies had touched his soul with a love of Him, the Son, and the holy Scriptures. His decision to enter the ministry probably came as early as the opportunity to enter Charterhouse. He evidently fulfilled all the requirements for his master's degree except further formal submission to episcopacy, which, in the course of his two years of graduate study, he found he could not abide. The year before Williams quit, Archbishop Laud began his reign of suppression for conformity and Charles I decreed "that all further curious search [into church doctrine] be laid aside."

It was another member of Parliament, Sir William Masham, one whom the king had jailed in 1626 for opposition to the forced loan (an extra tax decreed by the king upon every subject to finance the unpopular war with France), who engaged Williams as a household chaplain, sometime before February 20, 1629. On March 2 Charles dissolved Parliament as it defiantly rammed through a Puritan resolution against Arminianism, which the king with Laud's advice had made the test of loyalty to Church and Crown. This dissolution—which Williams likely witnessed—removed the last legal or effective sounding board of Puritanism until the Short Parliament eleven years later, especially since Laud and his pursuivants ferreted out and silenced the Puritan preachers one by one and stifled the freedom of inquiry in the universities that had largely catalyzed Puritanism in the first place.

At about the age twenty-five, then, Williams had completed all the formal education he would have, had definitely committed himself to the Puritan cause, going even as far as abjuring the perfunctory rite that would bring the M.A., ordination, church preferment, and permanent security, and had planted himself in the thick of high-level strategy planning in the Puritan underground.

This underground had developed on a large scale in Thomas Cartwright's time in the form of secret meetings or presbyteries, called conferences, and continued to operate in other forms in the early seventeenth century. In 1626 it revitalized a 1618 organization of clergymen, lawyers, and merchants known as feoffees, who purchased establishments which went under the legal name of lay impropriations, and hired Puritan preachers to preside over them. Outwardly they were private adjuncts of the Church of England, but in reality they were centers of Puritan subversion—as Laud quickly perceived; in 1633 he had the attorney general suppress the feoffees. It proved harder, however, to suppress family household gatherings, which often turned into Puritan conventicles. The first Earl of Warwick essentially supported such a conventicle when he engaged the great Cartwright as chaplain of his hospital. The Pilgrims at Scrooby essentially coalesced in such a conventicle in the manor household of the bailiff, Elder Brewster. Winthrop gives glimpses in his diary of an annual conventicle he attended beginning in 1613. The New England Company, the Massachusetts Bay Company, and the Providence [Island] Company served as effective directive organizations for the Puritan cause once they materialized; their business meetings tended to be indistinguishable from conventicles or even, on occasion, from the earlier Presbyterian conferences.

It is not divulged exactly how Williams came to be engaged by Masham or came to know men like Hooker and Cotton, but not much imagination is needed to infer that mutual Puritan fervor drew those of that persuasion into family-like parties through the long-established underground network. Masham's manor stood about ten miles outside London at Otes, Essex, and Otes lay only ten or twelve miles from Chelmsford, where Thomas Hooker enjoyed great fame, not having yet been obliged to flee to Holland. Williams took frequent trips back to London and probably back to Cambridge while he held his chaplaincy in the Masham manor, but the manor patently served as an underground rendezvous too.

Puritanism had not at this time quite crystallized into the clear-cut division between Presbyterian and Congregationalist, although the pioneers of nearly every shade of Puritanism had some time earlier raised their respective banners. The Pilgrims, for that matter, had been eight and a half years in America by late spring 1629. But a distinct party of nonseparating Congregationalists had not got beyond an emergent stage at that date. This is the party which most of the men of affairs Williams associated with at the Mashams' found themselves gravitating toward. Another group of nascent nonseparating Congregationalists cohered as followers of the Oxford alumnus Henry Jacob in London; by mid-century they had been given the name Semi-Separatists. William Ames, the influential theologian from Christ's College, Cambridge, systematized the nonseparating-Congregationalist point of view, and he, rather than Jacob, became the acknowledged mentor of the mainline group which included the Masham circle. Williams never quite became one of either nonseparating group in theology, though he became one of both socially. If he and his friends had reached the degree of clarification of their views in 1629 that they arrived at five years later, Williams would have been unable to move in their company.

He shared the gentry Puritans' disposition to salvage a passing medieval order (in this sense they were counterrevolutionaries against modern times) and their simultaneous determination to resist the obsolete medievalism of the ruling aristocracy (whereby they were leading the revolution to modernity), and he shared their ideal of Stoic discipline, good manners, and sound scholarship. Yet, no matter how long it took him to realize it fully, his pinched years in the narrow, winding, stinking, congested streets of pre-fire London had caught him up in the subterranean revolt of the lower classes against social suppression, which he saw represented in orthodoxy and in every form of pretense. This past-junking futuristic movement plunged toward sectarianism, which flatly rejected the state church. Respectable gentry Puritanism, which jealously professed to remain within the established church, converged at crucial points with this outcast sectarian variety but also hopelessly diverged. Williams showed the conflict of the two in himself as when he, later in Rhode Island excoriated the Bay magistrates and ministers and at the same time anybody who dared demean those same magistrates and ministers. Whenever it was that he consciously recognized his intransigent Separatism, it became an allegiance he hotly held against all real and imaginary foes ever after.

He appears to have been in the process of turning Separatist when, as Puritan preachers usually did, he fell violently in love. The girl was Jane Whalley, heiress-to-be of a baronet, sister of a regicide-to-be, and niece of Lady Joan Barrington, with whom she lived not far from the Masham estate. The imperious aunt, Lady Barrington, mother of Masham's wife Elizabeth, had warned Williams about seeking marriage above his class. Despite her warning, and despite clear signs of a bad temper and spiritual waywardness in Jane, he made persistent suit for her hand in the spring of 1629. He admitted to Lady Barrington in an April letter that he was poor, with but some seven score pieces undisposed and "a little (yet Costly) studie of bookes. Thus possessing all things haue I nothing, yet more then God owes me, or then my blessed Saviour had himselfe." He could expect very little from his aged mother, then an enterprising landlady who, he said, would not tell him just what he could expect. He also admitted he did not see how his scruples would allow him to accept a pulpit in England, although he said he had lately received a call from New England and that he had received other offers of church livings. He added that he had learned one lesson: "to still my soule as A weaned childe & giue offence to none."

Perhaps he had learned such a lesson, but not very thoroughly. A few days later, when Lady Barrington had closed her door to him, he wrote her a letter dated May 2: "We hope to live together in the heavens though the Lord have denied that union on Earth." Then he switched to the subject of Lady Barrington herself, and his blistering tirade is our earliest disclosure of his highly charged personality:

What I shall now expresse to your Ladiship hath long lyen like fire in my bones Jer. 20:9. . . . & I was weary with forbearing & could not stay.

Good Madame, it is not for nothing, the God of heaven hath sent such thunderclaps of late and made such great offers at the dore of your Ladiships heart. . . . If euer (deare Madam) when there is but the breadth of a few gray haires betweene you & your everlasting home let me deale vprightly with you.

I know not one professor [of Christianity] amongst all I know whose truth & faythfullnes to Jesus Christ is more suspected, doubted, feared, by all or most of those that know the Lord. . . .

If euer (good Madame) cry hard, & the Lord helpe me to cry for you. . . . I beseech you lay to heart these few Considerations.

1. First Job 34:[1]9. He with whome we deale excepteth not the persons of princes nor regardeth the rich more then the poore: for they are all the Worcke of his hands. . . .

3. The Lord will doe what he will with his owne. He owes you no mercy. Exod. 33:19. I will be gracious to whome I will be gracious, & will shew mercy to whome I will shew mercy. . . .

6. Remember I beseech you your Candle is twinckling & glasse neere run the Lord only knowes how few minutes are left behind.

Williams thereupon fell severely sick. At the height of his fever, when the Mashams thought him bound for another world (as Masham wrote Lady Barrington), Williams wished his services to her Ladyship remembered to her. Masham offered this communication as proof that Williams had only her soul at heart in the recent shocking letter. It took the old dowager ten months to relent and forgive her young Jeremiah. She found her niece a rising rector who had been to Massachusetts and who eventually became chaplain to Cromwell. After the wedding, Jane fell sick, but she wrote her aunt in gratitude for the alternate selection.

In late July 1629, not long after his recovery, Williams and Hooker took horses north together to Boston, Lincolnshire, picked John Cotton up there, and proceeded to the Earl of Lincoln's estate near the village of Sempringham. Winthrop emerged as the pivotal figure in the *coup d'état* decided on at that epochal conclave, which we shall look at closer a little later.

Williams's patron Masham had been a client of Winthrop's from the spring of 1628 to February 13, 1629, when Winthrop won Masham's case concerning the withheld inheritance of Masham's foster-daughter, in the Court of Wards and Liveries. Masham may also have engaged Winthrop earlier on behalf of Sir Francis Barrington, Lady Masham's father, another member of Parliament jailed in 1626; Barrington died in 1628. Winthrop instructed his son John Jr. on one known occasion to visit Sir Francis in prison. Winthrop represented Cotton on a probate matter in the Court of Wards in January 1629. Two of the most important Puritan sponsors, Sir Nathaniel Rich and his sea-dog cousin Robert Rich, second Earl of Warwick, knew Winthrop well and had become close associates of Masham and personal friends of Williams. Masham's mother-in-law, the widow of Barrington who closed her door to Williams, lived near Otes at Hatfield Priory. She was an aunt of John Hampden, who had visited New Plymouth in 1622 and who at the outbreak of the civil war in 1642 acted as one of the five leading members of the Puritan Long Parliament. Lady Barrington was also an aunt of Oliver Cromwell.

We do not know whether Williams knew either Hampden or Cromwell personally from their visits to Otes while Williams served there; but Hampden could have whetted his interest in Plymouth, where Williams not too coincidentally became a resident in less than two years; and Williams's almost casual relations with the inner circle of the Cromwell regime during his second mission to England from Providence suggest possible cordiality in this early era, when innumerable interconnections did implicate him in the intrigue to transfer the Puritan virus full strength to New England. Before Williams ever reached New England, he knew the principal ministers and magistrates of the Bay colony in a familiar way—probably including Endecott, Francis Higginson, and the Earl of Lincoln's long-time chaplain Samuel Skelton, who were already in Salem by the time of the Sempringham conference of July 1629—and he knew many of the powerful Puritans who remained behind and became yet more powerful in the English scene. Even this extraordinary advantage Williams proved willing to dissipate as readily as his certain hopes of success in the English Church, all because he could not quite agree. "I desire not to sleepe in Securitie & dreame of a

Nest which no hand can reach," he wrote Winthrop from Providence in 1636 or 1637.

What Williams argued about with Cotton and Hooker as they jogged to Sempringham and back to Boston in July 1629 evidently did not yet involve Separatism but the comparatively staid question of prescribed prayers. Williams recalled in 1652 presenting arguments from Scripture on this occasion "why he durst not joyn with them in their use of *Common prayer.*" All the answer Williams could remember Cotton giving was: "He selected the good and best prayers in his use of that *Book,* as the *Author* of the *Councel* of *Trent* was used to do, in his using of the *Masse-book.*" That Cotton, who for nearly a quarter of a century had held forth as a Presbyterian vicar who "could not digest the ceremonies," should have failed to relinquish that Puritan bugaboo the Prayer Book as late as July 1629 attests his slowness to change or even to realize the full implications of the Puritan position he had long committed himself to. In another couple of years, when he and Hooker had wholly accepted Williams's old-orthodox-Puritan position on the Prayer Book, Williams had gone on to radicalisms they were constitutionally unable to catch up with.

That same summer of 1629, Williams cultivated a romance with Mary Barnard, the maid or companion to Joan ("Jug") Altham, daughter of Lady Masham by her first husband.

It had been on Miss Altham's behalf that Masham engaged the services of Winthrop; for until she came of age, the Crown greedily tied up her inheritance from her father, Sir James Altham, in the name of her uncle, Sir Edward Altham. The complex suit for reversion, which involved a subsuit of attachment, was harrowing, protracted, and undoubtedly extortionary, but Winthrop brought it to as satisfactory and early a settlement as possible. The fact that he won when the defendant failed to appear to contest indicates that the latter had been satisfied, along with the corrupt judges and the chancellor of the exchequer, beforehand.

As for Mary, Williams's indulgent references to her slowness of writing—she could not in fact write her own name—betray her lack of education, but without question she had to be patient and long-suffering to put up with the life her husband led her for the next four and a half decades. She was meek and modest, according to Cotton, and every indication is that it was a happy match. Williams once addressed her from his bayside trading post in the Narragansett country: "My *Dearest Love* and *Companion* in this *Vale of*

Tears." One might be tempted to read into his marrying her and into his Separatist revolt a kind of dedicated reaction against not merely Lady Barrington and Joan Altham but the whole disgusting system of social privilege which had worked to exclude him in part and to wreck his health. Be that as it may, the wedding of Master Williams and Goodwoman Barnard took place in the parish church at High Laver, near Otes, in December 1629.

For the next eleven months or so their life is a complete blank to us. Did Williams not concur in the decisions of the Sempringham conference? Had his Separatism solidified to the point of keeping him and his bride from sailing with Winthrop on the *Arbella* in the spring of 1630? The attitude of Winthrop and others in 1631 intimates no such thing. Neither Cotton nor Hooker, after all, chose to sail in 1630. Williams may have felt with them that his first duty lay on the Puritan frontier at home as long as it was tenable.

Not quite one year after the wedding, in any case, Roger and Mary Williams rode horseback into the chill wind, probably in company with other emigrants and escorting friends, along the Thames toward the port of Bristol ("Bristow," Williams calls it). At Windsor they passed within a few miles south of the thousand-acre, forested estate of Justice Coke at Stoke Poges, and it was "bitter as death," says Williams, to have to go on without telling him of his conscience and flight. At Reading they struck down the Avon, crossed Berkshire (probably stopping over at Newbury), then crossed Wiltshire to Bath and the hills of Somerset, and came at last to the great river port.

Here, for the first time, so far as is known, Williams met John Winthrop, Jr., who would have been Williams's age or a couple of years younger. Together they drank a cup of western metheglin (a drink distilled from fermented honey), as Williams recalled in a letter to him thirty years later. Young Winthrop was an engaging lawyer-physician-entrepreneur, stout, gentle, cheerful, with heavy-lidded, weary eyes, ample nose, trim mustache, page-boy haircut, and a white, square Puritan neckpiece. He had come to Bristol to expedite the formidable job of gathering two hundred tons of supplies to be loaded, which was taking too long.

On December 1, 1630, the newlyweds sailed for Boston on that fateful stormy voyage of the *Lyon* which raised the siege of starvation in Massachusetts.

2 : *How The Bay Had Begun*

WHEN Williams was in his third year at Charterhouse School, Roger Conant, of Sir Walter Raleigh's home town, Budleigh, Devonshire, reached Plymouth in New England at the age of thirty-one with his wife Sarah and their servant Caleb. This was April 1623, the third year of Plymouth's existence. They did not find the village congenial and in 1624 moved on to Nantasket (later Hull) at the tip of the peninsula pointing to the site of Boston. Conant's preacher-historian friend William Hubbard, who knew him in old age and thought him "a religious, sober, and prudent gentleman," says he moved from dislike of the Pilgrims' principles of rigid separation. At Nantasket Conant joined the unctuous preacher John Lyford and the surly trader John Oldham, who had been banished from Plymouth as proved defamers and subversives. It is clear from Hubbard that Conant disliked the hot-tempered and, to him, un-Christian little Captain Myles Standish (whom Oldham once drew a knife on). Circumstantial evidence strongly implicates the quieter Conant in the anti-Pilgrim sentiments, if not the conspiracies, of his associates. All three appear to have thought of themselves as crusaders for Presbyterianism against the Pilgrim subversives of the Church of England. A likely previous connection with Thomas Weston, ironmonger entrepreneur, whom William Bradford regarded as the first betrayer of the Pilgrims, would further have divided Conant and Governor Bradford. Conant had probably crossed the ocean in one of Weston's fishing yachts. (In 1644 one of his four sons, Roger Jr., married Weston's daughter Elizabeth.) Conant failed to receive a land grant at Plymouth, whether because of his private plans—he was a "particular" on his own apart from the Pilgrim joint-stock enterprise—or because of Bradford's antipathy. He was by trade a salter. His brother, Christopher Conant, who had been a grocer in London, joined him in July 1623 and was allotted a plot of land by Bradford, though he too chose not to stay.

At Nantasket, where a few people had already settled, Roger Conant built a house, planted a vineyard and, on Conant's—later Governor's—Island, an apple orchard, and presumably prepared for the birth of his first son. He named the son Lot, perhaps thinking of the departure from Plymouth as a parallel of Lot's fleeing Sodom. In 1625 he pushed north with his family to the commanding promontory, Cape Ann, to which other such families had been gravitating, several of them being persons who remained in the area from the abandoned Gorges colony at Wessaguscasit (later Weymouth). (Prince Charles, who succeeded to the throne that very year, had renamed the Tragabizanda promontory on Captain John Smith's map in honor of his mother, Ann of Denmark.) At Cape Ann the Lyford-Oldham men pre-empted the fishing stage the Pilgrims had built there. When Captain Standish hotly demanded the trespassers vacate, they refused; but Conant interceded and arranged a peaceful negotiation if not a just solution. The Pilgrims, after building a second stage, found themselves obliged to write off Cape Ann for other reasons anyway. Meanwhile, a group of prominent citizens in Dorchester, England, under the guiding spirit of the compelling Presbyterian rector-promoter John White, had undertaken to plant a fishing-and-fur-trading colony and Indian mission at Cape Ann; which made it appear a place of opportunity for a pious fish-salter and fur-trade prospector like Conant.

Men who knew White described him as grave, subtle, and moderate. He sat in the Westminster Assembly long later as a notable moderate, but he controlled his diocese dictatorially. He was known as the Patriarch of Dorchester. He and the company he largely instigated—commonly called the Dorchester Merchants—started with the primary purpose of making bigger profits from the fishing business by establishing a year-round station on the mainland where employees, instead of losing most of their time in transit, could be constantly useful, fishing during the season and fur-trading and farming the rest of the year. The promoters learned to their sorrow, however, that fishermen would not farm and farmers could not fish, and they learned all over again the costly lessons that the Virginia Company had gone bankrupt learning: that just any able-bodied man would not do; that the profit motive was not, of itself, sufficient to sustain such a venture; that the government in the colony had to be stringent; and that the hazards and costs of planting a colony dwarfed anything at that time grasped by English capitalists.

In 1623–25 the company planted forty-six men and a small boat-load of cattle on Cape Ann, but the men had such bad luck fishing and disposing of the one haul they did take that the Merchants finally parted with their three ships at a 60 per cent loss. Most of the men at Cape Ann returned to Dorchester when sent for. After providing transportation home and paying up all wages, the bankrupt company went virtually out of existence.

"But," recounts White of the Cape settlers, "a few of the most honest and industrious resolved to stay behind" and to take care of the cattle that had been sent. The total population numbered perhaps thirty, counting noncompany squatters like the Conants. Another brother of Conant's—John—happened to be the rector at Lymington and a close associate of White; also, he was a member of the collapsed company. White was an alumnus of New College, Exeter; the Conant brothers had an uncle who was at this time rector of Exeter College, Oxford. A timely letter from Roger to John brought the Dorchester Merchants back to life, as White and the treasurer (i.e. director) John Humfrey seized on Roger Conant as governor over the remnant in the colony.

Conant felt cramped at Cape Ann, which, chosen for fishing convenience, offered little promise even of that. The boats had to go too far to find the fish plentiful, and, back of the harbor, good ground proved too scant for farming. Conant indicated his wish to transfer to a more commodious and convenient place, which he planned, says Hubbard, as a receptacle for those who would be coming on account of religion. Such a purpose struck fire with White, who had long cherished a similar notion. So in this trying time when the question had come to be not how to make profits but how to survive, the primary motivation for the colony shifted from commerce to religion.

Empowered from Dorchester to govern, Conant led the Cape Ann people about ten miles southwest by water in the fall of 1626, relocating them, after many trips fetching cattle and goods, at the plague-depleted Indian site called Naumkeag (literally "eel place"). There, backed against the North River, on the neck later known as Beverly, they put up little thatched cottages like the Pilgrims'. These fronted a marsh, and the settlers had to smoke the mosquitoes out of their houses at night. (Bradford said, "They are too delicate, and vnfitte to begine new-plantations, and collonies that cannot enduer the biting of a muskeeto.")

White and some of his fellow-adventurers decided to send over another twelve kine and bulls to the hangers-on and "conferring casually with some gentlemen of London," he says, "moved them to add unto them as many more." When these gentlmen caught the fever, the whole business, as White puts it, "came to agitation afresh in London," with the result that White wrote Conant not to desert, promising more men, provisions, trading goods, and a patent. But Conant had a hard time counteracting the bleakness of wilderness, winter, and an uncertain future. Most of the men had a mind to follow the disgraced preacher Lyford to Virginia; others wanted to go back home with the annual fishing fleet. Conant, however, says Hubbard, resolved "to wait the providence of God in that place . . . yea, though all the rest should forsake him"; "and when," Conant himself related in May 1671, the infant colony "was in great hasard of being deserted . . . I was a means, through grace assisting me, to stop the flight of those few that then were here with me."

Several Puritans in England offered to invest in the reviving scheme if (says White) "fit men might be procured to go over." After some inquiry, the hope-fanners lit at last on John Endecott, whom White identifies vaguely as "a man well known to divers persons of good note." Endecott answered the Londoners' religious requirements, and his military bearing must also have convinced them of his fitness for command. Joshua Scottow, writing an apparently reliable history of the first thirty years of Massachusetts Bay late in the seventeenth century, said that Endecott was the younger brother of a house of honorable extract whose ambition exceeded what he could expect under the system of primogeniture at home. His rank of captain suggests he saw service in the Netherlands, as does his fluency in French (confirmed by a Jesuit emissary Endecott entertained on an occasion of state in January 1651). The Captain had an illegitimate son and, possibly related to that fact, wore a skull-on-a-pike signet ring. "This Death's Head tells that loving hand that sealed it," Williams refers in August 1651 to a letter from Endecott, "and [tells] mine that opens your letter, that our eyes, our hands, our tongues, our brains are flying hence to the hole or pit of rottenness: Why should not therefore such our letters, such our speeches, such our actings be, as may become our last minutes, our death-beds [?]" To the colonial leader and historian Edward Johnson, who knew Endecott over many years, the Captain was undauntable and austere but also sociable and cheerful. He could, in fact, show courtesy on occasion, but typically showed highhandedness and tactlessness. Once, in March or April 1631, while presiding as judge over Salem Court, he struck a defendant at the bar. A portrait of him in his magisterial robes late in his career reveals a heavy man, with a high brow, wide face, long nose, baggy eyes, and a trim mustache and goatee. He does not look austere but rather cheerfully infallible. A pious elder, Samuel Clap, thought "he had a graue and godly face." The "cott" ending of the Captain's name, and the fact that he sailed to Naumkeag with a Dorset crew, imply West Country origins. He was, further, a brother-in-law of Roger Ludlow, the leading magistrate aboard the *Mary and John*, which carried West Country emigrants at the time of the *Arbella* voyage. He was also a cousin by marriage of a major London merchant of the Skinners Company, Mathew Cradock.

The likeliest liaison between White's West Country group and Cradock's London-Lincolnshire group would have been the titular head of the old Dorchester Merchants, Humfrey, who maintained a house in the important little transit port of Sandwich, Kent, as well as in London, and of course knew the Earl of Lincoln's retired bailiff, William Dudley, having married the Earl's daughter Susan— which happily made him, also, a brother-in-law of Sir Isaac Johnson. Young Johnson, who was gladly sinking his fortune in the cause of Congregational Puritanism, may have been the galvanizing spirit behind the new Massachusetts company, while from about 1627 Dudley was devoting his retirement to the enterprise. Although White gives the impression that some of the West Country men communicated to men in London their renewed plans for a colony with now a distinct religious objective, Dudley puts the initiative rather in Lincolnshire about 1627. Wherever the idea originated, a coalition of six members of the original Dorchester Merchants together with eighty-odd Londoners and others of eastern England formed the New England Company, its patent from the Council for New England dated March 19, 1628, and drawn "with large encouragements," White says. The titular head, called governor in the new patent, was Cradock.

The forty-year-old Captain Endecott and his wife Anna sailed from Weymouth, England, on the *Abigail* in June 1628 with at least

two other families and perhaps twenty-five men. After anchoring at
the mouth of North River in Naumkeag, they located on the river
beyond the Old Planters farther upstream. A few rods from the
water, on the highest site, Endecott had what the minister Francis
Higginson calls a "fayre House" re-erected for himself. It had been
built at Cape Ann for the Dorchester Company in 1624. Endecott
ordered it pulled down and transferred, mainly by the Old Planters.
His military severity, as he himself wrote in 1628, caused Conant's
men to fear he meant to enslave them. Thomas Morton, the ab-
sconded Anglican lawyer of Merrymount notoriety (he ring-led
dangerously antisocial behavior in the vicinity of his settlement,
Merrymount, below the site of Boston, for some years before the
Winthrop migration), bitterly called Endecott *the Cowkeeper of
Salem* and *Captain Littleworth;* "this man, thinking none so worthy
as himselfe, tooke upon him infinitely." Soon the Old Planters broke
into controversy with Endecott, but once again Conant's "prudent
moderation" came to the rescue and "quietly composed" the altercation, according to Hubbard on Conant's authority.

In June and July of 1629 the so-called Higginson fleet of six ships
and about three hundred passengers arrived, of whom a third
proceeded to Charlestown. (Charlestown the year before had been
laid out semicircularly south and southeast of Town Hill—forming
the later-called Bow Street—by the New England Company engineer, Thomas Graves.) The *Abigail's* passengers had found "sundry
houses" at Naumkeag and the few Indians entirely friendly. The
Higginsons, who got put up at the "fayre House" when they arrived later, delightedly noted "about half a score Houses" besides
the big one, also an abundance of multicolored maize, good peas
growing in the Governor's garden, a brick-kiln begun, and an acute
shortage of carpenters. With forty goats and forty cows giving milk,
settlers could buy a quart for a penny even before the two cattle-
boats of the same voyage arrived. Most of the newcomers were
servants, who seem to have become quickly demoralized. An epidemic, probably dysentery, killed more than eighty persons at
Salem in the winter following, including Anna Endecott, who lay ill
on her arrival in the *Abigail*. The clergyman Higginson, an alumnus
of Jesus and St. John's Colleges, Cambridge, from Leicester, despite
all his enthusiasm for the Promised Land—and he must have been
the person who gave Naumkeag (which sounded Hebrew to him)
its "translated" name Salem—died August 6, 1630, at the age of

forty-two, leaving a widow and eight children in the new Haven of Rest. The letters he wrote before tuberculosis felled him circulated widely in England as potent propaganda.

"By this time," says White of the period of the Higginson settling, "the often agitation of this affair in sundry parts of the kingdom, the good report of Captain Endecott's government, and the increase of the Colony, began to awaken the spirits of some persons of competent estates, not formerly engaged." In one of the great undercover maneuvers of history, the New England Company secured a charter on March 4, 1629, which transformed it into the extraordinarily powerful Massachusetts Bay Company with title to all of Massachusetts Bay (notwithstanding its being already largely granted out) and sovereignty over it. The Higginson fleet sailed in late April and May under this vastly expanded authority. The Earl of Lincoln's uncle, Viscount Saye and Sele (William Fiennes), a sly gentleman of great ability and influence who wanted not only to curb the king but also to establish a hereditary aristocracy for himself and friends in America, abetted the subtle business of swinging the new incorporation. His "cordial advice and true affection," the substantial West Country leader, Israel Stoughton, expressly confirmed, did much to that end, as did the concern of the Earl of Warwick and the "wise handling" of the Earl's cousin Sir Nathaniel Rich, Stoughton added. We can also safely presume the assistance of Winthrop's neighboring Suffolk squire Sir Robert Naunton, Master of the Court of Wards and nine years Secretary of State, who appointed Winthrop an attorney of the Court of Wards in 1627. One of the most expensive items in the drawing and passing of the charter was the unprecedented omission of a headquarters designation in the instrument, leaving the company legally free to choose its own capital or capitals later. Instantly this raises our suspicion that a scheme to transfer the company government abroad had already ripened, but the first documentable broaching of such a scheme does not occur for nearly another four months.

Then on July 28, in the home of the deputy-governor, Thomas Goffe, at the corner of Philpot Lane, London, Governor Cradock proposed to a general meeting of the stockholders (called the General Court) that the government of the colony be transferred to the inhabitants of it.

This was the identical day that Williams, with Cotton and Hooker, attended the conference near Sempringham which Isaac

Johnson had called and which Winthrop, mud-encrusted from a fall in a bog near Ely on the way, solemnly reached by horse in company with his brother-in-law Emmanuel Downinge, an Inner-Temple attorney and Johnson's liaison with Winthrop in London. Whether Winthrop, approaching through the long shadows of that late summer afternoon, looked quite like Joshua returning out of the mists of the past, he must have symbolized what hope for the future the twenty-five-year-old Williams could feel two months after the shattering of his courtship and his health. Williams developed more respect for Winthrop than for any other man he ever met besides Coke. This conference at the Sempringham castle was a time of fundamental reorientation for both Winthrop and Williams.

The fourth Earl of Lincoln (Theophilus Clinton), the leading Puritan peer of all England, happened not to be at home that day, having gone to Germany commanding three hundred volunteers under Count Mansfield, for Protestantism. His wife, Lady Bridget, would have been present as hostess, however, along with her daughter and Johnson's wife, Lady Arbella. A neighboring manorial lord, William Coddington, likely attended; also Sir Richard Saltonstall, the forty-three-year-old lord of Ledsham Manor near Leeds in the West Riding to the north. Saltonstall's uncle of the same name had been Lord Mayor of London in 1597; he had also been alderman of the conventicle-ridden Aldgate Ward and four terms master of the Skinners Company before his death in 1601. The Yorkshire Saltonstall concentrated his entrepreneurial activity in the West Country; the subsequent attitude of his largely West Country followers and employees in New England, together with his own moderation as a councilor and his permanent return to England after less than a year in America, suggests he never in his heart departed from the Presbyterian middle ground. Although he might have been attending the Company meeting in London this July 28, he (like Johnson) more probably represented Cradock and the transfer faction of the Company at this equally critical meeting closer to home.

Dudley surely would be present at the castle. The Earl of Lincoln had induced him to return to Sempringham from his retirement, which Dudley had spent in nearby Boston, under Cotton's ministry at St. Botolph's. He and Cotton resided in Boston near a lawyer with a Cheshire-cat smile named Richard Bellingham, who had for some years been recorder of the borough of Lincoln and in 1628 represented Boston in Parliament. Between June 1637 and August 1639 Williams singled out Dudley and his family in at least seventeen letters from Providence to Winthrop for regards to be conveyed. On fifteen of those occasions he also included Bellingham and family, as in this typical postscript: "my best respects to good mrs. Wintrop mr. Duptie [Dudley, the deputy-governor] mr. Bellingham & theirs." The reactionaries Dudley and Bellingham were the last members of the Council we would expect Williams to feel special fondness for. Only family friendship that developed in England during meetings such as this one at the Sempringham castle, preceded by stopovers in Boston, could satisfactorily explain such gulf-bridging. Williams mentioned long later to John Cotton, Jr., having tenderly loved and honored his opponent John Cotton, Sr., "as I did the persons of the magistrates, ministers & members whome I knew in Old England, & knew their holy Affectjons & vpright Ajmes & great selfe denjall, to enjoy more of God in this wildernes." Williams's long-later addressing of Simon Bradstreet as "my much honoured kind friend" indicates that that friendship began in Lincolnshire too. The Suffolk gentleman Bradstreet (born 1603 at Horbling) succeeded Dudley as the Earl's bailiff, then became steward to the Countess of Warwick's family. Williams's ties with the Earl of Warwick and Warwick's cousins may mean that he knew Bradstreet in Warwickshire. Bradstreet married Dudley's gifted daughter Ann, so he would have been periodically back in Boston and as likely met Williams there. They may all have met before at Masham's manor. In fact, being mostly Cambridge men, they may all have attended the meeting, during the Cambridge commencement of a few weeks before, which authorized Johnson to call this Sempringham meeting at Winthrop's convenience. The whole Massachusetts venture has about it a clannish, if not conspiratorial, air that forces us to assume, in any case, a long prior association, strengthened by religious communion, among the magistrates and clergy of the colony. It is necessary to know this in order to appreciate the in-group's ambivalent attitude toward Williams in the Bay.

The castle conference, which must have lasted far into the candle-lit night that July 28, apparently decided nothing less than to take over the Massachusetts Bay Company as an instrument for making Massachusetts a Congregational commonwealth under Winthrop's direction. We get the impression that the Lincolnshire intriguers had been mulling such a move for many months and had been persuading Winthrop to lead their cause since lighting on him during or sometime before the recent Cambridge commencement.

On August 26 Winthrop caucused at Cambridge again with eleven others. Half of the twelve (including Johnson, Humfrey, and Saltonstall) were in and half (including Winthrop and Dudley) were still out of the Company. They here contracted to embark by the following March 1 if they could secure a legal transfer of the Company government and patent to America before October, scarcely a month away. Two days later, twenty-seven members, or about one-sixth of the Company membership met in special session at Goffe's house; and the following day, Saturday, August 29, the proposal to transfer carried. The culmination of the *coup* came October 20, when the General Court elected Winthrop governor, Humfrey deputy-governor, and the full Cambridge-faction slate to the board of directors (called Court of Assistants or Council) for the ensuing year.

"I was first chosen to be Governour without my seeking or expectation," Winthrop said on September 4, 1634, "there being then divers other gentlemen, who, for their abilities everyway, were far more fit." He was forty-three at his election and by no means at the beginning of his career. From his several portraits, one of which must date from about 1629, he was a responsible-looking gentleman with dark, slightly wavy hair hanging down to his Elizabethan ruff, with a neat mustache and short beard. The tapering beard, together with a long nose and high-arched eyebrows, accentuated his narrowness of face and an air of imperiousness, softened by an attitude of weariness and carewornness. A more striking portrait has the Governor's face yellow and ghastly in shadows; the usual careworn expression is present, but in addition there is a harrowed look, with a faint smile that is weary yet grim; he appears a pleasant person but remote, gentle but resolute. "Such was the *Mixture* of *distant Qualities* in him," says Cotton Mather, "as to make a most admirable *Temper*; and his having a certain *Greatness of Soul*, which rendered him Grave, Generous, Courageous, Resolved, Well-applied, and every way a *Gentleman* in his Demeanour, did not hinder him from taking sometimes the old *Romans* way to avoid Confusions, namely, *Cedendo* [Yielding]." Morton of Merrymount's epithet "Joshua Temperwell" backhandedly confirms Mather.

Lord of Groton Manor in Suffolk, Winthrop's intellectual superiority had been evident since his precocious childhood. A pious mother who could speak French, and a nearby vicar who prepared him in Latin and Greek, fostered his early bent for wide reading. At Trinity College, Cambridge, aged fourteen, he endured a long, traumatic illness which deepened an introspective disposition. At seventeen the "voluptuous heart" he had been worrying about led him to precipitate marriage and fatherhood at eighteen. In these young-married years he studied law at Gray's Inn and served as a notably courteous justice of the peace in Essex, where a village curate, Ezekiel Culverwell, brought him, as Winthrop says, "to bid farewell to all the world." He almost switched to the ministry but, at twenty-one, held his first manorial court at Groton. Yet he felt unaccountably sad and drove himself beyond his strength in his work. "Some need the spurre, but you the reine," his friend Humfrey warned him in 1630. On top of an inner struggle for peace of mind and an undue frequency of sickness, a succession of family deaths devastated him: in 1613 his father-in-law; in 1614 his fifth child, an infant daughter Anne; in 1615 another whom he had also named Anne, and his wife Mary Forth; then late in 1616 his second wife Thomasine Clopton and her new-born daughter; in 1623 his hospitable father Adam; in April 1629 a close brother-in-law, Thomas Fones, and his mother Anne. But his April 1618 third marriage to Margaret Tyndal (daughter of the then lately assassinated master in Chancery, Sir John Tyndal, of Great Maplested, Essex) seemed to lift the gloom of his life. He lived in a lonely apartment in the Inner Temple during court terms in London, where he fell more dangerously ill than usual late in 1628. In late April 1629, certain that England was heading inexorably to disaster, he wrote Margaret to keep faith to the end of the race. A month and a half before the Sempringham meeting, he lost his attorney's privileges for his Puritanism. On June 22 he wrote his wife: "Where we shall spende the rest of our short tyme I knowe not." That his decision to throw in his lot at Sempringham constituted the guarantee of the intrigue's success is admitted in Dudley's reminiscence some twenty months later: "Mr. *Winthrop* of *Suffolk* (who was well known in his own country, and well approved here, for his piety, liberality, wisdom and gravity) coming in to us, we came to such resolution, that in *April,* 1630, we set sail from Old *England.*"

The captors of the Company worked as efficiently and quietly as possible to make good their getaway with the charter by March 1.

They did not miss this deadline very far, for it was the day after Easter, March 29, 1630, that Winthrop's flagship the *Arbella* (350 tons, thirty-eight guns), together with three sister ships, and three Dutch vessels on their way to the West Indies, weighed anchor at Southampton Water and headed down the Channel. John Cotton sent the passengers off with a farewell sermon assuring them that this expedition had divine sanction and protection. On March 10, at Plymouth, England, Patriarch White had given a similar sendoff to the passengers of the *Mary and John;* and the *Lyon,* William Peirse captain, left Bristol on about the same March day. These two ships sailed separately but in association with the Winthrop fleet. Seven additional ships sailed from Southampton about a month after the *Arbella.*

While the *Arbella* anchored temporarily at Yarmouth April 7, White and ex-Governor Cradock came aboard to get the sailing magistrates' signatures to *The Hvmble Reqvest,* i.e. a request to orthodox Anglicans not to misconstrue the Massachusetts Bay Company as leaving the Church. Besides being intended to allay public opinion, it might also have been a last effort of the Presbyterian minority of the old Company to forestall Congregational extremism. One of the signers was Dudley, who had been elected deputy-governor at a court held aboard at Southampton when Humfrey decided not to make the journey that year.

Somewhere on the Atlantic Winthrop delivered an address which Williams long later alluded to in a letter to Winthrop Jr. and which was entitled *A Modell of Christian Charity.* It restated the basic utopian conception of a holy commonwealth, a determination to make it succeed, a sense of divine mission, indeed contract, and the necessity of a loving interdependence in which "the publique must oversway all private respects." There was nothing in this broad philosophical statement with its frank recognition of class stratification, as well as of the obligation of the high to the low and *vice versa* in harmony, that Williams would not have subscribed to, excepting two assumptions—one on the inextricable relation of church and state and the other the relation of the state of the church to the prosperity of the commonwealth.

"Master Ludlow's ship," the 400-ton *Mary and John,* reached Massachusetts almost two weeks ahead of the *Arbella.* Roger Ludlow had been elected an Assistant of the Company on February 10, 1630, in London. An aggressive autocrat two years younger than

Winthrop, he had the same kind of background and education except that he came out of the West Country gentry (he was baptized at Dinton, Wiltshire, March 7, 1590) and attended Balliol College, Oxford, for two years (1610–12) instead of Cambridge. He studied law in the Inner Temple instead of Gray's Inn and probably practiced it in London mostly during court sessions, as had Winthrop, residing the balance of the year on his country estate. Before boarding the *Mary and John* at Plymouth, Ludlow and many of the passengers formally "gathered" as a congregation, John White presiding. White installed his West Country disciples John Warham and John Maverick as pastor and teacher respectively. Various bits of information from succeeding years confirm their loyalty to White's Presbyterian position.

Roger Clap, a quiet, twenty-one-year-old Devonshire lad in this newly formed congregation, relates that Captain Squibb mercilessly unloaded the passengers and their goods at Nantasket Point, "a forlorn place," where the *Mary and John* landed May 30. Left to shift for themselves, about ten men of the group got to the Charles River by a boat that some of the Old Planters at Nantasket loaned them. The "vacant wilderness" abashed the well-armed party; Captain Richard Southcot, their leader, retreated to England the summer of 1631. At Charlestown they saw some wigwams and, a short distance up the Mistick, one English house, palisaded, where they found the blacksmith Thomas Walford, a leftover of the abortive Gorges colony at Wessaguscasit, who had no bread but generously gave them his solitary boiled bass. (Walford and his family, loyal Anglicans, were banished by the General Court the summer of 1631.) Southcot's vanguard proceeded up the Charles until the river grew narrow and shallow, and there, with much labor, they unloaded their boat up the steep bank. As night came on, the desolate little band learned that three hundred Indians had approached and were close by. An Old Planter who was guiding the neophytes advised the Indians to stay away until morning. In the morning some of the Indians came and stood at a distance a long while looking. Some more joined them, holding out a great bass. Southcot sent one of his men with a biscuit and, in a while, many more bass had been exchanged for as many biscuits. After a few days, in which time the ten pioneers had built a shelter for their goods and thus more or less founded Watertown, Ludlow called them down the bay to Mattapan (which the Dorchester colonists soon renamed

Dorchester), where a neck of land provided a good place for their cattle. (In 1804 Dorchester Neck came to be called South Boston. That was five miles farther south than the South Boston of today.) The West Country people who settled Dorchester and, to a considerable extent Watertown and Newtown, tended to maintain something of a separate identity in the Bay, which preserved the split that had been developing within the Company between West Country and East Country members.

At about 4 A.M. Saturday, June 12, meanwhile, the *Arbella* drew near Salem, shot off two pieces of ordnance, and sent a skiff to Peirse's *Lyon*, which had ridden in the harbor some days. An hour afterward, Isaac Allerton, on his way in a shallop from Plymouth to Pemaquid, came aboard, and Peirse's shallop met and convoyed the *Arbella* between Bakers Isle and Little Misery; she probably came to anchor at about 10 A.M. within a half mile of Plum Cove. Peirse boarded, then fetched Endecott, who came aboard at about 2 P.M., along with the Earl of Lincoln's former chaplain and now pastor of Salem's Congregational Church, Samuel Skelton, and Captain Christopher Levett, down from Maine. They escorted the *Arbella*'s captain (Peter Milbourne), the magistrates, with other gentlemen and some ladies, back to Salem, "where we supped with a good venyson pastrye, and good beere," says Winthrop, "and at night we returned to our shippe, but some of the women stayed behind" (at Endecott's fayre House, no doubt). Meanwhile, most of the passengers went ashore on Cape Ann and gathered strawberries. On Monday the fourteenth the *Arbella* came to final anchor in the mouth of North River in Beverly Harbor. "In the afternoone we went with most of our Companye on shore, and our Captain gave vs 5: pieces," says Winthrop.

Dudley's daughter, Ann Bradstreet, says her "heart rose" in revulsion at what Higginson had claimed to be the Promised Land. Dudley, in a report to Lady Bridget ten months later, described Salem, which he said, "Pleased us not. . . . We found the colony in a sad and unexpected condition, above eighty of them being dead the winter before; and many of those alive, weak and sick; all the corn and bread amongst them all, hardly sufficient to feed them a fortnight." Winthrop's reaction went unrecorded or, rather, is recorded only in a large blank that comes in his *Journal* between the entry cited above about going ashore, and the next, dated Thursday the seventeenth: "We went to mattachusetts [Boston Bay] to find out a place for our sitting downe. We went vp mistick river about 6: miles." It had not taken long to decide against lingering in the Haven of Rest, but to swarm on, any or most of them, first to Charlestown. On July 2, the "very hot" day the *Talbot* docked, Winthrop's son Henry, who came on it and survived an epidemic of smallpox aboard, drowned while swimming across the river for a canoe; the coldness of the water probably caused his fatal cramp. (He was Winthrop's wayward son, aged twenty-two, who at eighteen had shipped off to the Bermudas. He left a pregnant widow at Groton.) Every boat reached port, and on July 8, says Winthrop, the voyagers "kept a daye of thanksgiving in all the plantations."

Endecott had had no adequate warning of the inundation of Salem; he did not have resources to prepare even for the more modest number he did expect. Many of the settlers misunderstood that houses would be awaiting them if they had put money in the common stock, but the Company did not intend to provide housing for any but ministers and Company servants; and the inadequately supervised servants who had been sent with the Higginson fleet to prepare lodgings had fallen into a lazy stupor or critical illness or both. Dudley does not say how many of the 180 servants so sent survived to July 1630, but he says that the provisions for them had been unloaded at a wharf in England and entrusted to another ship, which left them behind. So the Company found itself unable to feed the servants and forced to free them, "who had cost . . . about sixteen or twenty pound a person, furnishing and sending over." For interminable months in the primitive, congested, cramped village, where work had come to a standstill, where every family knew at least one death and nobody could shake the deadly dysentery, Salem must have presented a nearly hopeless prospect. Hundreds preferred to press elsewhere; another hundred or two gave up and went back with the returning ships.

Hardly a year before, Higginson had warned his friends at Leicester in a letter from this Promised Land that "when you are once parted with England you shall meete neither with taverns nor alehouses, nor butchers, nor grocers, nor apothecaries shops to helpp what things you need, in the midst of the great ocean, nor when you are come to land here are yet neither markets nor fayres to buy what you want." But while he was writing this letter, he goes on, his wife brought him word that the fishermen had caught sixteen hundred bass at one draught. Not only was milk plentiful and cheap;

little children of five, he says, could get their maintenance abundantly by setting corn during one month of the year. It took a decade of hard toil for the town to realize this kind of well-being again, but the basic conditions Higginson enumerates did begin to re-emerge gradually.

By the end of the summer of 1630 almost one thousand people and two hundred head of cattle had landed. Dudley says a total of seventeen ships came in the twelve months after the *Arbella* set sail. But in the heat of the summer another terrible epidemic of bacillary dysentery killed more than a quarter of the settlers. Twelve deaths occurred in Winthrop's own household, i.e. besides Henry, a surgeon and ten servants. Before December, says Dudley, "there dyed by estimation about two hundred at the least," among them Mrs. Coddington and a sister of Hooker's. Edward Johnson, one of the Winthrop-fleet settlers, says that almost in every family "Lamentation, Mourning, and woe was heard, and no fresh food to be had to cherish them . . . and that which added to their present distresse was the want of fresh water." Samuell Fuller, the Pilgrim physician, threw up his hands. "The sad news here is," he wrote Bradford from Charlestown August 2, "that many are sick, and many are dead. . . . I here but lose time and long to be at home, I can do them no good." Lady Arbella herself died in Salem sometime late in August. Isaac Johnson moved in grief to Charlestown, where Dudley and Winthrop, *et al.*, had started building, when his old classmate, William Blaxton, living as a hermit on the southern slope of the later-named Beacon Hill since the break-up of the Gorges colony at Wessaguscasit, apprized him of the suitability of that location, which had a good spring in the direction of the Charles. Johnson with others then transferred to this narrow, woodless neck, known as Shawmut ("abundant springs") or Blaxton's Neck or Trimountaine, "where people began to build their houses against winter," as the ancient *Records of Charlestown* says, "and this place was called Boston."

There, on September 30 at 2 A. M., Johnson himself died, not yet thirty years old, the wealthiest, the highest in social rank, a universally beloved man of principle, and the expected successor to Winthrop as governor. Dudley calls him "the greatest furtherer of this plantation," and says he died "willingly, professing his life better spent in promoting this plantation, than it could have been any other way." His death can be viewed as the biggest single shock sustained by the colony in its first five years' existence. Edward Johnson remembered around 1650 that "there was not onely many weeping eyes, but some fainting hearts, fearing the fall of the present worke."

Scurvy did not, apparently, become the critical disease until winter. "The poorer sort of people (who lay long in tents, Ec.,)," Winthrop noted in February, "were much afflicted with the sckirvye, & many dyed, especially at *Boston* & *Charlestowne*." Yet, in spite of everything, Winthrop could say in his first letter to Margaret from "Boston in Mattachusets," on November 29, 1630: "My dear wife, we are here in a paradise."

Winthrop had farsightedly sent the thirty-eight-year-old Captain Peirse back with the *Lyon* in early July for provisions. Peirse headed for Bristol, his home port. With increasing urgency, the whole colony depended on his return, but autumn came and went, and December and January, with no sign of him.

3 : *Boston*

SOME WOMEN grubbing for mussels on the beach near Nantasket caught the first thrilling sight of the *Lyon* as she hove over the horizon on February 5, 1631. It had been a tempestuous crossing; a sailor had been lost. The freighter carried about twenty passengers in addition to the two hundred tons of goods. Winthrop tersely noted that "she brought mr Williams (a godly minister) with his wife." He also notes that many "recovered speedylye" from the scurvy with the lemon juice Peirse brought. On February 9 the *Lyon* shifted from Nantasket and came to anchor before Boston, riding easily despite a great drift of ice. The next day, said Winthrop, "the frost brake vp." On February 22 the colony held a day of thanksgiving.

The Williamses probably stayed with Winthrop, as the Higginsons had stayed with Endecott on their arrival in Salem three years before. Winthrop had a reputation for open hospitality, besides being the official head of state; and a Puritan state held Puritan clergymen in high honor, even if Williams had not been an old acquaintance of the head. Winthrop would have had room, what with the death of so many of his household and the arrival of the larger part of his family another eight months away. But it was probably by way of the *Lyon* that he learned that his third eldest son, Forth, a promising minister of twenty, had died from an illness at Groton. It is possible that, out of consideration for the Governor's bereavement, the Williamses put up at the parsonage with Pastor John Wilson (who had not been able to induce his wife to cross the Atlantic with him).

Wilson hoped to leave the pulpit of Boston Church in Williams's care while he went back to England to persuade Mrs. Wilson to brave migration. His and Winthrop's—and the whole congregation's —expectation seems to have been that Williams would assume the teachership. (The Puritans insisted, when possible, on a dual ministry—a pastor for exhortation and a teacher for scholarly explication; there was some tendency for the teacher to gain the greater prestige, but the offices were equal in rank and often lost any clear differentiation in function.) After Williams's undoubted guest-preaching for a few Sunday afternoon services in the thatched meetinghouse at the head of the one street, perhaps even relieving Wilson in a Sunday morning service, and holding mid-week "lecture" services, the call of the congregation was unanimous. To their astonishment, he refused. Because they would not renounce their connection with the "false" Church of England, he renounced them.

So from his first weeks in America Williams openly raised the banner of "rigid Separatism," contending that the line by which the Anglican Church traced its authority over the keys to the Kingdom from Jesus and the Apostles had snapped in the long, corrupt reign of the Roman Catholic "Antichrist" and that the first step to finding the lost Zion must be a dissociaton from all taint of the state church. Winthrop drafted a rejoinder: "The Corruption of a thinge dothe not nullifie a thinge so longe as the thinge hathe a beinge in the same nature, that it had, when it was in the beste beinge." Williams could no longer stomach the state church of England; Winthrop could not yet bear to part from her.

Boston's inhabitants already knew of Williams's radical tendency, but his outright Separatism seems to have taken them by surprise; or perhaps what surprised them was that such a gentle man should have let his wilder talk make any real difference. The preacher-historian Hubbard talked with many who knew Williams and reported about 1680 that he had been "of good account in England for a godly and zealous preacher, but after he came here he soon discovered himself." Back in Essex, according to Hubbard, people were wont to say of him "that he was divinely mad; as if his too much zeal, as Festus said of Paul's too much learning, had made him beside himself." "He is passionate and precipitate," said Sir William Martin, "but I hope his integrity and good intentions will bring him at last into the waye of truth." "A good man and a good friend," Masham said of him in 1629. Possibly seasickness on the way over completed his cast-off of Anglicanism (his sickening at sea is one of the mortal trials he enumerates to Dame Sadleir), but in all likelihood he had been an unequivocal Separatist for a year and a half before he left.

The rupture with the Boston church must have occurred in March 1631. On April 12 the church at Salem called Williams to take the place of Higginson, who had died the August before, as an associate of the ailing pastor Skelton. If Williams left for Salem on that date, he had resided in Boston for sixty-six days; but he had probably already been some time in Salem unofficially assisting his congenial and perhaps long-standing friend. Williams later told Cotton Jr. that he wrought hard at the hoe in Salem and Plymouth, so evidently he did not tarry long enough in Boston in the early spring of 1631 to prepare a garden or a crop. But for a short while he did reside there.

He would have found a chaotic bustle in Boston as planters strove to erect frame, thatched cottages rather at random on the seven-hundred-acre Neck, the many wigwams and tents gradually giving way to more substantial but still modest and unpainted structures (though Williams must have witnessed some of the building of Coddington's house at the north side of a little square a few years later. Coddington reputedly had the first brick house in the town). Winthrop's large frame house, which his servants had originally erected at Charlestown, stood a short distance from Coddington's, which was also a short distance from Wilson's parsonage and from the steep-thatched meetinghouse, nearly opposite the town spring.

Samuel Maverick, an Old Planter (i.e. a pre-Endecott, non-Congregational settler) who did not live far from the Neck before the Puritan migration, said he knew the site of Boston "for some yeares to be a Swamp and Pound." Though treeless, the Neck, according to Edward Johnson, had "hideous thickets" that nurtured bears and wolves. The Indians who had done the tree-removing had all died in the plague—probably smallpox—of about 1615–19. Maverick said the hillsides abounded with blueberry and blackberry bushes, grapes, and strawberries. Beacon Hill, rough and steep, rose nearly a hundred feet higher then than now. Since Winthrop himself was reported working in shirtsleeves in this period, we can presume that Williams turned to the community labor of thicket-clearing and wall-raising, also thatch-gathering in hay "loyters" on the nearby islands, and wood-gathering both for building and burning, as well as perhaps for fencing (at first it was only the wolves the Bostonians worried about, which could be kept off the entire peninsula by one good fence). The replenished pig population (Maverick mentions "a very few Goats" in the area; they probably also were replenished) roamed at will despite the belated town vote of 1634 that this should not be allowed.

William Wood, who apparently came over with Higginson just to observe, had the impression in 1633 that there were only thirty or forty houses in the town. The compactness of the settlement and unevenness of the terrain may have made it seem that there were fewer dwellings than there actually were. They would not have been numerous in any case, but Wood notes that the Neck already looked cramped and that the inhabitants had begun building farm-houses at Mistick River two miles back of the town. They kept their cattle and swine there while corn grew on their Boston plots. In winter everybody's cows and hogs stayed in town. The Neck, says Wood, had the advantage of being free of rattlesnakes and mosquitoes, as well as wolves, by the time of his visit. A windmill, he says, had already appeared on the north side, and we need have no doubt that a brewery had put in its appearance as early. The old Puritans could endure almost any hardship of pioneering except having to drink water. A tavern opened in the first few days of March 1634, and the Court of Assistants ordered a market established that same month, to be kept on Thursday, when the country people came to town for the weekday "lecture" (church service). Wharves must already have been conspicuous, because Wood says that Boston, though not yet the biggest or richest town in the Bay, had clearly become in 1633 the chief trading mart of the colony, coinciding with its having won out as the colony's political capital. Two years later the town meeting had grown self-assured enough to appoint a hogreeve to impound stray pigs.

Some wealthy private citizens started a free school; the first colony-wide compulsory school law in America came a decade after that. (Sir William Berkeley, governor of Virginia, reported to the Commissioners of Plantations as late as 1671 that in Virginia "I thank God, *there are no free schools* nor *printing* . . . for learning has brought disobedience, and heresy, and sects into the world, and *printing* has divulged them, and libels against the best government. God keep us from both!") A bookbinder's shop opened in Boston the year after Williams fled; only two years afterward, in nearby Newtown, the first college in the colonies opened its doors, providing no narrow dogmatic curriculum but a broad liberal education. The first printing press in the colonies began its busy history in the same year at Cambridge, which is what Newtown had meanwhile been rechristened. These events were taking place or being actively planned in Boston in the time that Williams knew the town both as resident and occasional, not always voluntary, visitor.

The "corrupted" church there, which had moved from the open air to a rude, solid house of wood, presented a vigorous semi-democracy in which the members of the congregation as a whole made certain decisions by majority vote, as they did in the town meeting, which had already taken ineradicable root. The church was also functioning as a harmonizing medium, smoothing most disputes in the boom-town society without recourse to embittering public litigation. This, and the function of grammar schools, book-binders, college, and printing press, which Williams would most urgently require to underpin his own "free" society, he did not have or get in Providence. He furthermore quit a stable government, within which almost everyone could get a grant of land (easier than in Williams's town not much later) and could help develop the element of democracy which was nearly as resolutely guaranteed in Puritan theory and gradually in practice as the aristocracy that it insisted must be mixed with democracy to keep both from disintegrating.

If Williams had looked hard through the dust of the "lane which goeth to the Cove," in the days he walked it from time to time before his banishment, he might have seen more than an impure church connection in Boston; and if he felt any repression in the village as yet, or a need for more democracy than it had, he did not at the time take notice of either or address himself to such subjects. Salem disappointed the Winthrop-fleet Puritans, but to Williams, whose first taste of the New World was the starving, grieving, semi-sheltered population of only a few score huddled helter-skelter on the cold Boston Neck, Salem's settledness may have offered an attractive escape—if he ever paid that much heed to material conditions.

Williams's arrival in Massachusetts at the end of its time of horror, and his temporary departure from it during the most critical phase of its consolidation, help explain why he failed to grasp the enormity of the Bay's political problem. The multiple swarming of the Winthrop-fleet settlers from Salem before government had been effectively imposed upon them, let alone according to Winthrop's preconceived pattern, threatened to throw the whole enterprise beyond the ability of Winthrop's administration to control it. Controlling it at this stage would not have sufficed, because the Great Migration was on, and it did not abate until about 1640. The founding of Newtown in 1631 brought the number of full-fledged towns to ten, and Winthrop estimated the population of Massachusetts on May 22, 1634, as "about 4000 soules and vpwarde." Concord achieved town status in the fall of 1635, when the population of Boston must have been pushing 900. In 1640 Boston had grown to about 1200 and in the next ten years almost doubled that. In 1643, when the General Court divided the commonwealth into four counties or shires, no less than thirty-one towns had materialized; the colony as a whole had perhaps 15,000 inhabitants. Edward Johnson speaks of "this remote, rocky, barren, bushy, wild-woody wilderness . . . now [1642] . . . become a second England for fertilness in so short a space, that it is indeed the wonder of the world." The wigwams, huts, and hovels that the settlers dwelt in at their first coming, he says, have turned "into orderly, fair, and well-built houses, well furnished many of them, together with Orchards filled with goodly fruit trees, and gardens with a variety of flowers."

If Johnson was correct, certain basically democratic conditions already obtained despite social and religious discrimination in land tenure and suffrage, for he said "the poorest person" in the towns "hath a house and land of his own, and bread of his own growing, if not some cattle," and "many hundreds of labouring men, who had not enough to bring them over, yet now [are] worth scores, and some hundreds of pounds." But it was appallingly hard for poor people in the first years; they are the ones who did most of the dying. They also included most of those who, to the magistrates' incredulity, came without any particular concern for the holy experiment. The implacable Dudley told Lady Bridget on March 12, 1631, that "we have found by experience that [the poorer sort] have hindred, not furthered the work: and for the profane and debauched persons, their oversight in coming hither is wondred at, where they shall find nothing to content them."

Winthrop called meetings of the Court of Assistants, some eight or nine men, who met first on Monday, August 22, 1630, under a tree at Charlestown. They at once proceeded to establish their authority, directing chief attention to any who denied it to them or dissented from the nonseparating Congregational ideal. "These [Assistants] are the men that come prepared to ridd the Land of all pollution," the Anglican outlaw Morton said sarcastically. Morton answered the August summons to the September Court of Assistants "though hee decline their Iurisdiction." His sentencing came September 7.

There they all with one assent put him to silence [Morton himself related], crying out, heare the Governour, heare the Govern: who gave this sentence against mine Host at first sight: that he should be first put in the Billbowes, his goods should be all confiscated, his Plantation should be burned downe to the ground, because the habitation of the wicked should no more appeare in Israell, and his person banished from those territories.

Something like twenty persons had been banished from Massachusetts by the time Williams was; compared to his predecessors, Williams was handled with kid gloves by the government. Endecott started the banishings before the Winthrop fleet sailed, and Separatism was one of his grounds. He had no precedent in English common law; banishment is something the New England Congregationalists, like the Scotch Presbyterians, picked up from Calvin's practice at Geneva.

Israel Stoughton, a substantial settler of 1632 in Dorchester (six miles south of Boston), wrote his rector-brother John at Aller, Somerset, in 1635:

When I came into the Country for one whole yeare after, the gouernment was solely in the hands of the assistants. the people chose them Magistrates, and then they made lawes, disposed lands, raisd monies, punisht offendours etc. at their discretion.

Stoughton agreed with the Watertown delegation of protestors who had been fined in February 1632 for saying the General Court did not have the power to tax or legislate without the people. When conditions stabilized, Winthrop proved to be among the first to relent, to allow the people a full knowledge of their powers and the government's, to resume admitting freemen (116, including Edward Johnson, were admitted in May 1631), and to grant representation from each town in the General Court—first two deputies per town, later three, elected by the local freemen. Freemen admitted in 1631 included the most prominent of the Presbyterian Old Planters who had settled before the Congregationalists sailed. This act recognized the need to broaden the base and consent of government and also recognized the Old Planters' pioneering services. But at that same Court of May 18, according to its *Records:*

. . . it was likewise ordered and agreed that for time to come noe man shalbe admitted to the freedome of this body politicke, but such as are members of some of the churches within the lymitts of the same.

Here was the most crucial statute of seventeenth-century Massachusetts for effectively implementing the church-state concept of the commonwealth, especially in that only "nonseparating" Congregational churches were countenanced.

The statutes of the General Court and Court of Assistants prove clearly the intention of the Massachusetts magistrates to make their commonwealth autonomous as well as to bring it to heel. Their non-statutory actions also attest this, particularly their refusal to obey the Commission-for-Foreign-Plantations order (learned in July 1634) to send the charter back to England. Winthrop obtained both a unanimous opinion from the clergy that "if a general governour were sent, we ought not to accept him, but defend our lawful possessions (if we were able;) otherwise to avoide or protract"; and a decision by the Court of Assistants, meeting on Castle Island July 29, 1634, to fortify the island against the arrival of a royally commissioned governor-general. Higginson had warned his Leicester friends in 1629: "If you linger too long, the passages of Jordan through the malice of Sathan, may be stopped, that you cannot come if you would." When the full implications of the Bay's charter power and transfer finally dawned in England, all kinds of actions began against Massachusetts: besides the order to return the charter and the actual royal appointment of a governor-general who would supersede the Company authority, came lawsuits for prior title, appeals from banished persons on the ground that the Bay had violated the English constitution, and vigorous opposition by a revived Council for New England under Sir Ferdinando Gorges. In December 1634 an order went out from the Commission for Foreign Plantations at Whitehall to the officers of the Port of London:

We . . . expresly charge and command you . . . not to suffer any person . . . to imbarke . . . [except] he hath taken the oath of Supremacie and Allegiance . . . and Conformity to the orders and discipline of the Church of England.

This hit directly at Congregationalists, both in their religious dissent and in their political intention (in the Commissioners' words) "to liue as much as they can without the reach of [royal] authority."

The Massachusetts loyalty oath, passed in April 1634 and adminis-

tered to every male resident over twenty on pain of banishment for
a second refusal, left out any reference to the king or to the authority of the British government. The resident had to swear he
acknowledged himself lawfully subject to the authority of the government of Massachusetts and accordingly submitted his person,
family, and estate to the jurisdiction of "the lawes & constitucions
therof." The British flag did not fly at Boston until visiting seamen
protested.

That the church, too, operated independently of English jurisdiction despite its nonseparating shibboleth is equally evident from
Massachusetts statutes. The test would be whether a person in good
standing in the Church of England could enter a Bay meetinghouse
and receive Communion or present his child for baptism. It was not
until May 22, 1646, that the statute book openly recognized the long-
standing and long-reported fact of "many persons liveing in the
country who have bene members of the congregations in England,
but are not found fit to be received at the Lords table here," and
that (the statute continues) "in most churches the ministers do
baptize onely such children whose nearest parents, one or both of
them, are setled members in full communion with one or other of
these churches." The Bay Puritans did not call their churches
Anglican churches, as presumably they would if they really had
not seceded from the Church of England. They called them
Churches of Christ in New England. Since, in any case, their Congregational theory held each congregation to be a law unto itself,
immune to interference from any other congregation (though they
found ways of forcing conformity on each other), it would be only
a matter of time before they would draw the analogy that their civil
government was a law unto itself, immune to interference from any
other government. That would follow anyway if, as they adamantly
held, the primary purpose of the government was to uphold their
church. The analogy, however, did not have to wait to be drawn,
because the civil practice of independence was identically the
church practice from the beginning. Independence from England
did not, of itself, necessarily bring more individual freedom or more
democracy.

When Winthrop heard of Salem's official invitation to Williams
in April 1631, he called together such of the Assistants as could
conveniently be assembled, including Williams's presumed friends
Bradstreet, Coddington, and Ludlow. Fearing, says Cotton Mather,

that Salem Church would soon come to nothing of Salem (Peace) in it, and that the whole political and ecclesiastical constitution of the country would suffer by the employment of a minister of Williams's undermining persuasion, they advised the Salem congregation to desist from laying hands too suddenly upon him.

Theoretically, neither the civil government nor another congregation had any authority over Salem Church, but this pressure from the Council sufficed for the time being to deter either the Church or Williams or both. Williams had not, after all, set out on a course of deliberate wrecking—at least not yet. He and his wife shortly turned up in Plymouth, whence they undoubtedly went by boat.

Williams appears to have emigrated to Boston assuming that certain basic questions of church and state remained open and that he would find there a dedicated society truly motivated by religion. Whatever his expectations of the American experiment, or his obtuseness in entertaining such expectations, it seems a reasonable inference that they were disappointed. His later decision to turn Indian missionary is surely a sign of intense disappointment. That he sailed from Bristol with the idea of becoming an Indian missionary, or that he left Boston for Salem or Salem for Plymouth with that idea, is extremely improbable. Every indication is that he conceived the idea in Plymouth after the Boston and Salem disappointments and after having become disappointed with Plymouth in turn. Even then he chose to postpone such a course and returned a second time to Salem.

4 : *Williams Joins the Pilgrims*

WHETHER invited or not, Williams was welcome in Plymouth. The Pilgrims had got used to a high standard of preaching in Holland which Elder Brewster had tried to maintain in his ponderous style. They had had a succession of disappointments in their pulpit, including a minister who proved to be insane and another a lecherous subversive. A well-meaning mediocrity, Ralph Smith, held the Plymouth pastorate at the time Williams arrived. Endecott had banished Smith from Salem in 1629 for rigid Separatism. Williams and Smith agreed so well that they began to form a radical little minority which threatened dissensions of the sort the Pilgrim leaders had long avoided in horror. As Williams found out to his dismay, the Pilgrims had developed a moderate Separatism not far removed from the non-Separatism of the Bay and in some ways milder; whereas Williams in these days, in church matters, stood for the utmost stringency. He and the Pilgrims nonetheless had a great deal in common—enough that his imperious conscience allowed him to remain two years or more among them.

These two years comprise a decisive turning point in Williams's career. Here he reached his decision to turn Indian missionary, learned the Indian language and Indian diplomacy, also likely the Dutch language, got used to the Pilgrim system of government which consciously or unconsciously became his model for the state he later founded, wrote a treatise on land rights, and in other ways developed his ideas about political power. He appears at this time in Plymouth to have taken his first serious notice of politics and for the most part to have approved the way the Pilgrim leaders ran both church and state. Here, too, he followed in his father's footsteps as a businessman, dealing principally in textiles, while at the same time getting his thorough introduction to farming—hoeing his acre of corn and purchasing cattle through Winthrop. For the rest of his life he remained willy-nilly a politician, diplomat, trader, and farmer, as well as a preacher.

It may be here—we do not know where or in what year—that he lifted the load which left him with the hernia he complains of in later years. The "old pains and Lamenesses" which also plagued him later probably had their beginning in the long hikes with pack loads and his heavy farm labor in this Plymouth period. We, incidentally, do not know what he looked like, other than that his hair turned white by 1664 at the latest. It is almost certain that he would have been clean-shaven. Beards, goatees, and heavy mustaches were common among Puritan magistrates, but not the fashion for post-Cartwright-generation Puritan preachers, who wore no more than a thin mustache, if that. Williams did serve in time as a magistrate. But no matter how much modern commentators may wish to make him into a secular attacker of Puritan religiosity, he remained a devout Puritan preacher and his mental habits always preacher-oriented. Remembering this fact of his being primarily a preacher will more than anything else clarify his perplexing career. The well-known imaginary portrait of him seriously errs in crowning his cranium with a periwig, something Puritan preachers did not affect in Williams's lifetime.

The hillside town of Plymouth, overlooking its half-moon bay, was bigger when Williams went there than Boston just then. Only the May before had the last emigrating group of the Leyden congregation reunited with their brethren in Plymouth. With settlers also spilling over into the town from Massachusetts, Plymouth, while Williams resided there, attained probably its largest size of the century—possibly three hundred, of whom only about half would have been members of the church and about a quarter unfree indentured servants. Williams lived in Plymouth just as it broke beyond its old limits and went on to colonize new settlements, beginning with Duxbury and Marshfield. By 1643 Plymouth, partly with the help of Massachusetts migrants, had spawned ten new towns in New Plymouth Colony and had itself lost proportionately in size and importance. It kept losing population at least until 1670 and, into the twentieth century, stayed a comparatively small community.

So Williams caught Plymouth at a crucial turning point in its own history. The revolutionary changes began when the founding of

Massachusetts finally brought security to the older colony. As late as October 1627 the secretary of New Netherland, Isaack de Rasieres, had found the settlers at Plymouth on constant guard against attack, even marching to Sunday services armed and in military formation, holding services atop the hill in a combination meetinghouse and fort which mounted six cannon. When Williams joined the Pilgrims, they surely had relaxed this tense wariness. They had relaxed their religious tension as well.

Massachusetts provided not only a bulwark of protection but an immense market. Prices for the Pilgrims' corn and cattle hit the sky. More than a decade of bleak struggle suddenly gave way to a semblance of prosperity. Many battened on the inflation, which may have helped Williams accumulate capital to lay out for trading goods. In 1632 came the distribution of meadow lots beyond the town limits, under pressure of new population and new prosperity. This distribution marks both the beginning of the dispersion of Plymouth and the turning of primary attention from religion to commerce. Adversity had slain its thousands, said Hooker, but prosperity would slay its ten thousands. Williams himself records the waning of religious interest during his residence in Plymouth, while Bradford's comments on the scramble for land sound much like Williams's later expostulations about land having become the god of New England. Bradford, however, also deplored the breaking-up of the original church, which he fervently wished to keep intact. Numbers, expansion, power—these carried little weight with him. Yet it was prominent citizens like Brewster, Standish, Winslow, and John Alden who led the desertion of Plymouth for greener pastures nearby. As Bradford laments:

. . . ther was no longer any holding them togeather, but now they must of necessitie goe to theire great lots. . . . And no man now thought he could liue, except he had catle and a great deale of ground to keepst them, all striuing to increase their stocks by which means they were scattered all ouer the bay quickly, and the towne in which they liued compactly till now was left very thine, and in a short time allmost desolate.

And the church, Bradford's fundamental concern, was left, he says, "a widow"; "she that had made many rich, became her selfe poore." Williams preached ("prophesied") to the congregation before it thinned but after it began to be bored with religion during the rapid economic transition. Seeking the Lord further—Williams wrote

Winthrop from Plymouth (in a letter arranging a second shipment of cattle to himself!)—is "a dutie not so frequent with Plymmouth as formerly."

Williams reached the town about the time of the "reckoning" which showed that Isaac Allerton's mangement, despite the flourishing of their fur-trade station on the Kennebec in Maine, had run a £600 debt to £5000. No matter how naïve the Pilgrims may have been about business, the evidence, even without Allerton's ultimate confession and the treasurer James Sherley's confirmation from London of June 24, 1633, clearly bears out Bradford's belief that Allerton had monstrously defrauded the Pilgrims, in collusion with certain of the merchant partners in London. The new outward prosperity therefore but camouflaged a new inner financial desperation on the part of the little group of leaders who had underwritten the debt to the London merchants originally incurred by the Pilgrims' purchase of their independence and of their second patent. Williams likely knew little of this terrible burden; the cost of freedom and self-government was something he grasped only later and gradually, though he proved as willing as Bradford to pay whatever price they might cost.

In 1631, however, Williams might have found himself swept up in the Allerton altercation, for in the year of Williams's arrival in Plymouth, Bradford finally got enough evidence against Allerton and enough support from the hitherto-divided oligarchy (he was a son-in-law of Elder Brewster) to dismiss him as Pilgrim agent and to force his resignation from the holding company (the underwriting group; they called themselves "undertakers"). It has not escaped the older historians that Allerton left Plymouth approximately at the same time as Williams a couple of years afterward and moved to Marblehead, which then lay within the parish over which Williams presided as minister of Salem; and in the March following Williams's flight from Massachusetts in exile, the Massachusetts General Court notified Allerton he must go, too. But there is no known connection; Allerton found it increasingly untenable to remain in Plymouth, independent of Williams's decision to leave, and his non-religious operations with Cradock's unruly fishermen sufficiently account for his ejection from Massachusetts. His 1631 fall in Plymouth happens to have been only inside the oligarchy, which managed the colony's affairs largely in secret. The freemen brazenly returned Allerton to office as Assistant in 1634! He catered to the popular "progressive" element which believed the best way out of the colony's plight to be large-scale deficit spending rather than Bradford's and Brewster's rural thrift. The fact that Allerton was exploiting the colony for his private collusion prevented a test of the bolder philosophy. Williams must have been present on the occasion sometime in the fall of 1633 or the succeeding winter when Allerton, at last brought to account by the Pilgrim church, confessed his fault in organizing trade competition to cut off the Pilgrims' Kennebec enterprise "and other . . . gross miscarriages," then promised "betterwalking" and that he would "wind him self out of these courses" as soon as he could.

The fall of Allerton in the inner elite meant the more rapid rise of Edward Winslow, who ably replaced Allerton on the Council. Williams consequently formed his friendship with the polished, thirty-six-year-old ex-printer Winslow as Winslow "arrived." Winslow most probably would have been the one who initiated Williams into the mysteries of the Indian tongue and Indian diplomacy. Winslow held the palm as the first notable Indian diplomat in New England, although he yielded to Standish in understanding of the native language. Standish, as a matter of fact, was something of a scholar in other lines, to judge from his library; he also knew Dutch and was second only to Winslow in diplomacy, even if his methods were anything but diplomatic. So Standish may also have been an important teacher of Williams. Williams's introduction to the Wampanoag chief, Massasoit, most likely came through Winslow, who had saved Massasoit's life when the chief lay dying of gluttony back in 1624. Williams must also have picked up from Winslow some of the latter's secrets of treating Indian ailments; Williams often later served as a physician to the Indians. For all we know, Winslow, the long-time Pilgrim "merchant," had an important hand in the shipments of goods that Williams must have arranged with his brothers in England which set him up in his Indian-trading business. Winslow had brought the first cattle to New England in 1624 and would at least have advised Williams in the cattle purchases we know Williams made in Plymouth.

Winslow might have been the one who taught Williams Dutch; but a large number of the Plymouth population could speak Dutch, including the forty-seven arrivals from Leyden in 1629 and 1630. Bradford, Brewster, Standish, Fuller, Winslow, *et al.*, had lived a dozen years in Holland; thirty-three of the Pilgrims had become

Dutch citizens in that time (including Bradford), since citizenship was requisite to guild membership. Williams had proved himself an expert linguist in Greek, Hebrew, and Latin but probably had not got round to systematic study of Dutch before coming to America and had no likely occasion in America before or after living in Plymouth; yet he knew it well enough to teach to the great John Milton in 1652–53 during his second mission back to England. We know that he owned a Dutch Testament but not when he acquired it. Ola Elizabeth Winslow points out that, down any London street from Williams's childhood home, refugee Dutch and French Calvinists would have been close neighbors. About 450 families of them formed a conventicle privileged to maintain their own form of worship in their Church of Austin (i.e. Augustinian) Friars next to Drapers' Hall. This closely parallels the Pilgrim conventicle in Leyden of the same time. Williams *could*, therefore, have picked up Dutch in childhood or youth, or at least gained a familiarity with it that facilitated his later serious study. He might also have learned a precedent this early for somewhat different forms of worship cohabiting in harmony. Not only the Pilgrims but many other of Williams's acquaintances in America, besides the peripatetic traders and crewmen from New Netherland, spoke Dutch. Holland had been a crucible of English Congregationalism, including Anabaptist strains. Williams was one of the very few Separatists of note who had not lived some of his life in Holland. His conversance with Dutch, whenever he learned it, confirms his closeness to the Dissenting tradition co-stemming from Holland, doubtless related to his closeness to the cloth trade with the Low Countries. He made his first voyage back to England in a Dutch ship out of New Amsterdam and might have occupied the dreary months at sea with Dutch study as well as sectarian writing.

The Puritans, who took the Indians for the lost tribe of Israel, quickly noted the similarity of Indian to Hebrew. Williams thought the Indians' "Barbarous, Rockie Speech" nearer Greek than Hebrew. He had already learned to speak an Algonquin dialect before returning to Salem from Plymouth. William Wood refers to a minister at Salem who, alone, had acquired facility in the native tongue; Williams is obviously the one referred to. Williams confided his intention to become an Indian missionary to Winthrop in a letter from Plymouth in 1632 alluding to an earlier one of Winthrop's which seems to have urged Williams as a young elder to reconsider the Boston teachership. (Winthrop was arguing for youthful elders!) Williams clarified that he was not at the time a formally installed elder (i.e. "teaching" elder or clergical officer as distinguished from "ruling" elder or highest lay officer) "nor ever shall be, if the Lord please to grant my desires that I may intend what I long after, the natives souls." Winthrop probably responded to this letter (late summer or early fall) with his suggestion that Williams settle among the Narragansetts. Winthrop, with Dudley and Maverick, had made a successful foraging expedition among the Narragansetts in October 1630 and could have given Williams information no one else yet had in 1632 about penetrating their country. Williams undoubtedly conducted his original negotiations with the Narragansett grand sachems, as well as with Massasoit, while he lived in Plymouth, and probably that early secured their permission to settle in their territory.

Williams undertook to learn something of the art of physic from Samuell Fuller, the Pilgrim deacon and physician. Fuller mentions in his will of July 30, 1633, a "booke for phisick" Williams was indebted to him for, which "I freely give him." It is a good bet that Williams also learned the Ainsworth version of the Psalms from Fuller, who, as deacon, presumably had the deacon's usual charge of leading church-service psalm singing. The warmhearted Williams and softhearted Fuller became fast friends. Fuller says in his will that Williams had formerly refused to take a plot of land at Strawberry Hill that the deacon had offered him but which would still be his if he accepted it. Fuller could have been Williams's teacher of Dutch. Or perhaps it was Bradford, who about this time finally found leisure enough to study Hebrew, in which Williams might have exchanged instruction for Bradford's in Dutch. Bradford's library of eighty or so hefty volumes would certainly have attracted Williams.

Bradford was forty-one when Williams reached Plymouth. Only the year before had the constant crisis there relented enough to permit the governor to turn at last to writing poetry, his Dialogues, and his History, while studying Hebrew. Williams describes him as "prudent and godly"; Winthrop described him in 1632 as a "very discreet and grave man"; Bradford in one of his poems describes himself as "a man of sorrows." The later excellent general and governor Josiah Winslow (son of Edward) remembered Bradford as "just and gentle, merciful and just." Bradford's belief that Williams

was unsettled in judgment and developed strange opinions, together
with an unshaken gratitude for Williams's insights despite occasional
sharp reproofs, tends to confirm a quiet judiciousness of temper.
Here are Bradford's exact words:

Mr Roger Williams (a man godly & zalous, hauing many precious
parts [abilities], but very unsetled yn judgmente) came ouer first to the
Massachusetts, but up on some discontente left that place, and came
hither. . . . And his teaching well approoued, for the benefite whereof
I still blese god, and am thankfull to him, euen for his sharpest admoni-
tions & reproues so farr as they agreed with truth.

Already, by the time of Governor John Carver's fatal sunstroke
in a cornfield on a hot April day in 1621, Bradford's quiet perse-
verance, steadiness, and firmness had brought him to undisputed recognition as the leading Pilgrim layman. Thenceforth to his death he
did most of the decison-making for Plymouth colony, which fell into
the habit of leaving the state in his sole discretion, despite his repeated efforts to decline the responsibility. He was a strong and
often arbitrary executive, but his arbitrariness tended to be concealed; it also tended to be forced upon him. His governorship had
the same quality of forbearance which distinguished the governorship of Winthrop.

Williams would have learned an easy equality of conversation
with Bradford, a close neighbor in a small community for a couple
of years, similarly devoted to studious interests and to reformed
religion and a man no more born to the aristocratic manner than
Williams. He and Williams even had a remote family relationship to
draw them together. One of the first Puritan victims of Bloody
Mary's reign, John Bradford, a celebrated prebend of St. Paul's, was
a great-uncle of Governor Bradford, and Williams had descended
from near relatives of the martyr, whose burning took place July 1,
1555, at Smithfield, where Williams later grew up. Governor Bradford's connection with the prebend, whose original Lancashire home
had lain near his own at Austerfield, did not go forgotten; one of the
poems composed at the governor's death pointedly alludes to it.
What is important is that Bradford's conception and example of
governing the little colony of New Plymouth provided the working
model for Williams's own governing in Rhode Island. It may be that
Bradford provided him a still more signficant model of magistracy
as a patient, self-possessed, half-weary, underlyingly sad, quietly in-
domitable personality.

Bradford's model of magistracy in turn had been William Brewster in his feudal management of Scrooby Manor, including the manorial court, as Roland Usher began to perceive a couple of generations ago. Holding to Calvin's principle of limited separation of church and state—a church officer could not at the same time occupy a civil office—Elder Brewster never took a magisterial post in Plymouth; but he remained a powerful influence on Plymouth government through having largely educated his virtual foster-son Bradford, through the magistrates' habitual consulting of him in all "weighty" affairs, through his unmatched place of honor as original organizer of the Pilgrim church, and through his membership in the oligarchic holding company. Bradford and most of the other magistrates, furthermore, believed with Calvin that the first object of government was to buttress the church; and it is probable that when New Plymouth switched to the Bay's General Court system it copied the crucial feature of Bay politics which made church membership prerequisite to suffrage.

For Plymouth's first five years of existence the Pilgrims expected their Leyden pastor, John Robinson, to join them. During that time Brewster presided over the church as its ranking officer and, after Robinson's death before he could ever sail, he continued to preside over the church regardless of who might be installed in the pulpit with the title of pastor. Although Williams, a sort of resident supply without even the title of pastor or teacher, could have chafed under Brewster's entrenched authority, his friction with the church, so far as we know, arose only over his animus to make it more devout and more purely Separatist. While Brewster's growing doubts about Williams could have sprung from a suspected threat to his ascendancy, Brewster, so far as we know, merely wanted to avoid any doctrinal extremism which might divide the congregation or divide it from the Bay or England. According to Bradford's nephew, Nathaniel Morton, secretary of both Plymouth Colony and Plymouth Church, Brewster sensed that Williams was heading through the same course of rigid Separatism and Anabaptism as their one-time associate John Smyth at Amsterdam. Brewster had, himself, lived in hiding in a Separatist London slum (Duke's Place, Aldgate Ward) before the *Mayflower* sailed; the Pilgrims had many associations in that east-end underground; and they watched numbers of their friends succumb to the powerful appeal of the Mennonite form of Anabaptism in Holland.

Williams would have had to spend much time in the company of Brewster, whatever the degree of their mutual estimation. Brewster's library of some four hundred titles must have provided a continual bulwark to Williams's ministry while he resided in Plymouth. Brewster's favorite author, by the way, was a non-Separatist Cambridge professor, William Perkins, of whom he owned thirteen volumes. Brewster, like Williams, was an alumnus of Cambridge; he spent two years in Peterhouse College, and he had a fabulous store of recollections of the first-generation Separatists. Perhaps Brewster taught him Dutch. No one can say what effect two years of close association with the cheerful old Elder of deliberate utterance, who had known Elizabeth's court from the inside for five years and had met the great Cartwright in person while a pageboy in the Low Countries, might have had on Williams's thinking in subsequent years.

It is clear, at any rate, that in this fresh ferment in Plymouth—its most exciting time in nearly a decade—Williams's mind stirred in equal ferment, extending itself amid battle-tested impressors along several lines at once, with permanent consequences for himself and the rest of New England.

He joined the Pilgrim church—so Bradford expressly states—and therefore subscribed to the covenant its founders had first pledged in the private chapel of Scrooby Manor when Williams was about four years old, the same Brewster presiding on each occasion. The Plymouth congregation did not officially elect Williams teacher although he fully assumed the duties of teacher. He may have scrupled to accept an official call, having decided never to be an elder in any church, but to turn Indian missionary. Or the failure of the congregation to call him could possibly have prompted this resolution. In the less likely latter case, Brewster's suspicions of Williams's tendencies to Anabaptism developed earlier than we had thought. But when Williams suddenly wanted to quit Plymouth, the congregation, despite his jeremiads, tried to detain him. Only then, so far as we know, did Brewster openly advise that it might be best to let the young Jeremiah and his most zealous followers go in peace. Which they did, honorably dismissed.

At the height of Williams's profitable stay in Plymouth, however, Governor Winthrop's momentous visit of state occurred.

5 : *Winthrop Visits Plymouth*

MARGARET WINTHROP had been four months pregnant when the *Arbella* sailed. By the time she followed, the baby was about a year and a half old. Despite the death of two earlier infant daughters named Anne, Governor Winthrop named this one Anne, and suggested that Margaret leave her behind in his sister's tender care, but Margaret could not bear to. She managed to get away on Peirse's trusty *Lyon* about the first of September 1631 with the baby, a son Samuel and a daughter Mary, also John Jr. and his wife. Deane, another son, remained in England to complete his education; he made it over in 1635 in the *Abigail*. Two other sons, Stephen and Adam, had gone with their father in the *Arbella* when they were about eleven and ten respectively. Among the total of some sixty passengers with Mistris Winthrop came the estimable young minister John Eliot, a Hooker disciple. Little Anne died at sea, as did a child of another passenger.

The ship reached Nantasket (which by this time had acquired a mean, ghost-town aspect) in ten weeks, on November 2. A contrary wind held the vessel up at Long Island (in Boston Harbor), but the next day John Jr. got ashore. The Governor went aboard that night. The wind came fair the morning of the fourth, and the *Lyon* moved to anchor before Boston. Winthrop and his family landed with the Captain in the ship's boat, the ship giving them six or seven pieces, and the local militia captains with their companies formed an honor guard amid re-echoing volleys. The Bostonians and most of the people of the nearby plantations brought and sent fat hogs, beef, venison, poultry, geese, partridges, etc.; "so as [says Winthrop] the like joy & manifestation of Love had never been seene in N: E: it was a great marvyle, that so muche people & such store of provishions coold be gathered togither at so few hourse warning." On the eleventh, he concluded, "we kept a daye of thanksgivinge at Boston."

On the seventeenth Peirse fetched Governor Bradford to Boston to join a further festivity of three days, Bradford lodging aboard. (Williams did not, so far as we know, accompany him.) From this time forward, the Bay grew strong and prospered as Cotton said it would at Southampton.

Not quite a year afterward, affairs in the Bay had got well enough in hand that Winthrop could repay Bradford's compliment. He, the pastor Wilson (whose continued delay in going for his wife stemmed partly from Williams's unavailability, although Eliot also declined the Boston teachership), two military captains—John Underhill, who later attempted to arrest Williams in Salem, and Daniel Patrick, whom Williams entertained at Providence during the Pequot War—and some others comprised the party that on a Thursday in late October 1632 went aboard the *Lyon*, whence Peirse ferried them in his shallop to Wessaguscasit at the bottom of Boston Bay, where they stayed overnight. Peirse returned to his ship and unexpectedly to some perilous adventures at sea, while the Governor's party proceeded the rest of the way, about twenty-five miles, to Plymouth afoot, "and came thither within the evening," says Winthrop.

Bradford, Brewster, "and some others" greeted them outside the town, which Winthrop could descry in the dusk rising ahead on the right as his escort led him along the edge of Plymouth Harbor. "The Street" ran from the seaside 1,150 feet straight up the incline. For the first ten yards the going was steep; then came a plateau of gentler slope, which gradually steepened again as it swept on to the hilltop blockhouse 165 feet above the sea. Midway up, another broad street, "the Highway," intersected "the Street" at right angles. Along the two trampled roads the Pilgrims had placed their little peasant cottages of hewn planks and thatched roofs, complete with attic and stone fireplace, each with a garden in the rocky soil behind and to the side, enclosed by hewn planks. The windows had linseed-oiled paper panes that looked orange at evening from the fireplace glow and from cotton-yarn wicks burning in oil lamps. The cottages, standing trim in orderly rows, may have numbered fifty.

Perhaps the Governor's house was already in process of conversion to a solid half-timber structure. Here, in any case, the Pilgrim

dignitaries conducted Winthrop and his party. It was by far the
biggest dwelling and stood on an extra-large lot in the upper corner
on the right, fronting both roads, enclosed by a square stockade
with guns mounted at each corner to enfilade the streets. The Bay
men "were very kindly entertained" in this house, says Winthrop,
"and feasted every day at several houses." Brewster's house faced
the junction of the roads to the left on the uphill street. Standish
and Alden occupied lots directly above Bradford's, on the right-
hand side of this street; Winslow's house stood across the street
farther uphill. Brewster, Standish, Alden, and Winslow were all
moving from Plymouth at this time.

Harvested cornfields lay over the hillside to the right of the
houses. Captain John Smith in 1631 published information he received as early as 1624, when Plymouth numbered about 180 residents, that the town already owned many swine and poultry and
some cattle. At that time, he says, it consisted of thiry-two houses,
though seven had burned. Each of the three open street ends had a
wooden gate; as early as 1622 the secretary of Virginia, John Pory,
reported that a strong palisade 2,700 feet in compass surrounded the
village.

Sunday morning, in lieu of a bell, the beat of a drum summoned
the inhabitants. With grand solemnity they formed a procession
uphill behind the full-robed governor, black-cloaked clergymen,
and scarlet-cloaked captain, together with the honored guests. The
lower part of the thirty-foot-square blockhouse at the hilltop served
for a meetinghouse. The floor above—made of thick sawn plank and
stayed with heavy oak beams—served as a fort commanding the surrounding country. Smith preached, Fuller led the psalm singing out
of Ainsworth, and Williams assisted with scripture reading. The
Bay men partook of Communion; as in the Boston church, this
involved genuine wine, from a single chalice.

At the afternoon service, Williams propounded a question for discussion; this was the Pilgrim custom in their less formal second
service. His question: whether an unregenerate person should be dignified by the title "Goodman," that being the way free, respectable
citizens were addressed who ranked below gentleman, gentlemen
being addressed "Master." Smith spoke briefly to the question, taking the negative. Williams then preached the sermon, elaborating
the negative. He and Smith had, in fact, begun to disquiet the town
with their insistence about this issue, which grew out of the radical

economic transition Plymouth found itself undergoing, in which the Pilgrim leaders raised everybody one social rank higher than he had or could have affected in England. The two Separatist clergymen did not object to raising social rank, but they contended that it went against Scripture for the state to designate who was a good man, goodness being a state of the soul and beyond state jurisdiction.

Elder Brewster spoke following Williams's sermon, then several others of the congregation; and Brewster (who undoubtedly had taken the affirmative) invited Winthrop and Wilson to speak to the question. Winthrop distinguished between a theological and a moral goodness. When juries were first used in England, he said, it was usual for the crier, after calling the names of persons fit for that service, to bid them all, "Attend, good men and true"; whence it grew to be a civil custom in the English nation for neighbors to call one another "Good man such an one"; and it was a pity, Winthrop concluded, now to make a stir about a civil custom so innocently introduced. What Wilson added went unrecorded, but he doubtless seconded Winthrop and Brewster. Anyway, says Cotton Mather, Winthrop's prestige was such that his speech put an end to the dispute. Williams held his peace after once fully stating his view, but in Providence later he saw to it that everybody called each other "Neighbor."

Deacon Fuller "put the congregation in mind of their duty of contribution," says Winthrop, who with his fellow visitors, joined in walking down to the Deacon's seat, dropping in their offering, and returning to their places for the benediction.

In the course of the entertaining, Williams and Winthrop had ample opportunity to indulge in reminiscences, resume an old argument or two, transact some business about cattle, and further discuss Williams's Indian-mission intention, which they had already talked of by mail.

After four days in Plymouth, Winthrop and his party left at about 5 A.M. the fifth day (Wednesday the thirty-first), Bradford, Brewster, and Smith (Williams is not mentioned) going with them nearly half a mile out of town in the dark; others went another ten miles along the way, and Bradford lent Winthrop his own mare. The woods would still have been crimson, the sea air not yet cutting. Winthrop says the Wessaguscasit planters "bountifully entertained" that evening again, "with store of turkeys, geese, ducks, etc.," and the next day, he concludes, his group "came safe to Boston."

6 : *The Ghosts of Separatists Past*

To us Williams is unique, but to the Pilgrims he would have been curiously familiar. If the pattern of his thought reminded Brewster of John Smyth, his doctrinal positions and dauntlessness must have recalled to the Pilgrim old-timers half a dozen or more of the stalwart Separatist preachers their own tradition had been bound up with. He must have reminded them of their revered pastor Robinson in his inflexible younger days, and of themselves in the first fury of their covenanting. Time tamed the Separatists. Almost to a man, the original Separatist leaders who had scandalized English orthodoxy wound up mellow and moderate, even if remaining un-reconstructedly stubborn at the core: they all stayed Puritan. If Williams reminded the older Pilgrims of themselves a quarter of a century earlier, it would have been selves they had largely out-grown. They had come a long way on the road to the ultimate moderation which the notorious Separatists a generation earlier had trod.

One would hardly have guessed in 1632 that Brewster himself had shared their original radicalism. He long lived in the ramshackle, thirty-nine-room, moated manor house at Scrooby. Because neither the seldom-visiting Archbishop of York, who had slickly filched the Scrooby fief from the Crown, nor his lessor and eldest son Samuel Sandys, to whom he had indentured it, occupied it in person, Brew-ster in effect reigned as lord of the manor and thus the biggest man in the sleepy Scrooby vicinity. Since succeeding his father as bailiff, he had tended to go beyond his means in helping to procure Puritan preachers for the churches in that fenland. When he gath-ered the grave little congregation of mostly youthful tenant farmers from the surrounding northern Nottinghamshire villages who in the winter or early spring of 1607 pledged to "walke in all his wayes, made known, or to be made known" and thereby became a revolutionary band, Brewster was a family man of forty, seasoned by nineteen years in the responsibility of his manorial stewardship. Bradford says he had a "humble and modest mind" and "a peaceable disposition, vnder vallewing himself." "Sweet Brewster" was the characterization of an unidentified contemporary in a poem preserved in Morton's *Memorial*. Brewster told Bradford that he got his Puritanism—was "first seasoned with the seeds of grace and vertue" —while a student at Cambridge. The congregation he at last gathered was not, of course, the same as the village congregation that met in Scrooby's small stone parish church but a selection of outright Puritans from villages of the whole area. It met in the semisecrecy of the manor chapel beginning probably sometime in 1606, when King James's government cracked down on Puritanism anew.

Richard Clyfton, whom Brewster engaged as the first pastor of his "underground" church, had evidently just been silenced in the royal crackdown; for Clyfton had long openly avowed Puritanism in his pulpit at Babworth, six miles southeast of Scrooby. John Robinson, M.A. Corpus Christi College, Cambridge, another freshly unemployed Puritan minister, drifted back to the vicinity of his home town, Sturton-en-le-Steeple, about ten miles southwest of Scrooby. For a while he attached himself to Smyth's congregation at nearby Gainsborough but finally threw in his lot with Brewster's as assistant pastor.

These rural idealists would at first have regarded themselves as nonseparating Presbyterians, but James's crackdown must have convinced them that no hope remained of further reformation of the established church from within. Given the choice of following James *or* Jesus, Brewster's group made the drastic break on the day they pledged to walk in all *His* ways. In pledging this covenant they secretly declared their independence of the Church of England and constituted themselves an autonomous little religious republic. This made these deep respecters of law and authority at once heretics and traitors; statutes since 1593 had defined the heresy of Separatism as treason. The Scrooby Separatists broke another statute when they tried to leave the realm without royal permission. They got caught. Later in Leyden, the pious and honorable ex-bailiff added the capital crime of sedition to his capital crimes of heresy and treason by his furtive propaganda-printing; he went ignominiously into hiding from authorities who hunted him both in Holland and England and sailed on the *Mayflower* under an assumed name (Williamson). Brewster in his forties confronted English authority in exactly the spirit that Williams confronted Massachusetts authority in his late twenties and early thirties.

Bradford's vagueness about the date, place, and circumstances of the covenanting at Scrooby increases a suspicion that Smyth's congregation, which met just across the Trent north of Scrooby, covenanted jointly with them. Smyth was the most renowned Puritan in the vicinity at the time of the Pilgrim covenanting. A thoroughly grounded scholar, he had worked his way through Christ's College, taken his M.A. in 1593, received ordination as an Anglican priest in 1594, and continued at Cambridge as a fellow. He must have shown an early impressiveness, because the city of Lincoln chose him preacher on September 27, 1600. But on October 13, 1602, the city deposed him for having "approved himself a factious man in this city by personal preaching, and that untruly against divers men of good place." Williams himself could hardly have brought on his own deposition quicker. Smyth's second published book shows him yet a long way from Separatism in 1605, but he soon suffered a nine-month period of doubt and soul-searching in or around Gainsborough, eluding the pursuivant and falling severely sick at the home of his disciple Thomas Helwys at Bashforth.

Robinson probably was but one of several members of the Scrooby congregation who had also been members of Smyth's at Gainsborough. His statement that Smyth's "instability, and wantonnesse of wit [unsettled judgment?], is his sin, and our crosse," dates from 1610, after Smyth's "betrayal," yet implies an earlier identification of Robinson's group and Smyth's. As for Clyfton, a letter of his to Smyth in 1610 reads as if it were acknowledging that Smyth had some years before converted him, too, to Separatism. Since both the Scrooby and Gainsborough groups made their way to Amsterdam during the same summer of 1608, it would appear that they jointly planned their exodus and intended to reunite, perhaps under Smyth, in Holland. Smyth's connections in Lincoln would help explain the selection of a point in Lincolnshire as the rendezvous for the first departure attempt, and might also help explain the assistance arranged for the Pilgrims by Lincolnshire families on the failure of the second attempt. A further possible inference that the two groups acted in concert is a letter of 1608 from the rector of Halstead, Joseph Hall, addressed to Smyth and Robinson as "Ringleaders of the late Separation in Amsterdam." Smyth's views published immediately before the exodus would authoritatively expound the Pilgrim position of that period. Smyth in fact gives a version of the very covenant in question in his *Differences of the Churches of the Seperation*, 1608: "It is our covenant made with our God to forsake every evill way whither in opinion or practice that shalbe manifested vnto vs at any tyme."

Almost on hitting Amsterdam, Smyth succumbed to the influence of the Waterlanders, the mild branch of Mennonites (Mennonites comprised the dominant variant of Anabaptism in the Netherlands, or "Waterland"). Smyth first caused a schism in his own congregation by persuading a majority of it in 1610 to submit to rebaptism. He started by baptizing himself, in the absence of anyone he could recognize as authorized to perform the rite. Later, he decided he had been mistaken in the matter of authority and evidently regarded this second baptism invalid. (Williams went through similar phases in Providence.) The reversal occasioned a second split, but the first had already been the irreparable one, because it brought the break with his able lieutenant Helwys.

Helwys held to the authority of the Apostolic succession, whereas Smyth, like Williams later, asserted it had lapsed. Smyth and a number of his all-the-way followers applied to be taken into the Waterlander church, within which he continued to reside at Amsterdam and to magnify first this doctrinal detail, then that. His persistent *seeking*, however, brought him ultimately to a peaceful composure of mind and a kindly tolerance. He came to see, he said, that it was a waste of time to be fighting about "the outward church and Ceremonies" and that such differences should "not cause me to refuse the brotherhood of anie penitent and faithfull Christian whatsoever." He died of tuberculosis at the end of August 1612. It is not probable that a single Pilgrim had forgiven him enough to travel from Leyden to Amsterdam to attend the funeral in Niewe Kerk on September 1.

Clyfton, who may have fallen more fully under Smyth's spell than the rest of the Scrooby group, also gets short shrift from Bradford. About fifty at the time he accepted Brewster's call to Scrooby, he was "a Graue and fatherly old man" with "a Great white beard," Bradford remembered him; "sound and orthodox hee alwaies was and soe continuewed to his end." This is laconic and skimpy praise for the Pilgrims' venerable first pastor, who led them out to Holland. The tradition is that Clyfton remained behind in Amsterdam because of being too infirm to make the further move to Leyden. But he was not too infirm to succeed Ainsworth as teacher of Johnson's church in Amsterdam. Francis Johnson had been a tutor of Clyfton's back at Cambridge, which association may have paved the way for the Scrooby congregation's merging with Johnson's church after the expected merger with Smyth fell through. When Johnson's church split, the Pilgrims sympathized with the Ainsworth faction—except for Clyfton, who left his Scrooby flock to side with Johnson.

An obscure author, John Dayrell, said in 1617 that Robinson left both Johnson's and Ainsworth's church. If this is correct, the Scrooby Pilgrims joined or communed in Johnson's church, seceded under Ainsworth, and then without a rupture resumed their individual identity in Leyden. Bradford does speak familiarly of Ainsworth as a pastor, and nothing would have been more natural for the newly arrived Pilgrims than to attend Johnson's flourishing church of some three hundred in the Bruinistengange ("Brownists' Alley"), Amsterdam. It had been holding forth there since the early fall of 1597 and was known as the Ancient Church, being both the earliest of the English exile groups in that booming silk-manufacturing city and also the core of the old Greenwood congregation of London, which had been called the Ancient Church. Brewster could have known Johnson at Cambridge. Anyway, the high esteem in which the Pilgrims held the Cambridge martyr Henry Barrowe would imply their honor of Barrowe's successor Johnson. Barrowe's blunt, scathing attacks on the Anglican establishment made him the leading Separatist until his execution, when Johnson carried on as the Separatist of most distinction before about 1610. Both men had been members of the congregation of John Greenwood, an alumnus of Corpus Christi, Cambridge, who turned Separatist sometime before 1589, viewing his congregation a successor of the Marian-exile companies rather than followers of Robert Browne. Bradford describes Barrowe as a flourishing courtier—the opposite type one would suppose as radically flouting tradition—yet Barrowe's treatises even more than Browne's laid the doctrinal foundation of later Separatism.

Before Johnson's congregation got to Amsterdam, it experienced at Campen, Holland, in 1594 the same defection to the Mennonites that the Smyth congregation later knew in Amsterdam. The real issue at that time, of course, was not rebaptism, which gave Anabaptists their name, but their belief in free will; and Robinson held firm with Johnson in the Cartwright-Calvinist position. Johnson was an estimable and even-tempered scholar. One wonders if Robinson did not find him a model for his own restraint. "A man of note," is Robinson's final reference to him.

Johnson had the reputation of being highhanded. The altercation between him and his associate Ainsworth drove him to contend that the Biblical injunction "Tell it to the Church" meant "Tell it to the Elders," whereas Ainsworth, backed by Robinson, said this meant "Tell it to the congregation." Thus the Barrowist position represented by Johnson came to be identified as oligarchical and the Ainsworthian as democratic. The Pilgrims sided with Ainsworth who, though a more selfless person than Johnson, was actually more rather than less strict. Certainly he was no democrat; "if the multitude gouern," he said in his book *Counterpoyson*, "then who shalbe gouerned?"—a question John Cotton safely repeated in a letter to Lord Saye in 1636. Robinson, though he intimated he might tolerate a democratic civil government, explicitly agreed with Ainsworth that the government of the church should be aristocratic. Cotton contended for more democracy in church government than this reputedly liberal Separatist faction, but the object of the Separatists, while they did inexorably tend toward democracy, was not democracy. Democracy waited for some time to become an object of Williams's Separatism long later—and then in civil government only. Confusing as it has been to many students of Williams, he never advocated democracy in church.

The crux issue at stake between Johnson and Ainsworth undoubtedly stemmed from even hotter matters than doctrine. It might possibly have arisen over their rival translation of the Psalms; both versions were distinguished, though mid-century Presbyterian spokesmen considered both of them hard and harsh. (Johnson reintroduced psalmody in the Ancient Church, which had dispensed with it in London.) But the trouble all apparently began with Johnson's brother-in-law George, who intemperately assailed Johnson in print for his religious convictions. Then the plain people who largely comprised Johnson's congregation talked about his wife's dressing too fashionably, with specific allusions to her plunging neckline. Johnson had married her, a widow, in 1594. His worst luck, however, came from a circumstance he was long unaware of: a member of his congregation, Mrs. Judith Holder, an attractive prostitute, had been making a killing among the pillars of the church. One suspects that Johnson thought such a matter improper to bring before the total membership and that the opposing faction merely wanted morbid excitement.

After the Ainsworth faction seceded, it engaged the help of the Dutch government in forcing Johnson's faction from the meeting-house. Johnson led his half on to Emden, Holland, but returned to Amsterdam in a few years and there died in 1617. In the fall of 1618 his elder, Francis Blackwell, took the pastorless congregation of 150 on its ghastly death voyage to Virginia. In the summer of 1619 Ainsworth at Amsterdam and the Pilgrims at Leyden learned the stabbing news that Blackwell together with 130 of their former brethren had died aboard.

THE ONLY clerical leader close to the Pilgrims, outside of Robinson, whom they did not break with before they left Europe was Henry Ainsworth. "Hee euer maintained Good Correspondence with mr Robinson att Leyden," says Bradford, "and would Consult with him in all matters of waight both in theire [Ainsworth's and Johnson's] differences and afterwards." It was Ainsworth's excellent psalter of 1612 that the Pilgrims took to Plymouth as their most used and treasured volume next to the Bible; through it their old friend exerted his constant influence upon the colony until Plymouth adopted the *Bay Psalm Book* (because it was easier in their then-decayed state) in 1681. Williams, who un-Puritanically reiterated that music was a gift of God, sang from Ainsworth's psalter both in Plymouth and Salem. He surely read Ainsworth's exegeses and tracts, though specifically mentioning only Ainsworth's *Annotations* on the Pentateuch; and he and Ainsworth had a number of mutual acquaintances besides certain of the Pilgrims—for instance, William Pynchon and Sabine Staresmore.

Staresmore in 1644 published notes on Ainsworth's last sermon and wrote a refutation of Cotton's letter to Williams printed in 1643. (Bradford preserved a letter of Staresmore's dated February 14, 1618.) A member of Jacob's non-Separatist congregation in London in 1616, Staresmore a few years later—having first served a jail sentence when Johnson's elder, Blackwell, betrayed him to the bishops—could not enter either Johnson's church (under the temporary pastorate of Nicholas Lee since Johnson's death) or Ainsworth's because he had not fully separated, but he was accepted in Robinson's church in Leyden in 1624 apparently without further covenanting. Robinson's repeated intercession for Staresmore did not induce Ainsworth to receive him without a total renunciation of the Church of England. So Staresmore at last formed an Independent (non-Separating) congregation of his own in London, but continued to commute back to Amsterdam.

Bradford recalls Ainsworth in 1648 with the greatest admiration and affection as "a very Modest & bashful man" who "Concealed his wants from others, . . . very learned, . . . Amiable and sociable, . . . Inocent and vnblamable, of a meeke speritt and a Calme temper void of Pasion and . . . not ezely prouoked and yett hee would bee something Smarte in his style to his opposers in his publicke writings; att which wee that haue seen his Constant Carriage both in publicke desputes; and the Mannageing of all Church affaires . . . haue sometimes Marueled." He was exceptionally gifted at explicating Scripture; "thinges did fflow from him with the ffacilitie plaines and sweetnes as did much affect the hearers"; though deficient of voice, his preaching was powerful. "In a word," Bradford concludes, "the times and place in which hee liued were not worthy of such a man." Here and there this description sounds strikingly like Williams, especially the learning, the amiableness, the blameless life, the eloquence, and the occasional, uncharacteristic smartness of style.

Ainsworth declined out of a Puritan conscience to take a degree though he attended four years at St. John's and Gonville-and-Caius, Cambridge. He developed into one of the ablest Hebrew scholars of his time; Cotton joined in commending his exegesis of the Pentateuch. Ainsworth improved his mastery of Hebrew by associating with Jews while at Cambridge, which reminds us of Williams's unconventional freedom from anti-Semitism.

On the question of whether the Church of England could claim legitimate authorization somehow from Christ, and so whether it was a true or false church, Ainsworth held precisely as Williams in Massachusetts and New Plymouth. Robert Browne, who more than any other single person originated the Ainsworthian, Williamsian, and Pilgrim version of Separatism, held the Church of England to be reformable, therefore essentially a true church. Browne eventually returned to the Church of England as a parish priest though never reconciling himself to bishops. Barrowe, about the same time as Browne's separation-with-optimism, concluded the Church of England to be a *false* church beyond reformation. The gallows soon got him. Smyth, until late in his career, agreed with Barrowe, but the Barrowist Johnson held otherwise, with Browne. Robinson in Leyden, as late as 1618, pronounced the Church of England false, while permitting private communion with Puritans who remained within it. Later he reached the fully tolerant position of Smyth. But Ainsworth adamantly to the last declared the Church of England a false church, renouncing religious communion, public or private, with anybody who had not completely severed all connection with it. Thus the Williams of Boston, Salem, and Plymouth days, on this issue which caused his sharpest immediate differences with his fellow Puritans, was an Ainsworthian Separatist. In other ways he was a Smythian Separatist, a Johnsonian Separatist, a Barrowist Separatist, a Robinsonian Separatist, and a Brownist Separatist.

Both Ainsworth and Robinson, and perhaps also Brewster, found themselves at various times closely exposed to the influence of Browne. Circumstantial evidence is strong that it lingered in the consciousness of Williams. If we may accept George Potter's inference of 1920 that Williams read the eminent Anglican apologist Sir Thomas Browne because he was the only writer then using the word "tenent," which Williams brought sensationally into currency, it may be more certainly inferred that he read Robert Browne, who introduced the word "hireling" in application to ministers, which is the probable origin of Williams's book title, *The Hireling Ministry*, whence the Quakers apparently took up the term. Much stronger, as circumstantial evidence of influence, is the congruence of Browne's and Williams's ideas in the same basic pattern.

Ainsworth was born in about 1570 at Swanton Morley, Norfolk, a yeoman's son the same as Bradford and Robinson. Just a year or two before Ainsworth went to Cambridge, Browne gathered his notorious Separatist congregation in nearby Norwich, which incidentally was Justice Coke's home town. Whether Brownism affected Ainsworth then or after his matriculation at Cambridge, it was as a Brownist that he shipped off to Ireland after four years. He was so poor that he subsisted for some time there, Bradford says, on "Rootes boyled." When his friends found out his true circumstances, they saw to it that he lived better; but "being a single younge man and very Studious [he] was Content with a little." It was not poverty, according to Bradford, but close scholarship that impaired Ainsworth's health. He presumably was still a Brownist when he struck up the ill-fated alliance with Johnson and became teacher of Johnson's church sometime late in 1597 or early 1598. He may never have disavowed his Brownism. In 1607 he married a young widow from Ipswich, Marjorie Appleby, and they had a daughter. The decision of his faction of the congregation to secede from Johnson's Barrowist half came on December 15, 1610, and went into effect the next day, following a full year of written and spoken debate between the two factions. Ainsworth's normal sweetness of temper lived on in his versification of the Psalms, but his actual career exhibited little of the "singing merth" he extolled, or of the conviction he intoned that "I shal to length of dayes, repose-me-quietlie." He died in acute agony, of the stone, in 1622.

Shortly after Browne had left, Robinson arrived as a preacher at Norwich—as Brewster had reached Cambridge shortly after Browne left there. Robinson found a remnant of Browne's original congregation still bravely holding forth at Norwich. Also, St. Andrew's, where Robinson preached, together with another church in Norwich, had the right by purchase of the patronage to elect their own ministers. Though the two churches stayed subject to episcopal discipline, this feature may have colored both Browne's and Robinson's congregationalism.

The Pilgrims did not like to be called Brownists, because Brownism popularly connoted radicalism, contentiousness, and rebellion, whereas the Pilgrims deeply wished to be conservative, peaceable, and respectable. Browne also had the unsavory reputation of beating his wife. He said he did not beat her as his wife but as a curst old woman. Finally, he betrayed his own movement and returned to the Anglican fold at a moment when the Pilgrims could not countenance reversion. But it was for the loosely used crime of Brownism that the High Court of Commission served a process on Brewster in December 1607, and in the Pilgrims' first precarious years as Separatists, they were in fact Brownists, whatever other name they wished to go by.

While temporarily turned schoolteacher after graduation from Cambridge, Browne had concluded that the world was out of joint and "the vvofull and lamentable state off the church" the basic cause. Facing facts squarely as he found them, he saw no eventual alternative but to bolt the church outright. In January 1581 in Norwich he covenanted his Separatist congregation and in 1582 in Middelburg exile justified the step with his famous *Treatise of Reformation without Tarrying for Anie*. In this *Treatise* he makes the following Williamsian statement: that the civil magistrates "may doo nothing concerning the Church . . . but onlie to rule the common wealth in all outwarde Iustice. . . . but to compell religion, to plant churches by power, and to force a submission to Ecclesiasticall gouernement by lawes & penalties, belongeth not to them."

Robinson in time approached this position. But Browne meanwhile recanted, rejoined the state church, and wrote his tract, *A New Years Guift*, which says magistrates do have the power of judging ecclesiastical causes (which the Pilgrims grant in their *Seven Artikles* drawn up for the Virginia Company in 1619) but that they should exercise their power as prescribed by God and see to the purity of ministers and membership. In other words, he ended up with the identical point of view on the function of the state as Calvin and Cotton. Williams, when he joined the Pilgrims at Plymouth, took with him *both* their pre-Leyden rigidity of Separatism *and* Robinson's post-*Mayflower*-sailing opposition to civil coercion of conscience. He held equally with Browne's first position, against civil coercion and for strict purity of worship. Browne gave up this position—just as Robinson gave up his earlier rigid Separatism—and adopted a position Williams argued epochally with Cotton against. So Williams was a Brownist and a Robinsonian, but he stands unique in holding to two extremes of Browne and Robinson without giving up one or the other as each of these men had relinquished one in passing from an earlier to a later extreme.

WILLIAMS drops many hints that his mind had been shaped in part by the writings of Robinson, and he came in for an extra heavy dose of Robinson's influence by way of the greenness of the revered pastor's memory among the Pilgrim nucleus dedicated to his precepts. But Williams's book which eventually became *The Blovdy Tenent* (1644) curiously began in July 1637 as a refutation (for the benefit of gleeful Bay clergymen who called it to his attention) of Robinson's *Treatise of the Lawfulness of Hearing of the Ministers in the Church of England*, posthumously published in 1634. In 1652 Williams called Robinson "a holy, wise, and learned man" and referred to a manuscript he saw, undoubtedly in Plymouth, in which Robinson observed that such persons as had turned Catholic, believing Popery to be the truer way to heaven, were ordinarily more conscionable, loving, and peaceable than thousands who went by the name Protestant. Robinson carried this line of thinking farther in his later works, and Williams followed him. Robinson concluded in his magnum opus, *Observations Divine and Morall*, published the year of his death (1625), that

the ancient Fathers . . . pleaded against all violence for Religion, true or false; affirming [Robinson's marginal note here cites Tertullian] that *it is of humain right and naturall libertie, for everie man to worship what he thinketh God: and that it is no propertie of Religion to compell to Religion, which ought to be taken up freely.*

"No authoritie of man," Robinson goes on, "may bring into, or uphold in the Church either Doctrine, or Ordinance of Religion, or person." Here he had come round to the original position of Browne's *Treatise of Reformation*. Robinson's final tolerant position is that

A man hath, in truth, so much *Religion*, as he hath between the Lord, and himself, in secret, and no more. . . . Yea who can say with how little, and unperfit Faith in Christ both for degree, and parts, God both can, and doth save the sincere in heart?

The proper end of religious actions, he says, is not civil society "nor is attainable but by faith, and devotion in the heart of the doers." Many other passages also take a viewpoint later found in Williams's works; for instance, this one, where Robinson equally brings to mind Jonathan Edwards:

We usually call obstinate Errour in the foundation Heresie: but the Scriptures many times seem rather to place it in the peruersnesse of the will, and affections [emotions], whether the matter be great, or small; then in the errour of the judgment.

Williams insisted on the same distinction, though he put it in his own way: "What is this Heretick?" he asks in *The Blovdy Tenent*. "[It] is no more . . . then an *obstinate* and *wilfull* person . . . and is not such a *monster* . . . as most *Interpreters* run upon, to wit, One *obstinate* in Fundamentalls."

Robinson, says Bradford, was a man "not ezely to be parraleeled for all things"; he had learning, "solled Judgment," and "a quick and sharp witt," also a tender conscience and great sincerity in all his ways, "a hater of hipocresie and desimulation" who would deal plainly with his best friends, yet who was courteous, affable, and sociable. His quickness and precision in debate impressed the Pilgrims, and he "was euer desirous of any light." He, furthermore, gave direction in civil affairs well, foreseeing dangers and helping those in need, "& so was every way as a commone father." The persons who most drew his ire were such as thought of themselves before the common good and such "as would be stiffe, and riged in matters of outward order."

He had so reluctantly turned Puritan in the first place that he temporarily resubmitted to the prelates' spiritual jurisdiction around 1605. But faced with further submission or complete revolt, he chose the latter, even though this meant that followers who resorted to him at his home in Norwich got excommunicated. (Compare followers of Williams resorting to his home in Salem after he had been sentenced to banishment.)

Robinson was a *wary* revolutionary. But once separated from the Church of England, he swung on far counter to his basically moderate nature. His longest treatise—507 pages in the small-print modern edition of his works—was *A Jvstification of Separation from the Church of England*, published in 1610. It was the most sustained of many men's replies to Richard Bernard's *The Separatist's Schisme*. Bernard waxed as the Puritan vicar of Worksop, Nottinghamshire; his attack stung the Separatists all the more in that he knew Smyth and Robinson as a neighbor and denounced their Separatist decision at the critical interval between their covenanting and their flight to Holland. Smyth also wrote a reply; he of all people charged Bernard with being "changeable as the moon." Robinson bided his time and so could incorporate a reply to Bernard's reply to the first defenses as well as to Bernard's opening blast. This major effort of Robinson's appears to have been what established him and decisively matured him. Before he produced it, he does not seem to have been taken with full seriousness even by the Pilgrims; afterward, he commanded international respect. The book is orderly, logical, and dispassionate. It does not have Williams's compelling vitality, but we could wish that Williams had followed Robinson's method of refuting by topic instead of by sentence.

In 1611 Robinson took on none other than the chief prophet of nonseparating Congregationalism, Dr. William Ames, in a running dispute which blossomed into their celebrated *Manvduction* exchange of 1615, when Robinson was thirty-nine years old. At one point Robinson punningly referred to Ames as "Mr. William Amiss." (Bradford once called him "doctor Amesse.") But Bradford says the argument in the end was "lovingly" composed, evidently alluding to the conferences with Ames, Jacob, and Robert Parker during their visits to Leyden, which many later claimed won Robinson over to non-Separatism. But Robinson seems to have felt cool toward Ames ever after; he completely ignored Ames in his final writings though citing other eminent theologians by the score. Except for championing the one work of Ames that Brewster published in Leyden, the Pilgrims never noticeably warmed to the ailing asthmatic.

By 1615 the issue they clashed over had shaken down to whether the servants of God—the saints—should commune spiritually with the apparently wicked. Ames's *Manvduction* attacks Robinson's inconsistency in opposing such communion while not scrupling to associate privately with "godly persons" who remained "polluted" in not, themselves, having made a clear-cut separation from the unregenerate. This is the identical issue, it hardly needs pointing out, that initially and decisively divided Williams from the Pilgrims and Puritans in New England and led inexorably to nonplus political controversy. Robinson's reply, *A Manvmission to a Manvduction*, recalls a sermon he had heard of the Cambridge preacher Robert Baynes which reiterated that God had separated between light and darkness and thus between the regenerate and unregenerate (or children of darkness). Robinson holds firm on the purity of public worship at the same time that he redefends the legality of seeking light from contaminated worthies, which contact, he argues, does not affect public worship. Robinson regretted that the Dutch, who allowed the Separatists refuge, did not strictly enforce the Sabbath. This is one of the reasons Bradford lists for the Pilgrim decision to quit Holland. In this stage of his thinking, Robinson definitely favored government enforcement of Congregationalism and of universal church attendance, including the majority who could not qualify for membership. Here Robinson took the exact position of Cotton which Williams came to deplore. But all three, along with Ames, felt that saints and sinners could profitably meet together in the same room—that the saints might in fact aid in the regeneration of the sinners. It was participating together in actual membership and in the sacraments which brought pollution.

Soon after the Pilgrims reached Leyden, Robinson began associating familiarly with the Leyden University faculty. He formally joined the University corporation on September 5, 1615, which membership entitled him to receive, free of town and state duties, half a tun of beer every month and about ten gallons of wine every three months. He led the curious dual life of leader of an exile minority group and at the same time a scholar-teacher amid a withdrawn but international society of distinction where his views coincided with the Dutch-Calvinist (equivalent of Presbyterian) majority.

The very scholarship that sent him in dogmatic righteousness back to the primitive church, rejecting all present "error," had the salutary effect of deepening his familiarity with the early church fathers, who probably, in the last analysis, brought the relaxation and partial reversal of his course—as when he discovered that Tertullian thought religion ought not to be compelled. His favorite author, incidentally, was Seneca.

The views of Robinson which proved hardest for him to moderate as he fully matured were those respecting the relation of church and state. In his final position he still thought that heresy was a crime and that the magistrate has the right to see to his subjects' spiritual conformity, yet that Christians are subject only to Christ with the right of civil disobedience, at least passively. This was an old dilemma. Williams took it by the horns and denied the right of the state to define heresy or stipulate it as a crime. But, for Robinson, this would have been to give up his most cherished ideal. Underneath his painful threading between the Scylla and Charybdis of his church-state convictions runs a constant longing for a commonwealth in which the civil government might enthrone the church of his conception and guarantee its effective direction of the whole society. This was the longing which also took Congregational Puritans to Massachusetts Bay.

THE EPITHET "rigid," often later applied to Williams, gained currency when Browne and others of that time repeated Cartwright's old attacks on bishops and "Popish disorders" but repeated them shrilly, if not savagely. "Rigid" connoted uncompromising, narrow extremism that threw off all of Cartwright's gentlemanly reasonableness. The "rigid" zealots lashed out like animals at bay but usually calmed down after a while if they survived. They were not by nature chronic malcontents but reacting equal and opposite to the situation of pain and frustration which trapped them. Though the

Pilgrims had once felt pushed to the wall, their Amsterdam experience of sectarian wrangling made them recoil from aggressive rigidity and to seek quieter hearths in Leyden. They, however, did not forget that much of the Separatists' fault in the turn-of-the-century commotions arose as a reaction to hard treatment:

> . . . for theire Ridged and Roughness of Speritt as some of them especially mr Barrows is Taxed [says Bradford] it may be Considered they were very Ridgedly and Roughly dealt with not onely by the Lords enimies and theire enimies but by some Godly persons [Puritans] of those times differing in opinnions from them.

Bradford therefore inclined to excuse much of Williams's excessive Separatism. The Pilgrims proved more willing than the Bay (outside of Salem) to give Williams a hearing, in spite of having been cured of much of their own youthful rigidity. They did not feel, either, by 1631 the desperation to get their commonwealth set in the proper mold before it got out of hand, which the Bay was then experiencing. But the Pilgrims also indulged Williams partly because they had been consciously dedicated from the first to finding new truth, whatever the source. To this extent they and Smyth alike shared Williams's innate Seekerism, which grew naturally out of a questing Separatism. This questing element grounded both Separatism's further growth and its disconcerting shifts of position. The Pilgrim covenant itself disclaimed omniscience. Robinson based his farewell sermon to the smaller half of his church, which was about to depart for Delftshaven and Southampton, on the dynamic implication of the covenant—not to stand still, deluded that they knew enough truth to be complacent, but to keep searching with open minds.

The Puritans' profession of liberty of conscience to choose freely always gave their various parties trouble when they persisted in sanctioning conformity. It was on the very basis of the Christian liberty which James I denied, that his loyal Pilgrim subjects departed the fold of the state church. Back in 1604 Smyth, at the time he was becoming the probable line-layer of the Pilgrims, appears to have had a hand in drafting *An Apologie for those ministers that are troubled for refusing to Subscription and Conformitie*, presented to James on behalf of the Puritan preachers of Lincoln diocese. It pleads for "Christian Libertie, *which Christ hath purchased for vs by his death, and which all christians are bound to stand for.*" "Stand fast in the liberty wherewith Christ hath made you free

(Gal. 5:1)" became a battle-cry text of Robinson, quoted on the
title page of *A Manvmission to a Manvduction* in 1615. Smyth and
Robinson clearly foreshadow Williams and William Penn (Penn
wrote a book *Christian Liberty*, as did Luther, *et al.*). "For you
were called to freedom, brethren," Paul also said in Galatians. When
Brewster and his congregation deliberately broke the law and the
unity of the realm, they did so because they felt that true Christians
had an unalienable right to liberty. They thought themselves as
much the Children of Israel oppressed in Egypt as the Hebrews
whom Moses led out in freedom to the Promised Land. As Bradford
explicitly states, the Scrooby Pilgrims

shooke of this yoake of Antichristian bondage. And as the lords free people, joyned them selues (by a Couenant of the Lord) into a church
estate . . . to walke in all his wayes, made known, or to be made known
vnto them (according to their best endeaours) whatsoeuer it should
cost them.

It was this covenant that Williams repledged with the Pilgrims
when he joined their church about twenty-four years later.

7 : *Salem*

IN SPITE of the circumstances of Williams's departure from Salem in 1631, he accepted the call of the church there to return in 1633 and made the move probably in June, well before the birth of his first child, Mary, in August. Samuel Skelton's approaching end from the tuberculosis that caused him to look shockingly older than his thirty-nine years, and that had already killed his colleague Higginson, made the church desperate for someone to assume most of the burden of five services a week. Williams vigorously leaped to the preaching breach but, true to the intentions he expressed to Winthrop in 1632, did so as a free agent and not as a formally installed elder of the church. Skelton lay on his deathbed in the early summer of 1634, thus leaving Williams in sole charge of the pulpit, whether he held formal office or not. Probably because no one then could legitimately administer baptism or the Lord's Supper, Williams finally saw no tenable course at the moment but to accept the congregation's election as teacher in July. The fact that the Governor's Council had him under question when the congregation went through with this election put Salem Church, not just Williams, in serious jeopardy from that date. Skelton died August 2, 1634.

It appears improbable that Williams returned to Salem out of a false conception of affairs in the Bay, or out of revenge for his previous treatment there, or for any reason except a growing dissatisfaction with what he diagnosed as waning religiousness in Plymouth and a desire to give emergency help to his old friend Skelton and Skelton's church. Once back, of course, it was inconceivable that he would preach any other view of the truth than his own, or preach it with any regard for his security. He did not likely alter his 1632 intention to devote himself to the Indians, although he might have wavered when Skelton's death left him holding the bag (or plum). He seems to have regarded this whole second stint at Salem as temporary from the first—or as only temporarily tenable—and to have continued preparing for his Indian mission all the while he occupied or co-occupied the pulpit. We know from Wood that Williams already had learned the Indian tongue by the time he returned to Salem. We know from Williams's deed of December 6, 1661, that he negotiated treaties with Ousamequin (Massasoit's new name) and the Narragansett grand sachems in 1634 and 1635 when he presided as sole minister of Salem and when he may have seen the handwriting on the wall. Finally, we know from his statement of November 17, 1677, that he continued from time to time to lodge with the Indians "in their filthy smoke holes" while he lived at Salem, as before, while he lived at Plymouth.

Skelton and Williams had a certain affinity in bias. They, for instance, together opposed the fortnightly meeting of Massachusetts ministers in October 1633 as a step toward Presbyterianism and a state church. Winthrop and others felt offended at the imputation, but time proved the Salem duo correct. Skelton even shared Williams's Separatism to some extent. Hubbard, at Ipswich, suggests as much late in the same century when he states that in one year's time Williams filled Salem with principles of rigid Separatism and tendencies to Anabaptism, leavening the people with "many strange notions" and "partly also confirming the people in some which they had imbibed from Mr. Skelton."

Skelton had hailed originally from Coningsby and probably attended the grammar school at Horncastle which the first Earl of Lincoln had founded. He worked his way through Barrowe's alma mater, Clare Hall, Cambridge, 1608–11, took an M.A. in 1615, and wound up back in the (now fourth) Earl of Lincoln's bailiwick. He baptized Dudley's daughter Mary at Sempringham on July 23, 1620, and must have performed the secret marriage of Isaac Johnson and the Earl's daughter Arbella at Sempringham in April 1623. (Though no one ever betrayed the way young Johnson managed his marriage over his father's objections, it could legally have been performed only by the curate of the parish where the license was issued—i.e. by Skelton.) Skelton naturally knew Cotton, the famous vicar of nearby St. Botolph's and served as chaplain to the Earl at both his Sempringham and Tattershall castles. Untraceable tradition holds that Endecott sat under Skelton's ministry in Lincolnshire—whether that meant a day or two or a long period. Lincolnshire may have got confused with Salem, where Endecott certainly did sit under Skelton's ministry and also Williams's.

On August 6, 1629, Skelton and Higginson, with Endecott, gathered the Salem church, the first Congregational church in the Bay. Bradford and others deputed from Plymouth, delayed by contrary winds, came in during the solemnities and gave the right hand of fellowship. It is quite unnecessary to postulate Pilgrim influence on Salem to explain the Congregational form of the Salem church, but it is true that Plymouth and Salem had already found a rapport. Fuller, who attempted to help Salem during the 1629–30 dysentery epidemic, if not before, admired Endecott as a second "Burrowe." Plymouth and Salem had had several years of commerce and mutual interest in Cape Ann before Boston existed; many of the 1633–34 inhabitants of Salem had first lived in Plymouth (whether amicably or not), including older ones like the founder Conant and newer ones like the group the Plymouth church dismissed to follow Williams. Through most of the seventeenth century Salem behaved in many ways more like Plymouth than Boston. To mention one symbolic illustration, Salem early adopted the *Ainsworth Psalter*, which the Pilgrims cherished, in preference to the traditional Anglican psalter popularly known as *Sternhold and Hopkins*, or to the *Bay Psalm Book*, which soon displaced *Sternhold and Hopkins* in the rest of Massachusetts. The *Ainsworth Psalter* got so entrenched in Salem that the congregation did not finally relent under conforming pressures and turn to the Bay book until 1667.

Who introduced the *Ainsworth Psalter* from Plymouth to Salem? Williams's close friend Fuller could have, since Skelton probably asked that valuable visitor to lead the psalm singing in Salem services. Higginson could just possibly have been using *Ainsworth*. But it is most probable that Williams, who in his old-age debate with the Quakers expressed a greater concern for music than any other Puritan of the seventeenth century, introduced this musically superior version, especially since Williams had grown used to the Pilgrim customs, which seem as a whole to have crystallized his thinking, and since he took with him a part of the Pilgrim church who had also grown used to its ways, including Williams's preaching.

By the time Williams returned in 1633, Salem must already have assumed an old established air with a habitual port activity, surely no longer lacking an alehouse and some sort of market, even if every householder remained his own butcher as yet and thought of himself as essentially self-sufficient.

William Wood noted in 1633, when Williams had settled in Salem, that the neck where most of the town's houses stood consisted of very bad and sandy ground, though he had to admit that for seven years together it had brought forth fine corn, being fished every third year. The number of springs he saw hard by the seaside almost seemed to belie the acute water problem of three years before. Beyond the river at the north, and the other at the south of town, the inhabitants had taken farms, planted corn, and regularly gathered hay. John Josselyn, Wood's observer counterpart of the second half of the century, mentioned thirty-five years later the store of meadow and arable land in the plain about Salem, as well as some very rich merchants then residing in the town.

What struck Wood most about Salem was its dwellers' custom of crossing the rivers to their farms and meadows in canoes, which they made of whole pine trees and which measured about two and a half feet wide by twenty long. In these, he said, they also went fowling, sometimes two leagues to sea. "There be more canoes in this town than in all the whole patent, every household having a waterhouse or two." If Williams had not already acquired his canoe skill while based at Plymouth, he surely would have now. He never owned a horse; so, when he did not walk, he characteristically canoed.

Broad Street (all of four rods wide)—long later renamed Washington Street—connected the two rivers of the neck where they came nearest to each other. In 1634, while Williams alone occupied the pulpit, Salem at last completed its first meetinghouse, by which time it had already proved too small for the growing population. It occupied the northern portion of the acre lot of the dead teacher Higginson which bounded Broad Street and South River. Higginson's widow turned the lot proper, with the residence, over to Williams. So it was in Higginson's former house that Williams lived in Salem. The house had two stories, two rooms per story. The meetinghouse stood fifty-six feet north of this structure. The parsonage, or pastor's house, stood on the same street still closer to South River. (One William Browne, Sr., acquired this Skelton house in 1643, but it had to be taken down in the late summer of 1644 because it seemed in danger of collapsing.) When the aggressive little preacher Hugh Peter migrated to Salem, he took up residence nearby on the same Broad Street, in a different house. Endecott was another of Williams's neighbors on this street, and the fort commander Samuel Sharpe another. (Sharpe had been one of the small founding group of Salem Church; his name appears first on the church's roll of full members, ahead of Endecott's, which is second; Roger Conant's is fifth.)

From sometime before Skelton's death Williams was holding both the long morning and the long afternoon service on Sundays in addition to three weekday services—not to mention baptisms and funerals—and correctly described his ministerial labors at Salem as "excessive." On top of this, as he told Cotton Jr., he wrought hard at the hoe for his daily bread, as he had at Plymouth. In his *Mr. Cottons Letter Examined* he elaborates that he toiled "day and night in my field with my own hands, for the maintenance of my charge"; then his frequent summonses to court at Boston or Newtown meant "travels also by day and night to go and return," all of which, he says, brought him "near unto death," under the care of two physicians. We know that, besides, he journeyed among the Indians many days away to negotiate, probably to give religious instruction as well as further his own language study, and to truck.

Presumably he fell into textile merchandising in the course of his wanderings among the Indians from Plymouth, which, at the time of his residence there, operated a little empire of trading posts. He greatly expanded his business with the enlarged wholesale opportunities of a port like Salem. Salem had quickly become a more consequential port than Plymouth in itself but, besides that, had readier access to Boston shipping. Williams told his old friend, Major John Mason, in 1670 of "the Yearly losse of no small matter in my trading with English & Natiues" from being exiled and "debard from Boston (the chiefe Mart & port of New Englands)." He hints at the scale of his operations out of Salem in the next clause: "God knows that many thousand pounds can not repay the very temporary Losses I have sustained."

Farming, traveling, trading, preaching, appearing in court, and progressive frazzling from his yeasty contentions with the Bay produced serious illness and, before that, a leechlike fatigue; chronic fatigue in turn helps explain his inflexible insistence on the pure primitive church at any cost, his seizure upon petty doctrines which he erected into major issues, and his irritable and narrow censoriousness. He did not preach liberalism or tolerance at Salem. In contradiction of some of his later-developed arguments, he preached

stringently for the correction of sin, which, he felt certain, invited
divine wrath upon the community. In his *Blovdy Tenent* of 1644 he
recalls an occasion at Salem

> when in the apprehension of some publike evils, the whole Countrey
> profest to humble it selfe and seek God, I endeavoured (as a faithfull
> Watchman on the walls) to sound the Trumpet and give the Alarum:
> and upon a Fast day, in faithfullnes and uprightnesse (as then and still
> I am perswaded) I discovered 11 publike sins, for which I beleeved (and
> doe) it pleased God to inflict, and further to threaten publike calamities.

While showing how unraveled his thought remained along some
lines as late as 1644, this also indicates something of the acerbity of
his Salem preaching.

As to his shotgun assault on women who did not wear veils in
church, men who took off their caps to pray, and anyone who addressed an unregenerate person as "Goodman" or falsified God's
worship by tendering an oath, or accepted the cross of St. George
in the British flag, etc., we must remember that this overworked,
overwrought extreme Separatist, who impetuously and uncompro-
misingly hugged a religious position already out of date in half its
tenets even in Puritan America, was after all only about thirty years
old in 1634. His petty radicalisms—which, of course, to him loomed
as integral parts of the all-superseding will of God—on the other
hand expressed a basic discontent, if not outrage, and the form it
took somewhat smoke-screened the underlying soundness or valid-
ity of its motivation. He felt the Bay system had been fundamentally misconceived and was fundamentally betraying its own ends,
but he had not clearly formulated his negative prognosis or distinguished the source disorder from the unrelated or relatively incon-
sequential side effects. Most of the Bay leaders, however, detected
the seriousness of his assault from the beginning.

The surviving documents are silent as to the reaction of the
young Separatist Williams and the ageing non-Separatist Conant to
each other when Williams lived in Salem. Church attendance was
compulsory at Salem even for nonmembers. Conant, however, had
been one of the original thirty members who solemnly consented to
Higginson's draft of a covenant on August 5, 1629. The prospering
fur trader would have heard Williams a minimum of five times
weekly and occasionally received him in the course of pastoral
visits.

The Old Planters had moved, about 1630 onwards, from the south side to the north side of Bass River to form the Salem subdivision called Bass River Side or just Bass River and later Beverly. This concentration of Presbyterian-sentiment West Country people did not prove disruptive at all. The large disruptive element must probably be sought, rather, in the unusually high concentration of ex-servants—people the Company sent over as a labor force but had to free when it could not feed them. They had not been recruited as religious emigrants and likely did not fully share the Puritanism of the leaders, let alone nonseparating Congregational Puritanism. The eighty persons Dudley says had died in Salem from the winter's epidemic before the Winthrop fleet arrived, plus the languishing survivors who died shortly after, were not all servants. But even if they had been, the remainder who suddenly escaped their indentures would have formed a sizeable semi-alien element in the community and in the church assembly, which the government obliged them to attend irrespective of membership. They provided Williams his most flammable tinder.

A quick consideration of those who ultimately followed Williams out of Salem to Providence confirms this. Four of his first twelve fellow householders in Providence had been members of the Salem church; the other eight had been church *attenders* only—voluntary or involuntary. One of the Providence householders, Francis Weston, had been eminent enough to be elected a Salem deputy, but eight of the twelve, though unbound in servitude, were not voting freemen in Salem; and the householders of Providence do not include the servants who remained servants there. No more freemen came in the first two years of Providence's existence, so that its population of about sixty was eleven-twelfths nonfreeman in origin. The history of Providence indicates that the Salem defectors to Providence consisted largely of people glad to be relieved of the church-going importunity, despite the side-by-side religious tenacity of a small, radical minority.

The *perfunctorily* religious ex-servants at Salem would have been highly susceptible to any appeal against the status quo; while the religiously excitable ex-servants would have been more susceptible as a group than others to narrow, radical evangelism. (It was rowdy, close-cropped *apprentices* at this time in London who agitated against bishops and royal officials and were derisively called roundheads, the name that soon denominated the Puritan party in the civil war.) Salem also had a high proportion of *non*servants who showed

Separatist susceptibility. Skelton may have encouraged tendencies in that direction, and we have noted that Endecott was banishing Separatists before any servants had been freed in Salem.

Salem as a whole presented a greater receptivity to radical appeal than any other place at that time in America, and Williams for a year or so had more authority and fewer checks upon his radical leadership than he would have had at Salem or elsewhere, or did have elsewhere, at another time. The consociation of churches had not quite materialized to bring strong interchurch pressures toward conformity; the central government had not quite consolidated its supreme civil authority over the commonwealth; Williams's colleague Skelton tended to agree with him and, anyhow, died, leaving Williams alone and unbridled in the pulpit; Endecott, the magisterial power of Salem and only feasible source of bridling at this time, later bowed to central authority but just now gave his full official sanction to Williams, fervently sharing his censorious sentiments. Williams drew people to his cause by his absence of opposition at home, also by his learning, zeal, eloquence, warmheartedness, and sterling character. In one year he converted Salem into a stronghold of radical Separatism and threw the entire colony into an uproar.

8 : *The Way the Sentence and Flight Came About in the Intensifying Political Crisis*

ON June 12, 1633, Winslow and Bradford pulled into Boston Harbor and stayed a week with Winthrop, primarily to press a joint enterprise to beat out the Dutch, who were about to build a trading house on the Connecticut and corner the beaver and hemp trade there. Winslow was now governor of New Plymouth, by Bradford's instigation.

Back in 1631, Dutchmen of New Netherland commended the Connecticut to the Pilgrims as a place to plant and trade but soon wished they had not, in view of a potential rivalry. Indians from the Connecticut brought the suggestion directly to Plymouth anyway, in April 1631. The sachem (i.e. chief) Waginacut of the Podunks and Natawanut of the Metianucks, tribes in the later Hartford-Windsor vicinity, personally invited Bradford to establish a trading and Pequot-resisting settlement there; but the Pilgrims had their hands too full to be more than halfhearted just then. Williams may have seen these sachems in Plymouth or, if he had not yet sailed south, in Salem, where they broached their suggestion to Endecott. Endecott sent them to Winthrop with the handsome young sachem the English called John Sagamore and other of the friendly Massachusetts Indians. Winthrop gave them and their escorts a dinner but sent no one back with them to the Connecticut.

In the early spring of 1633, however, some of the chief Bay men proposed a joint trading venture on the Connecticut to the Pilgrims. Bradford and the other members of the Pilgrim holding company (who had an absolute monopoly of New Plymouth commerce until the colony debt should be retired) were slow to respond. When they did begin to wax enthusiastic, the Bay men got cold feet—as

Bradford and Winslow now found out in the conferences that began in Boston on June 12.

Winthrop explained that three or four thousand warlike Indians inhabited the Connecticut, that only small pinnaces could get into the river because a bar at the mouth allowed but six feet at high tide, that it was a violent stream, and that ice made it unnavigable seven months of the year. So, Winthrop concluded on behalf of the Bay, "we thought not fit to meddle with it."

Another subject undoubtedly discussed was Captain John Stone, a hearty Virginian who was making merry in the bustling town of perhaps four hundred people as the distinguished magistrates deliberated. On his way to New England with a cargo of cattle and salt, Stone had touched at the infant settlement of New Amsterdam and got gay drinking with Director Wouter van Twiller in the Fort. With van Twiller's roisterous consent, he nearly made off with a Pilgrim pinnace which arrived during the party, but some incoming Dutch vessels intercepted. When Stone reached Boston on about June 5, the fiery little Captain Standish hove in hard on his heels to prosecute him for piracy. Winthrop bound Stone to appear in the admiralty court in England but asked Standish to advise the Pilgrim magistrates to withdraw charges. Stone and van Twiller, temporarily sober the day after the horseplay at Manhattan, had apologized in writing, but above all, the Bay hated to turn to higher or outside jurisdiction. The fact that Stone stayed the summer in Boston may indicate that the Pilgrims agreed to forget him very slowly.

Winthrop, Winslow, and Bradford all feeling some closeness to Williams (the four of them had, in fact, been together in Plymouth eight months before), they must have conversed at length about Williams's precipitate departure from Plymouth to Salem, which presumably had occurred by this date. It may have been in the course of this Boston conference that Winthrop learned of Williams's tract written at Plymouth which disputed the right of Massachusetts and New Plymouth to their lands. The tract asserted that all Englishmen here lay under a sin of unjust usurpation and that King James was guilty of a solemn public lie for claiming this territory as his. At whatever time Winthrop heard of the "book," he demanded to see it and Williams sent him the manuscript. Winthrop may not have got wind of the tract until late November, or he may have pigeonholed it while dealing with bigger matters that it might merely have complicated.

Bradford and Winslow returned home to a horrible epidemic of "pestilent fevers" which killed more than twenty in their colony, including Fuller. In spite of everything, Winslow decided to compete with the Dutch on the Connecticut without the Bay. The very month of the Boston conference, Captain Jacob van Curler raised a "slighte-forte" with two cannons near the site of later Hartford and called it Fort Good Hope or House of Hope. About August, Winslow boldly ordered a band of Pilgrim men under Lieutenant William Holmes to ensconce on the river *above* the Dutch fort.

As the "great new" Pilgrim bark neared Fort Good Hope, Captain van Curler bade it strike and stay or be shot. The Pilgrims kept going. Van Curler threatened hard (says Bradford), but the Dutch shot not. Holmes landed his band a mile farther on, at the site of later Windsor, bearing a house frame ready to raise. They quickly nailed and clapboarded it and landed provisions. Those remaining as a garrison—probably already from this moment under the direction of Jonathan Brewster, the Elder's oldest offspring—dismissed the bark back. By the time word could get to Manhattan and a force of seventy Dutch soldiers arrive to assault the Windsor post, the Pilgrims had it well palisaded and mounted, whereat the Dutch preferred a parley and quiet departure.

On July 4, meanwhile, Winthrop launched his thirty-ton bark, *Blessing of the Bay*, on the Mistick at Medford, the work of William Stephens, shipwright. Partly because the free-roaming hogs gorged themselves on the Bostonians' unabundant corn harvest this lean summer, Winthrop sent the new bark forth on a voyage of trade and investigation to the Connecticut after all, on about August 26.

Bostonians luckily found plenty of fish and fruit to compensate for their scarce corn, and on September 4 they thrilled to the arrival of the *Griffin*. John Gallop in his fishing shallop piloted the three-hundred-ton vessel in by a new route (thereafter called Griffin's Gap). The two hundred disembarking passengers included the clergymen Cotton, Hooker, and Hooker's close associate Samuel Stone, along with the exceedingly substantial gentleman, John Haynes, a devotee of Hooker and a future governor first of Massachusetts and then of Connecticut.

Hooker, the supercharged ("cholerick" is Cotton Mather's word) but highly disciplined forty-seven-year-old leashed lion of a preacher who had been used to swaying thousands, proceeded on to Newtown. It is interesting, in view of his reputation in America for championing the rights of common men, that he should have allied himself with the leading reactionary of the colony. Cotton stayed in Boston and accepted the teachership which Williams and Eliot had declined. Eliot, the day after he landed, had gone on, by apparent prearrangement, to Roxbury, as teacher in association with the pastor, Thomas Welde, who had preached in association with Hooker at Chelmsford. Roxbury, two miles southwest of Boston, presented in some ways a more respectable and exclusive prospect than Boston at that time. Wood says the inhabitants of Roxbury were "all very rich," with "fair houses, cattle, impaled cornfields, and fruitful gardens." They had more in common with Newtown than with Boston, sharing each other's lecture days, for instance.

Eliot, when fresh out of Jesus College, Cambridge, had served as usher in the "little academy" Hooker kept at Badow, near Chelmsford. Here, says Eliot, "the Lord said unto my dead soul, *live*." So many ministers from the neighboring towns (including Peter and Shepard) came to consult Hooker that he conducted a monthly meeting for them. Until the government silenced him at Chelmsford, even that un-Puritanical Earl of Warwick, faithful to his family tradition of protecting Puritans, would travel to hear him and doubtless is the one responsible for whisking Hooker to Holland ahead of the pursuivants. Hooker drew enormous crowds in and around London about 1625–26 before proceeding for four years to the Chelmsford pulpit, for he preferred to preach the Gospel to masses of the poor, says Cotton Mather.

The son of parents well-to-do for yeomen, he grew up in Marfield, Leicestershire, in an atmosphere of cultivation and courtesy; "a sensible *grandeur of mind*," Cotton Mather reports, caused those who knew the boy to predict greatness for him. While a fellow at Emmanuel, after taking a B.A. from Queen's, Cambridge University, he went through an especially wrenching religious convulsion which ever after gave him remarkable insight into the ministerial treatment of emotionally disturbed persons. He was a disciple of that Ramaean professor in Queen's College, Alexander Richardson, who died in 1602 at the age of forty-six. In his Holland exile, Hooker sought out Ames, another Richardsonian (and Perkinsian), who had been at Christ's while Cotton was at Trinity and Hooker at

Emmanuel. Back in England in order to take ship for America, Hooker hid out in the home of his fellow Emmanuel alumnus, Samuel Stone—in fact, was reproving Stone for smoking a pipe when pursuivants knocked at the door in their search for Hooker. (Stone sent them on a wild-goose chase.) Hooker had preferred Cotton before Stone as his co-minister in America; Cotton's remaining cordially independent of Hooker even in England is provocative.

Cotton was a short, dumpy man of forty-eight with a cool temper and a ruddy, cheerful countenance. Cotton Mather, whose mother and father both could give him intimate recollections of Cotton, claimed his face had an inexpressible sort of majesty which commanded reverence from all who approached him. The Connecticut Historical Society portrait that purports to be Cotton at sixty-five shows little of any such majesty but a rugged, coarse-featured, clean-shaven divine with an exceedingly alert, confident, and good-humored expression. He displayed a serene and impartial civility to all. Williams in 1652 recalled Cotton's even temper and "former sweet peaceable disposition." "All men that know Mr. Cotton," said Winslow in 1646, "know his moderation, wisdome and piety." He spent ordinarily twelve hours a day in his study legalistically unraveling Scripture, fragmenting and analyzing each sentence; he would "Anatomise the sense," as Edward Johnson said, which makes his sermons boring to read yet gave them a scholarly authority in actual delivery which gripped his listeners as much as Hooker's trenchant and colorful style. The noted librarian Zoltán Haraszti, in proving Cotton's authorship of the *Bay Psalm Book* preface, contrasts Cotton's "quiet flow" and "slow persuasiveness" with the "blunt force" of Richard Mather, to whom the preface used to be attributed. Cotton, however, had a liveliness in speaking that is lost in print. Wilson averred that in the pulpit Cotton seemed to become the very prophet or apostle he was expounding; his presumed portrait decidedly confirms an animating presence, under control. But his superrationalism or legalism, together with a dearth of imagination, filters his printed words of vibrancy. (When he pushed conventional Puritan allegories to an extreme, such as his interpretation of the tremulous *Song of Songs* in terms of the church institution, he did not become "the least legalistic" theologian in America, as Perry Miller says, but the most, showing up his unimaginativeness to the point of absurdity.) Like Ames and, to a lesser degree, Calvin, he missed the poetry and the mystery of Scripture. Yet these must have been a basic motivation of his anatomization, as of his habitual praying alone up to six hours at a stretch.

The son of a devout lawyer of Derby (126 miles northwest of London), he had gone through grammar school there and matriculated at Cambridge at the age of thirteen. The hardest Hebrew was already simple to him, and, he admitted, his studies became an addiction. He resisted the powerful pull that bold William Perkins, the celebrated fellow at Christ's College, exerted on him toward Puritanism, because he feared Puritanism would interfere with his studies. Walking in a field when he heard the tolling bell proclaim Perkins's hourly expected death, Cotton felt secretly glad to be freed of him; but a sense of guilt for such a feeling soon afflicted him, making him vulnerable to a sermon of Richard Sibbs, master of Catharine Hall, about regeneration; he became a posthumous follower of Perkins. (He confided these details to his close friend John Norton, who became the commanding minister of Ipswich.) Cotton gained fame in 1608 by an elegant funeral oration in Latin, with all the flourishes of the Ciceronian style, for Dr. Robert Soame, master of Peterhouse. This took place in St. Mary's, the University church, and earned him a return invitation. The second time, he did not "flaunt, as before," says Samuel Whiting, who may have been present (and eventually became pastor at Lynn, near Boston, Massachusetts), but made "a plain, honest sermon." His student audience registered disappointment, but Cotton on that day reached maturity if not stature and never after used his vast learning for show. He took three degrees from Cambridge—two from Trinity and one, the bachelor of divinity, then a rare and very high degree, from Emmanuel—and also served as head lecturer, dean, catechist, and tutor. He was the most learned man in America before Increase Mather of the second generation. Winthrop surely knew such a distinguished graduate student during his two undergraduate years at Cambridge; this was, of course, a full generation before Williams reached Cambridge.

The bishop of the diocese in which Boston, Lincolnshire, lay did not want Cotton to assume the Boston pulpit, because of his youth or his Presbyterianism or both, and Cotton nearly returned to the University. But somebody seems to have bribed the bishop (Puritans were pragmatists; they played to win, not just put up a righteous front), and that bishop's successor made life exceedingly pleasant for the young vicar. If Cotton held to the Prayer Book, he found himself unable to "digest the ceremonies," and his abandonment of them after three or four years in Lincolnshire encountered no barriers from above, until 1632. He married a girl named Elizabeth Horrocks in Balsham, Cambridgeshire, in 1612, having undoubtedly met her through her brother, a famous preacher in Lancashire. She died in 1630. They had had no children. On April 25, 1632, he married a widow, Sarah Story. She outlived him, and married the widower Richard Mather, whom she also outlived. She and Cotton had three sons and three daughters, all but the eldest born in America. It was the second son, John Jr., who had the brilliant record as reform pastor of Plymouth Church until adultery undid him. It was the youngest daughter, Mary, who wed Increase Mather, who grew up as practically a brother to her in the same house in Dorchester. *Their* son, Cotton, was born in John Cotton's old hilltop house in Boston in 1663.

A summons went out in 1632 to the High Court of Commission for Cotton and Hooker. Together, they "gat out of England with much difficulty," as Winthrop puts it, all the places being belaid to take them. They slipped aboard the *Griffin* with their families at the Downs and reached Boston, Massachusetts, in eight weeks. On the way across, the first Cotton child was born; his father, calling on all his imagination, named him Seaborn.

It is not likely that Cotton, any more than Williams, came to America prepared to accept the holy experiment as he found it. We shall see that he maintained the "Antinomian" heresy concerning justification against all his entrenched colleagues, to his peril. Yet he must have adapted rapidly, for him, if Williams's testimony is correct that Cotton clung to the Prayer Book as late as July 1629. Dr. Robert Baillie, an eminent Scotch Presbyterian historian in London, gave credible indications in 1646 that Cotton did not agree to Congregationalism until after he got to America. He, however, emerged as the principal apologist for the Bay "way" in the 1640's. His tremendous academic prestige, plus prior association with eminent Bay families back in Lincolnshire, plus his dominance of the church of the capital and his inevitable association with Winthrop, who sat on the magisterial bench of honor down front during Cotton's sermons, consolidated his authority, which was such, says Hubbard, that, even more than Hooker, anything he advocated in the pulpit soon became an order of Court or a church practice. When Cotton abortively tried to model the Massachusetts code of law after the "judicials" of Moses, he was obeying Scripture as he saw it, not his own will. His course toward bigotry and even cruelty did not come out of a cruel and bigoted nature but out of a dedication to "His ways" whatsoever that should cost. To be sure, whenever "crime" has been confused with "sin," the rule of law has become more severe. But it appears to have been the rule of law, not the rule of Cotton, that Cotton stood for.

Hubbard says that the Bay was not big enough for both Cotton and Hooker, but as the official historian as well as an orthodox clergyman, he may have been continuing the old policy of concealing the real rift, or even the fact of rift, in the inner structure of the colony. We shall presently glimpse something of that rift, which went deeper than any theological or temperamental differences between the two outstanding ministers who arrived in the Bay aboard the same ship.

Within a few days of their arrival, that restless enterpriser John Oldham and three companions returned from the Connecticut carrying hemp and black lead. He reported the distance overland to be about 160 miles and the Indians friendly all the way. Oldham, always dignified by the title "Master," had some kind of private affluence before coming to America, since he arrived a decade before with ten employees. His closeness to the Gorges interests gave him additional social and economic power, and he was an able and intrepid gentleman to begin with. The Pilgrims had welcomed him to the deliberations of their council after he overcame the anti-Separatist contempt he originally brought with him to Plymouth. Then in 1624 he fell under the subversive influence of the Presbyterian clergyman Lyford and got banished with him. A year or two later, he had another change of heart toward the Pilgrims. It came about when he started for Virginia on a boat that nearly did not negotiate the death-trap shoals on the back side of Cape Cod. In his fright he realized he had wronged his hosts. The Pilgrims gladly reinstated him in their good graces once more—even made him their agent in the deportation of a more incorrigible troublemaker, Morton of Merrymount. Oldham's land and business demands caused the Massachusetts government some exasperation both in London and Salem during the pre-Winthrop rule of Captain Endecott. But following at least three more moves after settling in Nantasket, he wound up an honored citizen of Watertown in the Winthrop regime's good graces—though in the better graces of those elements of Watertown, Newtown, and Dorchester which tended to dissent from the Boston-Winthrop leadership and who came close to dethroning it in the years 1633–37. Oldham survived malaria following a voyage to Virginia and prospered in an ever-wider trading circuit after returning to New England.

The evening of September 11, 1633, Captain John Stone threw a farewell party, and someone later caught him prone in a cornfield with one Barcroft's wife. Public-spirited Puritans haled him next day before Winthrop, who reluctantly required Stone to stay in town a while longer for trial. Stone left Winthrop's house only to seek out the highhanded magistrate Ludlow to badger for being a pompous ass. Ludlow reacted strongly, raised a detail, and returned Stone to Winthrop, who this time put him in irons under guard. When Ludlow was safely away, Winthrop directed the irons removed.

A "great jury" pondered the indictment for adultery, a capital crime. They found Stone *ignoramus* because of only one witness. For his "other misdemeanors" the Court fined him £100 but did not actually levy it and ordered him to return no more to the Bay without license of the Court, on pain of death.

Stone shoved off for Virginia, by a roundabout route. First he went north to Sir Ferdinando Gorges's settlement at Agamenticus (Bristol, Maine) to take on a Captain Norton, then coasted all the way back around to the Connecticut, intending to do business with the newly established Dutch post nearly twenty leagues upstream.

The *Blessing of the Bay*, long at large, got into the Connecticut all right. Its reconnoiterers also noted the treacherous appearance of the Indians of Long Island, who had canoes that would carry as many as eighty men, and enjoyed the hospitality of Director van Twiller at Manhattan. Van Twiller, however, sent along a letter to Winthrop warning him that Holland claimed Connecticut. The *Blessing* reached home on October 2. She had not encountered Stone's pinnace. For more than four months after Stone's departure from Boston Winthrop heard nothing of him.

On October 10 the Boston church formally installed Cotton as teacher. On the eleventh the Newtown church formally installed Hooker pastor and Samuel Stone teacher.

A sixty-ton pinnace, *Rebecca*, was launched at Medford in November. Winthrop shortly turned her over to Oldham to follow up his pioneer trade contact with the Connecticut by sea, on behalf of the Bay.

It was on November 11 that Skelton and Williams raised their joint objection to the fortnightly meeting of ministers which had begun to convene in each other's homes in rotation. The Salem clergymen felt that such a custom would lead to a presbytery and thus an abridgement of individual congregations' liberties. The timing of their protest, if nothing else, indicates that the recent joining of Cotton and Hooker had given these meetings a new turn, in the direction of a closer, more purposeful organization. Circumstantial evidence from many directions points to a determined play for power on Hooker's part in particular (on behalf of the Kingdom, of course, not himself).

HOOKER appears to have had a decisive hand in restoking the subsided hostility of Dudley toward Winthrop that November. The Court of Assistants had decided that the towns conveniently close to Boston Harbor should furnish the labor to finish the fort at Boston and that then the towns at an inconvenient distance should send a proportionable sum of money for the house, the building of which had to be hired out. Most of the towns near Boston had gone through their second round of dispatching labor gangs when Winthrop warned Dudley that Newtown had not yet complied at all. Dudley refused to send any Newtown men because (he said) Salem and Saugus had not yet brought in money for their share. Winthrop patiently explained the Court decision by letter and asked him to send in his neighbors for further discussion. Haynes and Hooker forthwith arrived in Boston to treat, bearing a blistering letter from Dudley. Winthrop said he would leave the matter to the Court and handed the letter back to Hooker with the words "I am not willing to keep such an occasion of provocation by me." He sent back with these emissaries a letter inviting Dudley to send for a fat hog; for Dudley had indicated his need of one or two. Dudley replied: "Your overcoming yourself hath overcome me." Skinflint though he was, he insisted on trading for the hogs (he got two). Two days later the Court ordered Newtown to go through with its work commitment.

Here is a quick review of Dudley's opposition to Winthrop before Hooker complicated it:

Everybody shifted as best he could in the desperate dispersion-time of the late summer and fall, 1630, to prepare against winter. But just as cold weather set in decisively, the Council agreed to locate a fortified capital at what came to be called Newtown, on the tacit understanding that all the leading men would settle there. Dudley, who did settle there, accused Winthrop, who did not, of breach of promise in August 1632. The *ministers* deliberated and found Winthrop at fault for moving abruptly from Charlestown to Boston without consulting Dudley and the rest of the Assistants. Winthrop acknowledged himself faulty—and remained in Boston.

Before Dudley's blowup that August he had been seething for many months. On April 3, 1632, he walked out of a meeting of the Court of Assistants and wrote Winthrop his resignation. Winthrop said simply that it was "not allowed." Dudley told the Assistants on May 1 that "his main reason was for public peace; because he must needs discharge his conscience in speaking freely; and he saw that bred disturbance." The Assistants decided unanimously that he could not leave his place but by the power that put him there. He nevertheless refused to continue to the General Court, which convened on the ninth.

What most infuriated Dudley was Winthrop's summoning him to an Assistants' meeting at his house about Dudley's "oppressing usury" in selling seven and a half bushels of corn to some poor men of the Boston congregation for ten bushels after harvest. Dudley retorted with "hot words"; if he had thought the Governor had called him there to give him such usage he would not have come; if the Governor thought his deal unlawful, "it was his weakness." Winthrop bore these speeches, he says, "with more patience than he had done, upon a like occasion, at another time."

The General Court re-elected Winthrop with Dudley deputy-governor, May 8, 1632, and chose John Winthrop, Jr., one of the Assistants. They also adjudged Dudley's resignation a nullity; but he and Winthrop had had one of their periodic reconciliations the day before, and as Winthrop records, "all things were carried very lovingly amongst all, etc., and the people carried themselves with much silence and modesty."

Winthrop notes under August 3 following, however, that Dudley was still discontented with him. The ministers Increase Nowell (who had sailed as an Assistant on the *Arbella* but had been persuaded that a clergyman should not hold civil office and had become pastor of the newly founded church at Charlestown), Wilson,

Welde, Warham, and John Maverick conferred with Winthrop and
Dudley this August 3 at Charlestown to attempt an amicable settlement "in a church way." First they found in Dudley's favor about
Winthrop's failure to move to Newtown. After dinner Dudley
wanted to know the bounds of the Governor's authority. Here the
hypocrisy first came into the open wherein men like Dudley, who
favored a severer regime, attacked Winthrop on the ground that he
had exceeded his authority.

Winthrop answered that he would challenge no greater authority
than he might by the patent. Dudley: Then he had no more authority than any other Assistant, except power to call courts and preside. Winthrop: He had more; for the patent gave him whatever
power belonged to a governor by common law or the statutes, and
(speaking somewhat apprehensively) demanded Dudley show
wherein he had exceeded that power. Dudley (beginning to be in a
passion): If the governor were so round, he would be round too.
Winthrop bade him be round if he would. So Dudley, as Winthrop
goes on to relate,

rose up in great fury and passion, and the governour grew very hot also,
so as they both fell into bitterness; but, by mediation of the mediators,
they were soon pacified. Then the deputy proceeded to particulars. . . .

1st. By what authority the governour removed the ordnance and erected
a fort at Boston. The governour answered, that the ordnance lying upon
the beach in danger of spoiling, and having often complained of it in
the court, and nothing done, with the help of divers of the assistants,
they were mounted upon their carriages, and removed where they might
be of some use: and for the fort, it had been agreed, above a year before,
that it should be erected there: and all this was done without any penny
charge to the public.

2d. By what authority he lent twenty-eight pounds of powder to those
of Plimouth. Governour answered, it was of his own powder, and upon
their urgent distress, their own powder proving naught, when they were
to send to the rescue of their men at Sowamsett. [While Williams was
residing at Plymouth, the Narragansetts started after Massasoit a hundred
strong. Massasoit fled with all his people to the Pilgrim tradingpost hard
by. Standish rushed to relieve the three Pilgrims there and sent back an
urgent call for more men and provisions to Plymouth. Bradford quickly
entreated powder from Winthrop, who supplied the messenger all he
could carry. This had been March 12, 1632. On March 16 the same
messenger returned to Boston with Bradford's report that the Narragansetts had retired in favor of a fray with the Pequots, as Winthrop could
verify from the flight of John Sagamore, the nearby sachim on the
Charles, and Chickatabot, near later Milton, with all their men in answer

to the Narragansett grand sachim's, Canonicus's call. Massasoit evidently on this occasion or shortly before adopted his new name Ousamequin (Yellow Feather), by which Williams and most others referred to him thereafter.]

Dudley brought seven such charges, which Winthrop answered in the same vein. When Dudley had at last finished, Winthrop reminded the mediators that not only had he not taken advantage of his authority for his own benefit but had disbursed all common charges out of his own estate, in the lack of a public stock, when the Deputy would never lay out one penny. The only conclusion was a commending of the success of the meeting by prayer. Winthrop "brought the deputy onward of his way, and every man went to his own home."

Throughout Thomas Dudley's life the domineering side of his nature got full development. He was born into a military tradition in the first place; his father, a captain, had died in battle, and he himself commanded as a captain at Amiens. He appears to have been brought up in the household of the Earl of Northampton, who may have felt indebted to the slain father or may merely have recognized young Thomas's talents. Thomas had been born in Northampton in 1574. He grew up with a patrician point of view—doubtless helped by the considerable inheritance of £500 when very young. Learning law as clerk to a judge of course strengthened his rigid conservatism. But he remained utterly unostentatious. To his adoring daughter Ann, whom he probably educated himself, he *"was both pious, just and wise. . . . A Magazine of History. . . . In manners pleasant and severe."* It was only the bad people, in her opinion, who feared him. He married Dorothy, a gentlewoman of means (who bore Ann). She fully exposed him to Puritan ministers, who "seasoned his heart." He moved in those circles which enabled him to get the recommendation of a couple of lords, among others, for bailiff to the Earl of Lincoln. In nine or ten years he overcame an astronomical £20,000 debt and put the Earl's estate on a profitable basis. No wonder he would sometimes have seemed irascible, inflexible, stern, and dictatorial in America! It is not too hard to see, either, why the Assistants usually chose him deputy-governor and sometimes even governor, and why Winthrop and Williams, among many others, would have been so fond of the intolerant old man (he was going on sixty in 1633). Winthrop pointedly alluded to Hooker, who did not just happen to be present at the time (January

18, 1636), when he disclaimed any alienation from Dudley since their reconciliation of August 1632 but observed that "of late . . . some new comers had estranged themselves from him, since they went to dwell at Newtown."

DECEMBER 1633 saw renewed ravages of smallpox among the Massachusetts Indians, John and James Sagamore among the fatalities. Cotton's ministry meanwhile caused more conversions among the immigrants and brought more new members into the Boston church than all the other churches in the Bay combined.

On December 27 the Court of Assistants met at Boston to consider the "book" Williams had written in Plymouth which disputed the right of Massachusetts and New Plymouth to their lands. It concluded that King James could have no title except by compounding with the natives. Winthrop betrays the Assistants' real worry when he says that if Williams loved the peace of these churches "he would not (for smale or no occasion) have provoked our Kinge against vs, and putt a sworde into his hande to destroye vs."

"Some of the most judicious ministers," says Winthrop, "much condemned Mr. Williams's error and presumption"; besides self-interest, international law stood solidly against Williams. The Court ordered him "convented" at its next session to be censured (sentenced). Endecott being absent, Winthrop wrote him the judgment with added arguments and asked him to deal with Williams. The added arguments took this tack:

> . . . and if God were not pleased with our inheriting these parts, why did he drive out the natiues before vs? and why dothe he still make roome for vs [through smallpox], by deminishinge them as we increase? why hath he planted his Churches heere?

This philosophy, incidentally, required very little stretching to justify the Bay's imperialistic pretensions against Rhode Island in 1645 which Winthrop concurred in.

> If we had no right to this lande, yet our God hathe right to it [said Winthrop in 1634], and if he be pleased to give it us (takinge it from a people who had so longe vsurped vpon him, and abused his Creatures) who shall controll him or his termes?

Endecott returned what Winthrop considered a "very modest and discreet answer."

Williams also wrote the Governor and Assistants "very submissively, professing his intent to have been only to have written for the private satisfaction of the governour etc., of Plimouth, without any purpose to have stirred any further in it, if the governour here had not required a copy of him; withal offering his book, or any part of it, to be burnt." At the next Court, Winthrop continues, "he appeared penitently, and gave satisfaction of his intention and loyalty. So it was left, and nothing done in it." Wilson and Cotton, when consulted, had helped the Assistants see that the passages in question, "being written in very obscure and implicative phrases, might well admit of doubtful interpretation" and were not "so evil as at first they seemed." Winthrop said in dismay that the treatise indeed exceeded all he had ever read in "figures and flourishes." The Court agreed that upon Williams's retraction or taking an oath of allegiance to the king "it should be passed over." This was January 24, 1634.

Not until the twenty-first, three days before, had news reached Winthrop from the Pilgrim post above Fort Good Hope via Plymouth of what happened to Captain Stone in September on the Connecticut. Two Pequot ambassadors the following November provided Winthrop more details; General Endecott and Captain Underhill learned still others from the Pequots during their punitive expedition of 1636; Captain Mason, Governor Bradford, and an anonymous writer extensively quoted by Increase Mather recorded a few more.

It developed that, just before Stone, a Dutch boat had stopped on the lower Connecticut and seized the grand Pequot sachem Wopigwooit when he went innocently aboard to trade. The Dutch yelled to the sachem's subjects ashore that they could ransom him. When the Indians sent the required bushel of wampum, the Dutch sent back their sachem, slain. The Dutch did this to avenge some Indians the Pequots had killed who were on their way to trade at the new Dutch fort. The Pequots in turn knew that the Indians who were accommodating the Dutch had been making overtures to the Europeans in hopes of acquiring an ally to drive the Pequots back out of Connecticut.

Stone arrived "suddenly after" the Dutch reprisal, according to a Pequot spokesman, as recorded by Underhill. Stone anchored about two leagues from the river mouth, and several Indians who lived in the vicinity—West Niantics, close allies of the Pequots—met the landing party. Stone seized and bound two of them for pilots upriver. But dusk overtook the voyagers before they could reach the Dutch fort, so Stone put the bound Indians and three of his own men ashore in the skiff to hunt fowl (according to the first Pilgrim report). The November ambassadors said that nine Indians— evidently including one or both of the ambassadors relating this to the Bay magistrates—had been watching every move since Stone's first landing downriver and, when the hunters fell asleep that night, killed them to rescue their bound kinsmen.

Wauphanck, whose name we know from references of Williams's, meanwhile led a dozen sannups (warriors) aboard at twilight as if to trade. The ship lay anchored near a steep rock which for at least a generation after this evening was known as Captain Stone's Rock. As the warriors roamed casually on and below deck, Wauphanck personally called on Stone in his cabin and stayed until the drink-saturated captain fell backward on his bunk asleep. Wauphanck then slipped a small hatchet from under his garment and sliced Stone's head.

The other Indians aboard sensed that the time had come for them to act—just as the remaining two to five white men perceived what probably was afoot and ran for the kitchen with the idea of firing the powder magazine and blowing the Indians up. But, as Winthrop had it by the first report, the Indians grabbed already-charged muskets they found in or near the cramped kitchen and trained them on Norton and the crewmen. An unskillful shot by one of the Indians accidentally set off the powder magazine and blew up the deck. Most of the Indians shifted overboard in time. Back in the woods, the nine stalking Indians had just finished the fowlers (the November ambassadors narrated) and were heading for the pinnace to take it when it suddenly exploded into the air. The Indians reboarded, easily dispatched the Europeans who still breathed, plundered the pinnace, and sank it. Ninigret, an East Niantic sachem in the Narragansett confederacy, ominously accepted a share of the spoils.

When the Court of Assistants met to censure Williams for his treatise on land rights, this intelligence about Stone must have worked as much as Cotton's mollifying to relegate the Williams case to minor consequence. Since Stone was a Virginia citizen, the Massachusetts magistrates, in no hurry to get embroiled with Indians on the faraway Connecticut, agreed to write the governor of Virginia moving him to undertake revenge, then to wait for his answer before acting further themselves if at all. One death so many hundred miles distant must have meant little to the harassed governor of Virginia. When, for instance, the squire of Noddle's Island in Boston Harbor, Samuel Maverick, returned from a trading voyage to Virginia August 3, 1636, he informed Winthrop that in the year past eighteen hundred people had died there and, with corn costing twenty shillings a bushel, all that sustained most of the population for a long time was the reddish weed purslane.

On January 20, 1634, the day before Boston's first news of Stone's calamity, Oldham's lieutenant Samuel Hall and two other Bay men who had gone to Connecticut overland on November 3 got back home after having been much of the way miserably lost. They reported that smallpox had spread as far west as any known plantation. Other communications revealed seven hundred Narragansetts dead of the pox, which spread northeast as far as the Indians of Piscataqua. This epidemic, especially among the awesome numbers of the Narragansetts, who had somehow escaped the plague which had decimated their neighbors in southern New England before 1620, came as good news to the Bay. The Lord was making room for His own.

Williams's campaign to veil women in church, in strict accordance with Paul's first epistle to the Corinthians, had progressed alarmingly enough by March 1634 for Cotton to tackle the issue in his lecture-sermon of March 7 at Boston, when Endecott would be present for the sitting of the Assistants. Cotton's common sense, as well as his natural inclination to allay, enabled him to find that the apostle had not commanded veiling in church, though that took some casuistry, since Paul is embarrassingly explicit. Endecott so heatedly upheld Paul, and thus also his pastor Williams, in the discussion period that Winthrop felt obliged to interpose lest the meeting end too discordantly. This is the significant occasion when Cotton first publicly committed his tremendous prestige against his Salem colleague.

On April 1 came the Court order for administering the loyalty oath which freshly fueled Williams's "subversion" for later.

The following month, the freemen of each town met to elect two deputies to the General Court which had been called for May 14. When the elected deputies convened on that date in the Boston meetinghouse, they wished to see the patent. When their reading disclosed that the document empowered them to make all laws, they asked Winthrop about such matters as the Court of Assistants' abrogating certain orders the General Court had made before, like the one for killing swine in the corn. Winthrop explained that the patent had been granted in anticipation of a small number of freemen, as in other business corporations, which would make their lawmaking power feasible; but the freemen (i.e., in the original charter sense, stockholders) had become such an unwieldy number in the Company, few of whom were competent for law-making—and the commonwealth could not afford to spare very many for this function anyway—that they must vest this authority in a select council, by which Winthrop did not mean representatives, or deputies of the freemen but the aristocratic magistrates, or board of directors. The deputies might, however, Winthrop continued, order that the governor appoint a commission to revise and reform laws found amiss and to consent to taxation and land distribution, though not make any new laws themselves; rather, to refer any grievances to the Court of Assistants. The paternal sound of this may be a little misleading. Winthrop's position is more liberal than William Penn's sixty-five years later; it did not reduce or intimidate the deputies into nondiscussion; they, in fact, refused to accept Winthrop's conception of their function; in practice, Winthrop proved amenable to freeman pressure for more power—he is the one who brought up the need to give in in private meetings of the Council. It is true that Winthrop was no democrat, much as he acknowledged a democratic component in the Puritan system. Yet no one—not even Williams —was advocating democracy at this date. As late as Jefferson's Presidential triumph, "democrat" remained a sneer; Jefferson called his aristocratic-democratic party "Republican." What emerges as more significant in the political crisis building in the Bay in 1634 is that Winthrop represented the humane and flexible tendency of the divided Council, and it was along this avenue that democracy had its only substantial hope of developing.

Not merely the deputies but the majority of those likely to be chosen magistrates could be detected beforehand in a mood of revolt. Hooker significantly declined to honor the Court's request to preach the election sermon, pleading unfitness. So the session opened on the fourteenth with Cotton preaching it. He elaborated the doctrine that a magistrate should not be turned out of office and so publicly "convict" without just cause. In effect he said: do not depose Winthrop. He had taken a public stand against Williams; he now for the first time publicly committed himself to the cause of Winthrop.

The deputies did dutifully return Winthrop to the magistracy, as they also returned Dudley and Ludlow and elevated Haynes to that circle. Then the invested magistrates brought Winthrop's reign of a little more than three and a half years to an end with the election of Dudley to the governorship and Ludlow to the deputy-governorship. A more ominous split than one developing between Winthrop and the freemen had developed within the magistracy, paralleled in the clergy. The deputies had, however, arrived for this session aroused. Hubbard revealingly notes that "after Mr. Hooker's coming over, it was observed that many of the freemen grew to be very jealous of their liberties."

Hooker's influence came out in the open the second day of the General Court session, when the deputies from Newtown complained of "straitness for want of land, especially meadow," and asked leave of the Court to enlarge or remove. Whether the Court fully perceived the underlying political discontent in this motion or not, both deputies and magistrates agreed to grant it, and Newtown shortly sent men to reconnoiter northeast in the vicinity of Agawam (which Winthrop Jr. had founded in March 1633 and which the Court later renamed Ipswich, also the river which ran past it) and nearly due north all the way to the Merrimack, presumably the vicinity where Andover later materialized.

The John Humfreys at last arrived early in July 1634, bringing a new supply of cannons, muskets, and powder bought by money donated in England; news of the warrant to stay the immigration of more of the "best" from England, but the release of this ship in order to bring sailors back from the Newfoundland fishing banks on its return voyage; and an ominous letter from Cradock that he had been ordered to give up the charter. Humfrey also brought sixteen heifers, given by an alderman of London, Richard Andrews, to be distributed one to each minister, the rest to the poor. (Wilson immediately gave his to Cotton.) Williams received not only a new heifer but all the Humfrey family as new communicants in his Salem church. In Humfrey he also gained an unflagging supporter of Indian missions. But the four years and four months since Humfrey had last seen the Winthrop-fleet passengers (who survived) had wrought changes which left some kind of unbridgeable gulf between him and them. He seemed disoriented; his impact on the Bay remained indecisive; and from the time he moved to Lynn, between

Salem and Boston, he sustained a series of disheartening misfortunes.

Following the arrival of the Humfreys—perhaps the same day, but before July 9—the *Blessing of the Bay* sailed to do business with the Dutch fort on the Connecticut, and six men of restless Newtown rode aboard intending to find a site for their community to move to on that river. This must have made Winthrop anxious; if he instead of a Newtown and a Dorchester magistrate were now governor or deputy-governor, he might have blocked the auxiliary mission. He must have felt far more anxious at the arrival of a second letter from Cradock (or the same one mentioned twice, which would confirm uneasiness) enclosing a copy of the official order to return the charter. On July 29 the magistrates and clergy resolved to fortify Castle Island, under Ludlow's command. On August 2 Skelton died, with the immediate effect of enlarging Williams's authority in Salem. The Salem problem must have loomed vexingly perplexing to Boston by this time. On August 4 Winthrop acquainted some of the ministers and the convened Court of Assistants with a letter which one of the Gorges Old Planters, William Jeffrey, had received from the twice-banished Morton of Merry-mount, which railed at the Bay and divulged the victory of his long lawsuit against it, that a governor-general had been commissioned to sail to Massachusetts. Winthrop's one-line next paragraph in his *Journal:* "This summer was hotter than many before."

On September 4 the General Court convened at Newtown, doubtless out of deference to the governor, who resided there with Haynes and Hooker for neighbors, and perhaps also as a gesture of conciliation to the people there. For the main business of the Court had developed to be the pressure of the planters of Newtown to move to Connecticut. They gave as their reasons: 1) they hadn't enough room for their cattle, so they could not maintain their ministers or raise more funds from newcomers to help; 2) the fruitfulness and commodiousness of Connecticut, which was in danger of falling to others—Dutch or English; and 3) the "strong bent of their spirits to remove thither." The adequacy of the Newtown area to accommodate an even larger population with much less audible distress later casts doubt on the first reason as the real one. As the magistrates opposing the migration pointed out, the people of Newtown could find an amplitude of meadow within the patent—on the Merrimack, for instance—if they were determined to transfer on account of land. Hooker made a speech to the Court in which he declared it a fundamental error to have set the towns so near each other. This was an indirect attack on Winthrop, who had been governor at the time of the spacing. Winthrop opposed the removal of Hooker's church, "this candlestick," because of the judgment it implied on the Bay's holy experiment and because Hooker's leaving would draw away large numbers and deflect many more from the Bay.

The deputies voted fifteen to ten to allow Newtown's departure. When the magistrates voted separately, Dudley and two of the Assistants favored, but Ludlow and the rest opposed permission. So came the historic dispute over the negative voice (veto power) of the Assistants, which ten years later resolved in the formation of a bicameral legislature.

Israel Stoughton and a young fellow-deputy from Dorchester, "a brother of our Church," Stoughton identifies him, conspicuously opposed Winthrop, who assumed the role of spokesman for the majority of Assistants. Stoughton denied that the Assistants had power, simply by their places, over the persons, goods, and lives of the inhabitants governed. "What is it so?" Stoughton had retorted at one point; "I had thought your poure had been so and not so" (Stoughton does not fill in the arguments his "so's" stand for). Managing to remain deferential toward Stoughton for the moment, Winthrop took the "young" deputy to task "somewhat harshly and unadvisedly," says Stoughton in his extended letter to his West Country brother in England; but Winthrop afterward went to Stoughton privately, apologized, and professed that though Stoughton and the young man had much opposed him, "yet the more he honored us both in his very hart," adding that "he saw our aymes and ends were good."

Next day, September 5, Winthrop had to undergo the indignity of an investigation into the finances of his administrations as past governor. This was doubly insulting in that the Court had appointed Ludlow and Stoughton, political opponents of his from rankling Dorchester, as investigators. The findings showed not only a perfect scrupulousness on Winthrop's part but the great burden the office had put on his private resources. What is significant for the mounting political crisis, however, is the suspicion and vindictiveness that ordering the investigation at all implies on the part of the reactionaries who had assumed control of the Council. When no way could be found out of the deadlock between deputies and Assistants over Newtown's removal, the Court adjourned for a week.

All the churches kept a day of humiliation on the eighteenth, the very day, apparently, that a copy of the commission creating Archbishop Laud's committee to regulate all foreign plantations came on the *Griffin*, together with intelligence from friends that Captain Woodhouse, about to sail with a fleet and soldiers ostensibly for Virginia, might be on his way to force the English Church establishment and a governor-general upon the Bay. This news strengthened the Assistants' hand against the deputies and also helped the new repressive leadership pass a set of sumptuary laws against tobacco, immodest fashions, etc., after Court reconvened the twenty-fourth. It also prompted an appropriation to speed the Castle Island fortification. Ann Hutchinson, with her husband and nine of her children, passed the fort on this ship appalled at Boston's mean appearance. One of her sons had come over with Cotton.

Hooker again declined to preach to the Court at its reconvening. Cotton again accepted the duty, and his sermon proved to be a model of mollification. He upheld the people's right to maintain their liberties against any unjust violence but went on to maintain that the people, magistrates, and ministers *each* had a veto, that a resolution should lie with all together. He did not satisfy all his hearers, says Winthrop, but no one dared rupture further. The Newtown congregation accepted the extra land which had been offered by Boston and Watertown; "and so the fear of their removal to Connecticut was removed," Winthrop concludes.

Winthrop Jr. stoically attended this Court through the last day— October 6—though he had reached his worst of many dead ends by the death of his cousin-wife, Martha Fones, and her newborn daughter in the late summer, and within days of the October adjournment at Newtown sailed for England with Wilson (who now finally got away) on one of the numerous startings-over which characterize Winthrop Jr.'s whole restless, questing career.

On November 5 the Court of Assistants heard a complaint from a delegation headed by one Richard Brown, significantly of Watertown, that the king's colors had been defaced in Salem during a recent militia-training day. The Court awarded an attachment against the Salem ensign-bearer, Richard Davenport, to answer to this complaint at the next Court. Thus one of the intensest controversies in early Bay history got underway. It evidently originated in Williams's crusade preaching. The argument was that the red cross of St. George the dragon slayer had been given the king of England by the pope as an insignia of victory, which made it a symbol of superstition and a relic of Antichrist. Endecott grew sufficiently incensed to cut or order the cutting of this cross from the ensign of the militia company he commanded.

While the Court was sitting, Oldham reached port in the *Rebecka* from a voyage to Connecticut. He had acquired five hundred bushels of corn from the Narragansetts on his way home and brought new information on the nature and extent of their country, which he found "full of Indians," notwithstanding the reported smallpox scourge earlier. He saw more than a thousand Narragansetts even with the bulk of the men absent hunting.

On the sixth Ludlow brought into Boston the two Pequot ambassadors previously mentioned; they followed an emissary of a couple of weeks before and offered large encouragements to Bay business with their people. Most of the Assistants being assembled anyway for the lecture of that morning, they met with the ambassadors and told them that the men responsible for Stone and company's murder must be delivered up. The ambassadors said that only two so involved had survived smallpox but that they would be delivered on demand. The two Pequots repeated this promise when Winthrop and a few other Assistants brought them to the Governor's presence in Newtown. Having gone to war against the Narragansetts over ownership of lands lying between Pawcatuck River and Wehapaug Brook, and simultaneously against the Dutch for the slaying of their old sachem, the Pequots badly needed Bay trade.

The morning following, news came from Neponset (near later Milton) that two or three hundred Narragansetts had come there to kill the Pequot ambassadors. The Assistants hurriedly met at Roxbury, raised a small force, and sent it to summon said Narragansetts. The hundreds turned out to be but two petty sachems with about twenty men visiting at Neponset to hunt according to custom, though later events made the original rumor of intent to assassinate ring true. Eliot, at Roxbury, became angry that the Assistants would protect the Pequots without the consent of the "people" (meaning representatives of the freemen) and said as much in a sermon.

The Court of Assistants convened at Dudley's house November

27 about the cross-cutting. Hooker, in his advice, took the Winthrop-like line which minimized the whole matter, whereas Cotton, carrying the majority of ministers with him, sided with Williams and Endecott! The Court had no doubt as to the illegality of cutting the colors, but wrote deploring the act (to Downinge, the Bay's legal counsel in London) in wary language because of an inclination to agree on the red cross's unfortunate signification. This Court incidentally appointed Hooker, Cotton, and Welde to deal with Eliot about his recent criticism of the Assistants.

And, in the throes of anxiety about the king's possible reaction to the cross-cutting incident, this Court learned, Winthrop reports, that Williams "had broken his promise to us," teaching publicly against the king's patent, against the "antichristian" churches of England, and against the sin of New Englanders in claiming a right by patent to this country. The Assistants intimated to the ministers of the neighboring churches their mind to proceed against him. These ministers, however, proved loath to concur in such action against a fellow clergyman before they had the advice of more of their colleagues. It becomes evident that the general clerical sentiment against the cross of St. George in the flag helped Williams's cause with them, though he had no support for his patent stand.

Cotton, who had come to the rescue when Williams's "book" first brought him to Court, did so again. He persuaded the broader circle of ministers, when they met, to request the magistrates to forbear their prosecution until they themselves had endeavored his conviction and repentance "in a church-way," hoping, he said, that Williams's violences issued rather from a misguided conscience than a seditious principle. It was ominous for Williams that Dudley instead of Winthrop now sat in the governor's seat. Dudley "foretold" the interceding ministers when they reported (according to Cotton Mather): "You are deceived in the man, if you think he will condescend to learn of any of you." But he allowed Cotton's request and passed up the case for that session. Williams merely got a summons to appear at the next court.

The ministers, evidently needing more time, must have managed to prorogue the case at the winter term, for Dudley again stayed his hand. The fear of a governor-general, the cross-cutting, the negative-voice controversy, and the renewed Newtown pressure to migrate to Connecticut made Williams's patent talk seem minor. It was on

January 13 that all the ministers (excepting only Nathaniel Ward of doubtless-too-distant Ipswich) met in Boston to advise the Assistants what should be done if a governor-general appeared and whether the cross could be countenanced in Bay banners. Williams among them, they called for resistance insofar as possible to a governor-general but hopelessly divided over the cross.

ON MARCH 4, 1635, Hooker, aggressively accepting this time, preached at the opening of a General Court at Newtown. He "showed the three great evils," Winthrop says laconically. Now the clergy of the colony, including Williams, had been convening in a meeting of their own to get straight on what to advise the government when consulted. A three-man delegation approached Stoughton on behalf of his Dorchester minister Warham requesting that he draw up his reasons for not granting the magistrates the negative. Stoughton had come to Newtown this term as a "speaker" (spokesman) in league with Bellingham as "chief speaker" of the deputies. Stoughton reluctantly put down twelve reasons. Without Stoughton's knowledge, Warham presented the paper to the ministers' meeting. Four of the ministers later came to Stoughton, says Stoughton, with thanks and applause for his brief, but Cotton took it home and sent it to Winthrop on the day Court convened. Whereby Winthrop and other of the Assistants could charge Stoughton with writing a "booke" against the magistrates, denying that they were magistrates or their power more than ministerial. Winthrop could not but recall that Stoughton had "used many weak arguments against the negative voice" back in September. In fact, says Stoughton, Winthrop "fell into such bitter tearmes against me as was much, if it had beene prooved," for Winthrop said:

This is the man that had beene the troubler of Israel, and that I was a worme, (such an one as Mr. Hooker had spoke of in his sermon) and an underminder of the state: and yet *saith he, who but Mr. Stoughton in the eie of the country.*

Stoughton denied this and repeated what he had said about ministers of justice in a court where there was no contradiction. When Winthrop produced the incriminating instrument, Stoughton put in an omitted comma (a maddening gesture to a magistrate already worked up) and confirmed his work:

The pattent makes their [the magistrates'] power Ministeriall according to the greater voat of the generall courts, and not Magisteriall according to their owne discression [Stoughton quotes himself]. These were my very expressions.

"But much ado their was," Stoughton goes on, and "at length for peace sake, and to show how little I esteemed ought of myne," consented that the paper be burned. The Court disfranchised him for three years. Stoughton claims that the majority of the deputies concurred in that sentence "meerly to give the Magistrates content." Bellingham and other deputies assured him afterward they regretted their vote. Cotton, Hooker, and Ward were prominent among the ministers who privately expressed to him their disapproval of the magistrates, especially of Winthrop, whom Stoughton learned had confessed both in court and privately that he had gone too far. Yet the May General Court confirmed Stoughton's sentence.

This episode had an important bearing on the development of democracy, with which Williams later came to be identified; but the impression that Winthrop's opponents were working toward democracy and Winthrop against it is deceiving. Let us look closer for a moment at the men who sympathized with Stoughton. First, Cotton, who betrayed Stoughton's and Warham's confidence in transmitting the damaging document to Winthrop. Finding some of Stoughton's reasons grounded on the charter, which he did not well understand (Cotton told Stoughton), he, "in the simplicitie of his hart," sent them to Winthrop to be resolved. It is difficult to believe that Cotton did not really know what he was doing, having been an architect of the church-state system since soon after his arrival and having worked in all that time to block encroachment on Winthrop's authority. Cotton could even have been the behind-scenes prosecutor of Stoughton—a possibility which becomes more and more plausible in the light of Cotton's subsequent operations.

Bellingham, whom Stoughton called "a great man and a Lawier," followed as his senior fellow-deputy, and supported for the magistracy, long fooled many of the Massachusetts electorate into thinking him a "liberal." But it is hard to find that he stood for anything but his personal esteem and control. He had the knack—until he got into power—of making everybody feel that, however he happened to vote in Court, in his heart he favored him. Thus he supported every regime that was in power and at the same time subtly connived at it. His slow and difficult speech added to this ambivalence.

When he became an Assistant he usually sided with Saltonstall Jr., and so shared Saltonstall's reputation for liberalism. But this identification may have been a deliberate sharing of Saltonstall's popularity and social prestige, because liberality was conspicuously absent in Bellingham's actions after young Saltonstall returned to England. Bellingham joined in voting in January 1641 to censure Winthrop for having been too lenient. That his long opposition to Winthrop, at first covert, sprang from an ambition to hold power himself and not from any liberal convictions, became obvious in 1639 when he beat Winthrop for the governorship by six votes. He then openly broke with Winthrop and openly cast off all the pretended liberalism. Despite his grounding in the law, Bellingham assumed himself above it and had so many disputes with the other magistrates that the Court withdrew his salary. He scandalized the colony while governor when the fiancé of Penelope Pelham entrusted her to him as chaperone and he married her himself (though old enough to be her father), performing the ceremony himself too. At the death of Endecott, he decidedly continued the excessively repressive policies in his gubernatorial regimes that Dudley and Endecott had laid down in theirs. Once, while he was deputy-governor under Endecott, he savagely horsewhipped a crooked-backed Quaker girl who was begging him for mercy (she nearly died from a split nipple in consequence). Besides sadistic tendencies, Bellingham had had hallucinatory tendencies, having been known to hide under his bed from an apparition before he left England. He died insane December 7, 1672.

The lawyer-preacher Nathaniel Ward, whom Stoughton enumerates among his private supporters, was a sour, conceited—and able —member of the "reactionary" group, who later openly identified himself with the Dudley camp. His *Simple Cobbler of Aggawam*, a vicious book that he palmed off as humor, calls for utmost mercilessness toward any who disagreed with his version of Massachusetts orthodoxy. The extent that democracy dictated his sympathy with Stoughton may be gathered from a letter he wrote Winthrop Jr. from Ipswich on December 24, 1635, bewailing the "multitudes" of "profane & idle" young workingmen and servants who were becoming property owners in Ipswich; "it sinks us almost to the grave to looke upon the next generation to whome we must leave [our children] & the fruite of our adventures [investments], labours, & counsells."

We have Hubbard's explicit disclosure in the next generation that Hooker was responsible for making the freemen jealous of their liberties, but we also have more contemporary documentation that Hooker actually agitated for a greater popular voice. Winthrop and he continued the debate after Hooker had gone to Connecticut. Winthrop says in a famous *addendum* of his *Journal* that on August 28, 1638, "I expostulated about the unwarrantableness and unsafeness of referring matter of counsel or judicature to the body of the people, quia the best part is always the least, and of that part the wiser part is always the lesser. . . ." Hooker sabotaged the Bay's efforts to form a New England Confederation for basically the same reason he had sided with the deputies against Winthrop in Massachusetts. Winthrop understood this clearly: "The differences between us and those of Connecticut were divers," he says; "but the ground of all was their shyness of coming under our government. . . ." Hooker disagreed with Winthrop over the discretion to be allowed either directors of a confederation or of a commonwealth. He wrote Winthrop in about December 1638:

> That in the matter which is referred to the judge, the sentence should lie in his breast, or be left to his discretion, according to which he should go, I am afraid it is a course which wants both safety and warrant. I must confess, I ever looked at it as a way which leads directly to tyranny, and so to confusion, and must plainly profess, if it was in my liberty, I should choose neither to live nor leave my posterity under such a government.

"Under such a government as Winthrop would be the one exercising discretion in," we might expand this conclusion of Hooker's which can be taken as the plainest explanation he ever put into writing of his reason for moving one hundred instead of ten or thirty miles from Newtown ostensibly for roomier meadows. That Hooker retained a personal spite against Winthrop in particular clearly emerges in the long, rhetorical letter he wrote from Hartford in about December 1638 accusing Winthrop of condoning Bay dissuasion of Connecticut-bound emigrants pausing in Boston.

It must be remembered that Hooker voted against Winthrop in January 1636 because of the leniency of his administrations, i.e. for Winthrop's absence of tyranny. Hooker virtually controlled both church and state in Connecticut, where he proved no more willing to grant the deputies greater power than Ludlow. He encountered no contradiction because there was no one not already predisposed to his leadership. The harmony of his church likely reflects his imperious grip on it. Perry Miller points out that the first doctrine of Hooker's renowned election sermon of 1638 in Hartford, that the choice of public magistrates belongs to the people, was a Congregational commonplace; that the second, qualifying that the people must not exercise their election privileges according to their humors but according to the will and law of God, had always been advanced by the Congregationalists as a safeguard against popularity; but that the third, that

> They who have power to appoint officers and magistrates, it is in their power, also, to set the bounds and limitations of the power and place unto which they call them,

is the significant doctrine. Yet Miller of all persons should have remembered that this was the conventional Calvinist—and Jesuit—position of long before; Hooker really advances *nothing* original and *nothing* in the nature of a departure from the standard Puritan line in this sermon. Winthrop and Cotton, as well as Williams, agreed with all three of Hooker's points. An admirer of Hooker and a conservative, Richard Mather, observed that Hooker allowed the people less voice than he.

Winthrop's sentence "I am willing to listen to advice, and my aim is the common good" is not so often quoted as the one which precedes it about the best being always the least. Other of Winthrop's writings, such as his *Discourse on Arbitrary Government* of July 1644, and above all his actual governing, leave no doubt that he abhorred tyranny and was no tyrant. Not that he was never arbitrary. But, as John Locke pointed out in 1690,

> We do but flatter ourselves, if we hope ever to be governed without an Arbitrary Power. No . . . the only point is, who shall have that Arbitrary Power . . . ?

Winthrop's equally patriarchal opponents were invariably more arbitrary and more tyrannical than he.

It is hard not to conclude that Hooker's real objection was that he or someone beholden to him did not hold the Bay reins. He must have felt that justice entitled him to be the (benevolent and high-minded) tyrant himself. His stance against the New England Confederation exhibited him as a small-time autocrat resisting every statesman-like vision for coping with the external crises of the age. Williams in great anxiety protested that Hooker had completely misread the Indian situation. Ultimately, with the help of the threatening Dutch across the Sound, Hooker saw the superior wisdom of what he had opposed, and was big enough to write his change of heart to Winthrop. The Antinomian controversy also changed his mind about Winthrop's "tyranny" within the Bay, which he did everything he could to strengthen. Whatever antagonism had existed between the two men, they died reconciled.

Hubbard's intimation that Hooker left Massachusetts because it was not big enough for both him and Cotton, tends to be confirmed in Hooker's sulky refusals to preach to the General Court. Even this degree of jealousy toward Cotton may have been occasioned by Cotton's siding with Winthrop instead of Dudley. But Hooker's *Survey of the Summe of Church-Discipline* complements Cotton's *Way of the Congregational Churches Cleared,* which tracts came to print bound together in 1648. The two men disagreed on several fine points of doctrine after Hooker's migration, but these had nothing to do, either in degree or kind, with democracy, church government, evangelism, or the other matters on which they are sometimes alleged to have clashed, and could not possibly be held to have caused the migration. Hooker's treatises show a somewhat greater Calvinistic strictness than Cotton's and a greater emphasis on sin than on reason, as in his *Soules Preparation for Christ* of 1632:

. . . The Lord will make all crack before thou shalt finde mercy. . . . We must looke on the nature of sinne in the venome of it. . . . suppose any soule here were to behold the damned in hell, and if the Lord should give thee a little peepe-hole into hell, that thou didst see the horror of those damned soules, and thy heart begin to shake in the consideration thereof. . . . many a man after horrour of heart hath had a love after some base lust or other, and is held by it so fast, that hee can never bee ingrafted into the Lord Jesus. This one lust may breake his neck and send him downe to hell.

Instead of reason he talked of broken hearts and horrors of heart, etc. "I can compare with any man living for fears!" he once told an anguished young minister. Cotton never got so stern in his Calvinism as Hooker in his *Soules Humiliation* (1638) when he argued that despite the covenant God might still consign the believer to hell, in which case the Christian should be content to be disposed as God wills. Hooker sounds more like an Old Testament prophet than Cotton (Cotton's published works show a far greater concern with the New than the Old Testament, incidentally). Hooker did much more toward organizing the coercing institution of synods than

Cotton. So it cannot be argued that Hooker left Massachusetts because Cotton was too strict and undemocratic in matters of doctrine, church organization, or church-state relations, however much he may have become personally irritated with his old friend.

Hooker's migration has every earmark of political rather than ecclesiastical secession. Yet the ease with which Connecticut Congregationalism merged with Presbyterianism compared to the situation in Massachusetts around 1700 revives our speculation on the possible endemic depth of West Country Presbyterianism in the Bay towns which largely pulled out, as a factor in their migration.

Back to Stoughton in 1635. A substantial enough gentleman to have financed the first water mill in the Bay, he would not likely be working against entrenched privilege in the interests of the outcast many. What he and his cohorts were working for in their opposition to the vetoing magistrates may be hinted in the fact that Stoughton, Bellingham, Warham, and that unidentified deputy who led the anti-Winthrop fight when it first broke out in Court—also Ludlow—were all men of Dorchester, which Wood called "the greatest town in New England" in 1633. Dorchester had got the jump on Boston in exploiting the fish wealth off the coast and, in addition, had received an influx of well-to-do settlers like Stoughton. It was such settlers that Stoughton represented, and they could not likely be considered a rising class of commoners clamoring for democracy either. Notice that Warham, the Dorchester minister who instigated Stoughton's ill-fated paper, pulled out with his congregation and went to Connecticut just as Hooker and his left Newtown. They both did so on the decisive defeat of their towns for leadership of the Bay.

AN ALARM sounded through the Bay towns on April 26, 1635. Fishermen had brought word to Marblehead that a 400- and a 350-ton ship hovered on the coast all day and then headed for Cape Ann. Dudley rushed to Boston to meet with the Assistants. They ordered a shallop to Cape Ann. The visiting vessels proved to be an eighty- and ten-ton pair bound for Richman's Isle; no governor-general and no army.

Four days later the Governor and Assistants summoned Williams. They no longer bothered about his patent talk, which from this time or many months earlier ceased to be an issue. Rather, as Winthrop puts it, he had taught publicly, that a magistrate ought not to tender an oath to an unregenerate man, for that we thereby have communion with a wicked man in the worship of God, and cause him to take the name of God in vain. He was heard before all the ministers, and very clearly confuted.

Endecott, adds Winthrop, held the same opinion, "but he gave place to the truth." An implication is that Williams did not give place to the truth but, so far as we know, the Court felt a clear confutation enough on this occasion. Williams never relinquished the attitude he expressed in 1635 on oaths.

On election day at Newtown, May 6, 1635, John Haynes was elected governor and Bellingham deputy-governor. The domineering Endecott and Ludlow did not make the magistracy at all. Ludlow, who felt certain of a promotion from deputy-governor to governor, protested the election as void because the deputies had agreed on their choices before they left their towns! (Back on May 1, 1632, the afternoon of the day Winthrop had argued with Dudley about usury, etc., Winthrop announced to the Assistants that the deputies—"the people"—intended to request at the next General Court that the governor be elected by the Court at large and not by the Assistants from among themselves, at which Ludlow flew into a passion and said "that then we should have no government, but there would be an interim, wherein every man might do what he pleased, etc." Winthrop says he "continued stiff in his opinion" despite the reasonable discussion, and threatened to go back to England.)

Haynes, "that heauenly man," as Williams recalled him in 1670, had been lord of Copford Hall Manor near Old Holt, Essex. It was in Essex that he came under Hooker's spell. He surely knew Williams in Essex also. A widower with two sons and a daughter when he sailed, he married Mabel Harlakenden in Hooker's Newtown and by her had three more sons and two daughters in Hooker's Hartford. Cotton Mather describes him as a "pious, humble, well-bred gentleman. . . . a great friend of *peace* while he lived." He showed his pacific proclivity, as also his wealth, in declining compensation for office in his inaugural address—an act which, at the same time, highlights the economic depression which had gripped the colony since 1633 and had constantly goaded friction and anxiety from other causes. Haynes was not so humble and peaceful, however, as to refrain from firm action on his anti-Winthrop (and anti-Williams) bias.

A committee of four magistrates plus a deputy from each town met for a couple of hours on Endecott's case during this General Court and reported back a recommendation that he be disabled from holding any public office for one year for the flag cutting. He had laid a blemish on the rest of the magistrates, implying they *would* suffer idolatry, and had given occasion to England "to think ill of us," and so on. The committee's merciless tone pointed to a heavier sentence, but they realized he had acted out of conscience and not any evil intent, they said. However, the Court found itself still unable to resolve the doctrinal question of the cross in the flag and had to defer again; so the question raged on.

So did the Connecticut question. Oldham and eight or nine companions from Watertown had put up temporary houses at Pyquag and spent the winter trading out of there. By the middle of May their number had grown to twenty-five or thirty. For a long time this settlement went under the name Watertown but eventually became Wethersfield, Connecticut. In mid-June, a vanguard group sent out by Saltonstall from England to begin a settlement on the Connecticut landed in Boston: a master carpenter, Francis Stiles, and Stiles's two carpenter brothers, with eighteen indentured servants, authorized to impale two thousand acres. They knew, and brought a letter from Saye affirming, that the ship of the intended governor-general had broken in two at its launching. The Stileses and company sailed in ten days for the Connecticut. But Ludlow, learning of their arrival in Boston, led a band of Dorchester pioneers, apparently reinforced from Newtown and Watertown, who struck out overland, and on about June 25, 1635, beat the Saltonstall vanguard to the best meadows around the Pilgrim fort. There Jonathan Brewster, the Pilgrim agent in charge, provided invaluable hospitality while watching the pre-emption of Pilgrim land with dismay. He says that settlers from the Bay arrived on Ludlow's heels almost daily. They took approximately fifteen-sixteenths of the Pilgrim Indian grant without leave, though they finally relented in May 1637 and paid Plymouth £27 10s. of the £100 Winslow demanded. Their mushroom settlement, together with the Pilgrim post and its two 40-acre meadows, constituted Windsor, which at first the Dorchester settlers called Dorchester. The Saltonstall voyagers found the Ludlow squatters already in possession of all but inferior or overgrown land on the northern outskirts, where they reluctantly settled.

Francis Stiles sailed the pinnace back to England to report. Even before he got there, Saltonstall and the other patentees of a Warwick grant to the lower Connecticut engaged Winthrop Jr., who was in England at the time, to look after their immediate interests in New England. This was June 7.

The General Court, already aggravated over the cross and the unauthorized exodus to Connecticut—and probably also by the heat—summoned Williams, who was present with the clergy, on July 8. For he had been preaching that the magistrate ought not punish breaches of the first table (the first four Commandments) other than in cases of disturbing the peace. Here his doctrine of separation from the established church decisively branched into its logical corollary, the doctrine of separation of church and state. Since the Bay clergy, magistracy, and deputies agreed with Calvin that the first purpose of government was to buttress the church, that the church should dominate society, and that this would be impossible without the coercion of the state, Williams in their view was trying to pull the rug out from under the entire order they had risked everything to erect.

Williams's growing arsenal of Separatist radicalisms salted the Court's exasperation. The most contentious of these at this point was his doctrine that opposed praying with unregenerate persons— even if wives or children—which persons would of course remain unregenerate in his definition so long as they failed to renounce any connection whatever with the Church of England. The controversy over this doctrine brought the Bay back to the same place it had left off arguing with him in 1631, and must have convinced his old friends that he would have to be written off as incorrigible.

In the "much debate" Winthrop says developed, Williams protested that one particular slanderous report wronged him in making him appear to hold it unlawful for a father to call upon his child to eat meat. The great Hooker hereupon got recognized to reply, according to Cotton Mather: "Why? You will say as much again, if you stand to your own principles, or be driven to say nothing at all." Williams expressed his confidence he should never say it, but Hooker went on:

If it be unlawful to call an unregenerate person to pray, since it is an action of God's worship, then it is unlawful for your unregenerate child to pray for a blessing upon his meat, it is unlawful for him to eat it, for it is sanctified by prayer, and without prayer, unsanctified: [1 Tim. 4:4,

5.]. If it be unlawful for him to eat it, it is unlawful for you to call upon him to eat it; for it is unlawful for you to call upon him to sin. [Brackets Mather's.]

Aside from the disadvantage of being a young dissenter striving alone against the massed learning, dignity, and maturity of the Massachusetts intelligentsia, and against their granite-embedded first principles, which he could hardly hope to budge, Williams had not clearly worked out or synthesized his position, which must have sounded like a hodgepodge of quibbling heresies to his hearers. "A Haberdasher of small Questions against the Power [of the state]," Cotton called Williams in a private conversation (quoted by Coddington to the Quaker founder George Fox in 1677).

What perhaps rankled the Court most was that the Salem church had gone ahead and elected Williams teacher while the Court had him under question for his opinions. "The said opinions," summarizes Winthrop, "were adjudged by all, magistrates and ministers . . . to be erroneous, and very dangerous, and the calling of him to office, at that time was judged a great contempt of authority." The Court gave Williams and the Salem church till the next General Court to consider this judgment, "and then either to give satisfaction . . . or else to expect the sentence"; for the clergy had "expressly declared" when requested to advise, "that he who should obstinately maintain such opinions (whereby a church might run into heresy, apostacy, or tyranny, and yet the civil magistrate could not intermeddle) were to be removed, and that the other churches ought to request the magistrates so to do."

The Salem deputies, it so happened, had picked this time to prefer a petition to be acted on by the July Court for some land in Marblehead Neck which they claimed belonged to Salem. But because of Salem's choosing Williams teacher, their petition was refused. The Salem church thereupon wrote the other churches, unquestionably at Williams's instigation, to admonish the magistrates and deputies for this "heinous sin" of coercing a supposedly autonomous Congregational church with a political lever. Such an attack on the government, especially after the Court had pronounced that the churches ought to request the magistrates to remove such a one as Williams, struck the magistrates as treason. They forbade Salem's deputies to sit at the next General Court until they had renounced the letters. (As between land and principle, there could be little doubt about which the holy people of Salem would choose.)

Williams worsened matters between the two sessions when, in August, too sick to speak, he wrote his congregation that he could no longer communicate with the churches of the Bay, including them, unless they too renounced communion with the rest; "but the whole church was grieved herewith," Winthrop adds.

The General Court convened again September 2, in Haynes's Newtown. It got in the mood to deal with Williams by invoking Massachusetts' first grand jury, which confronted more than a hundred offenses immediately. The following day the Court adjourned to the Thursday after the next meeting of the Court of Assistants, which did not convene until October 6. Haynes and the Assistants must have hashed out their final decision about Williams in this long interval of adjournment. The length of the interval points to a deep rift among magistrates and clergy as to his fate. We hear echoes of the possible inner-sanctum clash of this fall, in the callings-on-the-carpet that occurred in private meetings of ministers and magistrates both before and after the court session that finally sentenced Williams. Although Cotton claimed to Williams that he had no hand in that sentence, some of the members of the Court later tearfully told Williams they never would have voted for his banishment had Cotton not persuaded them it was the thing to do.

The General Court reconvened Thursday, October 8, in an implacable, solid-front temper. It jailed Endecott for justifying the Salem Church letter and released him when he retracted the same day. It sentenced a miller of Dorchester, John Smith, to banishment "for dyvers dangerous opinions which he holdest and hath divulged." Then Haynes called Williams before the Court and ministers assembled, about the church letter and his to the church.

"He justified both these letters," says Winthrop, "and maintained all his opinions; and, being offered further conference or disputation, and a month's respite, he chose to dispute presently." Haynes appointed Hooker as debater for the state, but Hooker "could not reduce him from any of his errors."

So the next morning, with all the ministers but one concurring (we do not know who that one was), Haynes read the sentence of banishment:

Whereas Mr Roger Williams, one of the elders of the church of Salem, hath broached & dyvulged dyvers newe & dangerous opinions, against the aucthoritie of magistrates, as also writt lettres of defamacion, both of the magistrates & churches here, & that before any conviccion, & yet mainetaineth the same without retraccion, it is therefore ordered, that the said Mr Williams shall departe out of this jurisdiccion within sixe weekes nowe nexte ensueing, which if hee neglect to performe, it shalbe lawfull for the Gouvernor & two of the magistrates to send him to some place out of this jurisdiccion, not to returne any more without license from the Court.

Haynes gratuitously added a quotation from Romans 16:17: "Mark them which cause divisions and offences, contrary to the doctrine which ye have learned, and avoid them."

When Williams returned home he refused communion with his own church, which, says Winthrop, "openly disclaimed his errors" (they had to to get that land); the congregation "wrote an humble submission to the magistrates, acknowledging their fault in joining with Mr. Williams in that letter to the churches against them, etc."

In consideration of Williams's severe illness, the Court gave him till spring to depart, provided he did not "go about to draw others to his opinions." He defiantly named his second daughter, born this very month, *Freeborne,* and went on about his magnetic mission. He would have said with Socrates that to hold his tongue would be to disobey God. "However in Civill things we may be servants unto men," Williams said a few years later, "yet in Divine and Spirituall things the poorest *peasant* must disdaine the service of the highest Prince: Be ye not the servants of men, I Cor. 14."

YOUNG Sir Henry Vane, son of the king's comptroller; Hugh Peter, a short, thickset, aggressive preacher-entrepreneur subject to psychotic depression, a good friend of Patriarch White and Hooker, originally of Fowey, Cornwall (and a prosperous and lusty background), recently of Rotterdam; Wilson, returning with his wife (having been assisted by John Dod and other persuasive clergymen; Dod told her she should be content with little things for a while); Winthrop Jr., returning with his bride, Elizabeth Reade, much younger than himself; another of the elder Winthrop's sons, Deane, on the smallpox-ridden *Abigail;* and the thirty-six-year-old preacher-scholar, Emmanuel alumnus, and close friend of Stone, Welde, and Hooker, Thomas Shepard and family on the *Defence,* arrived the same day at Boston just three days before the sentencing of Williams. Whether any or all of these men heard the proceedings of the eighth and ninth, or how they reacted to them if they did, we do not know. They all figured in Williams's later career.

Before Winthrop Jr. arrived and could assert his authority as the Warwick patentees' governor of Connecticut, about sixty men, women, and children of Hooker's congregation that October went overland for Windsor with their cows, horses, and swine. Finding the Windsor lands fully taken, they settled just south and across the Connecticut at Suckiaug—which they called Newtown before renaming it Hartford—preempting the Dutch grant just as their Dorchester counterparts had preempted the Pilgrim. Some of the soldiers of the Dutch garrison of fourteen or fifteen forbade these settlers to put plow to Dutch land, but a little band of Newtowners gave them a cudgeling that ended all resistance indefinitely. By November, 150 or 200 people had settled at Windsor, Hartford, and Wethersfield.

Winter set in early and bitterly that year. The Connecticut froze on November 15. Twelve men of the Newtown vanguard, who had accompanied it to help build houses and a palisade, had a hard ten-day return journey to Massachusetts after working a month at Hartford. One of their number died in a fall through the ice; the rest escaped starvation by grace of Indians along the way. Seventy men and women of the desperate Windsor settlement braved knee-deep snow down the Connecticut to meet relief barks that never came, but twenty miles above the mouth they discovered the *Rebecka* icebound. When a small rain freed it, it took on the seventy sojourners but grounded two days later on the bar at the river mouth and had to lose lifesaving time unlading while some of the passengers lay dying. At this very juncture, a Dutch sloop hove up to take possession of the mouth. The *Rebecka* men rose to the occasion by lugging two cannons ashore in time to deter the Dutch from landing. Five days later, December 10, the little ship made Boston. Back in Connecticut, the blizzard-blasted pioneers scrounged for acorns. The Dorchester people lost most of their cattle, to the value of nearly £2000.

In September 1635 Williams's scholarly friend William Pynchon, a wealthly magistrate of Roxbury who later got into trouble with the Bay for publishing an unorthodox religious book, reconnoitered the Connecticut farther up than his fellows and late the following April took a handful of men in two shallops to build a trading house twelve miles above Windsor at Agawam, which he shortly renamed Springfield. He hired the free-enterpriser Allerton, who was operating out of Marblehead, to freight sixteen casks of trading goods to the Connecticut mouth, and got Winthrop Jr.'s help to deliver various quantities of them upriver later. Pynchon built first on the west bank but moved to the east side after Indian cattle and hogs ruined his corn crop, as he told Winthrop Jr. on June 2 when acknowledging receipt of the goods. For some years this tiny outpost was regarded as part of Connecticut before finally getting redefined as inside Massachusetts.

That same spring of 1636, Warham led a large part of his congregation, including Ludlow and others who had returned temporarily to Massachusetts, to Windsor. Richard Mather and his congregation took possession of the vacated lesser half of Dorchester, where Stoughton had remained and cornered more of the land of that town. Fifty or so people of Watertown, in many family groups, by land and by sea, migrated to the Oldham outpost at Pyquag (Wethersfield). That April, a party of leading members of Hooker's congregation still at Newtown joined the earlier Newtown settlers at Hartford and organized it in accordance with the temporary agreement settled with Winthrop Jr.—Ludlow and others to be "commissioners" under Winthrop Jr.'s governorship. Shepard's congregation arranged to take over the already-vacated dwellings of Newtown together with the rest, which would be vacated when Hooker led the balance of his congregation west. This he did not do until Tuesday, May 31, 1637. Fifty persons (thirty-five of them men) and 160 cattle (furnishing milk all the way) comprised this rearguard, which in about two weeks settled mainly south of the previous settlers from Newtown, close to the Dutch fort, though Hooker and other dignitaries stayed in the northern, or main part of Hartford.

In early December 1635 (as the Bay learned months later) their appointed governor-general died before he could sail. He was Sir Ferdinando Gorges's closest colleague, Captain John Mason—not to be confused with Williams's later friend of the same name.

THE COURT OF ASSISTANTS met in Boston in January 1636 under Haynes expressly to consider further the case of Williams. They had been credibly informed that Williams had been preaching to company in his own home, even on points he had been censured for. This in itself may not have surprised or bothered the Court so much; but he had in effect organized a group of about twenty, "much taken with the apprehension of his godliness," for erecting a plantation, Winthrop says, about Narragansett Bay, "from whence the infection would easily spread into these [Massachusetts] churches." Many of Salem Church, "especially of devout women," had followed him in separating from all the Bay churches.

The Court therefore sent the marshal, James Penn, to fetch him presently, to be shipped to England on a vessel then ready to depart. Several Salem men returned with the answer that Williams could not come, being so ill, without hazard of his life. Whereupon the Court sent Captain Underhill in a pinnace then anchored at Nantasket to apprehend Williams and carry him aboard the England-bound vessel. When the officers came to the little two-story dwelling near the Salem meetinghouse, they found he had fled three days before; "but whither they could not learn."

The frustration of the ruling faction's will in Williams's escape looks to be the immediate mover of the "mediation" Vane and Peter took on themselves to arrange for January 18 ostensibly to compose the Dudley-Winthrop differences once again. Though both Dudley and Winthrop were out of either gubernatorial office, they remained the nominal heads of the clashing factions in the Bay, of which Dudley's was now the turned worm and could blame the "tyrant" Winthrop's failure to be tyrannical for Williams's dismayingly successful subversion and disruptive developments in general of late. Bellingham, Cotton, Hooker, Wilson, and Haynes were others present. Cotton's study may have been the meeting place, one reason being that the co-host, Vane, was living at Cotton's hilltop house (he built an addition and continued living here in a duplex arrangement with Cotton).

Politeness caused a slow start, both Winthrop and Dudley maintaining that their differences had long since been patched up. Finally, Governor Haynes got round to mentioning one or two passages wherein he conceived Winthrop had dealt "too remissly in point of justice." Winthrop admitted that his speeches and carriage had been at times mistaken "but withall professed, that it was his iudgment that in the infancy of plantation iustice should be administered with more leantye than in a setled state, because people were then more apt to transgress partly of ignorance of newe laws and orders, partly through oppression of business and other streights." This brought the conference to its real purpose. Haynes desired the ministers to consider the question by the next morning and to set down a rule in the case. The next morning they delivered their several reasons, "which all sorted to this conclusion,"

that stricte Discipline both in criminall offences and in martiall affaires was more needfull in plantations than in a setled state as tending to the honor and safety of the gospell.

Winthrop acknowledged himself remiss. "Whereupon there was a renewal of love amongst them, and articles drawn to this effect:"

1. That there should be more strictness used in civil government and military discipline. . . .

Winthrop refrains from mentioning what Williams learned privately in time (from Peter or Vane in England, or Haynes or Hooker in Connecticut), that Peter moved to send an excommunication after Williams into the wilderness. If, as is likely, this motion came at the January 18 meeting, it underscores the connection between the meeting and Williams's migration planning and escape, as also the punitive mood of one, at least, of the meeting's organizers.

9 : *The End and the Beginning*

WHEN I was vnkindly & vnchristianly (as I belieue) driuen from my howse & land, & wife & children (in the midst of New England winter . . .)," Williams wrote Major Mason from Providence on June 22, 1670, "That euer honoured Governour mr. Wintrop privately wrote me to steer my Course to the Nahigonset Bay & Indjans, for many high & heauenly & publike Ends, incowraging me from the Freenes of the place from any English Clajms or pattents. I tooke his prudent Motion as an Hint & Vojce from God, & (Waving all other Thoughts & Motjons) I steerd my Course from Salem (though in Winter snow which I feele yet) vnto these parts, wherein I may say as Jacob, Peniel, that is I haue seene the Face of God."

Thus Williams perfected into myth his flight of twenty-four and a half years before. The government of Massachusetts did not exactly drive him from his house in midwinter; the General Court, by protracted due process, found him guilty of a frontal assault on the foundations of the Bay system and sentenced him to banishment within six weeks, shortly extended to six or seven months. He deliberately forced the Assistants' hand by violating the terms of the extension. Even then he was not driven; he eluded deportation to England. The impression he gives of lawless bigots invading his premises and whiplashing him out into the snow is special pleading to begin with. Next Williams pulls the mantle of respectability over his ignominious escape by claiming the authorization of the revered Governor Winthrop. If Winthrop had really written him when he was "driven" from his home "in the midst of New England winter," Williams would not have received the letter, at least not at Salem in time to steer a course by it. Winthrop could conceivably have written such a letter shortly after the sentencing in October. If so, Williams again gives a false impression, this time that Winthrop secretly connived against the government after it had determined to deport him rather than after ordering him to depart with his destination left entirely open. It is *possible* that Winthrop did so connive after the decision to deport; he found himself at odds with prevailing government policy at this very time. But, especially while under fire, he would not probably have acted in a private capacity as Williams implies. Winthrop's *Journal* entries, dating from the weeks in question, contradict such a supposition, as does the invariable correctness of his magisterial conduct throughout his career. It is not as though he secretly agreed with Williams; he disagreed on every count that brought Williams before the bar. It was Winthrop, no matter how reluctantly, who called the meeting which examined Williams's charter attack and so started the chain reaction of court appearances for the harassed gadfly. The fateful letter, we have seen, would almost have to have been written while Williams still resided at Plymouth, where he was corresponding with Winthrop about Indian missionizing. If the letter originated in this context in 1632, Williams condensed the fact of the letter and the fact of the flight of 1636 into a single day.

Sharp details we should want to hear from Williams faded from the record. We can only partially restore them. He said on November 17, 1677, that he mortgaged his house and land at Salem, along with some hundredths, "for supplies to go through." He had had nearly all fall and part of the winter to arrange such things after he knew he must be gone, and he had been negotiating with the Indian sachems well before that.

He could have made Providence far more effective for democracy and freedom of conscience if, instead of pressing his petty and grand radicalisms, he had used the time the Court granted after his sentence of banishment to organize a slower transfer and if (as Henry C. Dorr long ago remarked) he had settled at the future site of Newport in the first place. But Providence (more propitious than the Newport site for *land* communication with Massachusetts, New Plymouth, and Connecticut) was not Williams's destination before he left Salem or until spring, after he left. Also, he *had* been organizing a group migration, according to Winthrop; the Council appears to have decided on a hasty deportation primarily to frustrate this. Yet on November 17, 1677, Williams testified: "My souls desire was to do the natives good, and to that end to have their language . . .

and therefore desired not to be troubled with English company." He contended that it was only "out of pity" that he allowed the company of half a dozen who pressed to join him to do so. If this version is correct, it squares with the intentions Williams expressed to Winthrop back in 1632, and means that he had no clear idea of founding a colony, let alone a democracy, but intended a private Indian mission which he would have preferred to be a solitary endeavor, with his family and servants.

Marshal Penn's appearance at the door must have been Williams's fire bell. The instant the marshal was out of sight with some of Williams's friends who would plead illness for his failure to answer the summons, Williams must have jumped into action, given hasty instructions to those who had been planning a spring migration with him, grabbed the knapsack his wife had scurried to cram, and taken grim leave of her and the two little girls. There is a possibility that Thomas Angell, a servant lad and distant relative of Williams's friend Richard Waterman, accompanied the ailing preacher with a heavy load of prearranged supplies. The wayfarer(s) must have left that same afternoon in order to have been gone three days when Underhill arrived to arrest Williams. Our available evidence, which can be read in more than one way, admits of no more exact dating of this flight than that January 15 would be the latest possible day and January 8 the earliest, with the eighth or ninth most probable.

Alone or attended, Williams obviously would have headed several days southwestward from Salem afoot, over trails he fortunately already knew, and would have had a real struggle at that season in his serious illness, which he sufficiently attests to in such allusions as the one twenty-four and a half years later about still feeling the winter snow of this trek. The Baptist elder, James Brown (1666–1732) preserves some early memories of Williams in a manuscript written sometime after June 1675, the last date mentioned in the document. Brown should be a good source because he grew up near the Williams house. He was seven when Williams died; but his father, and others of the neighbors and relatives of Williams whom young Brown knew well, had had a close association with the founder from the earliest years of Providence. Brown says in part that Williams

was forsed to great hardships so that If the Indians . . . had not hope him hee might have sufered deth but they was very kind to him and hope him a long in his Jurne tel hee came to a place senc caled mantons neck Where hee had much kines sheued him from the Indians there hee abode the latter part of that winter. . . .

Williams says that God gave him patience to endure the Indians' filthy smoke holes even while he resided in Plymouth and Salem; we get the impression of his enduring a succession of them in Massasoit's jurisdiction, gradually recovering his health, and winding up late in the winter at Manton's Neck, where at some previous time he may already have acquired Massasoit's authorization to settle. This might have been his destination all along—the place where he instructed those who insisted on joining him to converge in the spring. It was also conveniently close to the "palace" of Massasoit, where Williams most likely completed his convalescence.

IN THE FLAT meadow country about forty miles from Plymouth, at Pokanoket or Sowams (present-day Barrington, Rhode Island), Massasoit—by this time called Ousamequin—held sway over the Wampanoags. He is the same sachem whose initial visit of state to the Pilgrims on March 22, 1621, is familiar to every schoolboy. He must have been about twenty-five at that time; Bradford described him in 1621 as "a very lustie man, in his best yeares, an able body, graue of countenance, and spare of speech."

His face was paynted with a sad red like murry, and oyled both head and face, that hee looked greasily: All his followers likewise, were in their faces, in part or in whole painted, some blacke, some red, some yellow, and some white, some with crosses, and other Antick workes, some had skins on them, and some naked, all strong, tall. . . .

Samoset, the English-speaking sachem from Maine visiting in Massasoit's jurisdiction who boldly preceded Massasoit into Plymouth on March 16 and 18, was still living as late as July 1653 (when he sold land to three Englishmen and drew his bow-and-arrow mark in a hand tremulous with age) as Captain John Somerset at Pemaquid.

Bradford sent Winslow and Edward Hopkins, with Squanto as guide, to return Massasoit's visit on July 2, 1621. (Squanto was the sole survivor of the Indian village where Plymouth later stood; he escaped the plague which wiped it out because of having been kidnaped and sent to Spain and England.) The Pilgrim ambassadors found that thousands of Wampanoags had died about 1617—too many to bury; skulls and bones lay here and there on the ground, "a very sad spectackle to behould." Robert Cushman, visiting Plymouth five months after the mission of Winslow and Hopkins, said that Massasoit came to see the Pilgrims often, that his people looked dejected and affrighted, and that perhaps nineteen-twentieths of them had perished from the plague and in their wars and civil dissensions.

Canonicus, the wise old grand sachem of the Narragansetts, naturally looked jaundicedly at the Pilgrim pact with his satellite. In February 1622 he sent a messenger to the Pilgrims with a bundle of arrows tied in a great rattlesnake skin. When Squanto explained that this meant a declaration of war, Bradford sent it back filled with powder and shot. The Europeans never frightened Canonicus, but neither did they ever goad him to reckless action. Sensing that they presented a force which could not be dealt with in the ordinary Indian manner, he refused to receive the snake skin back. The Pilgrims, however, took the precaution of commencing their palisades and appointing a night watch.

They began to hear rumors of Massasoit's capture by the Narragansetts, of intrigues between certain of Massasoit's sub-sachems and the Massachusetts Indians, and of Massasoit's intention to join a band that set out to assault Plymouth while Captain Standish was away. This last seems to have been an invention of Squanto. When Massasoit learned about it from Hobomok's squaw, who had been sent to scout its truth, the sachem stormed into Plymouth in person to clear himself. After departing from Plymouth he sent a messenger to Bradford demanding Squanto, as a subject, or his head and hands. This put quite a strain on the governor's statesmanship, which statesmanship, however, enabled Squanto to die a natural death not long afterward, much lamented by Bradford.

Hobomok, Massasoit's *piness* (counselor) who came to live with the Pilgrims and enjoyed their utmost confidence, told Winslow on the way to the presumably dying sachem in 1624 that they would never see the like of Massasoit again among the Indians, that he was no liar and was not bloody and cruel, like other Indians, that his anger quickly passed; he was easily reconciled with those who had given him offense; he would not scorn the advice of mean men, and he governed better with a few strokes than others with many. Crediting Winslow with saving his life, Massasoit reaffirmed his friendship with the Pilgrims, which had wavered. The extent that both sides took this friendship for granted appears from an incident of August 1634 preserved by Winthrop. Winslow was just returning by boat from Connecticut and had anchored in Narragansett Bay with the intention of proceeding on to Plymouth overland. He dropped in to see Massasoit, who offered to conduct him home himself. But before they set out, Massasoit sent one of his men ahead to tell the Pilgrims that Winslow had died, with particulars as to how and where. The next day Winslow and Massasoit entered a sorrowing community. When the Pilgrims demanded of Massasoit why he had sent such word, he answered that it was the Indians' manner so to do, "that they might be more welcome when they came home."

By this time, everyone had got used to Massasoit's new name Ousamequin. Williams must have been negotiating with both him and Canonicus from 1632 on. He testified on November 17, 1677: "I spared no cost, to wards them [the Indians], and in Gifts to Ousamaquin, yea & to all his, and to Conanicus & his, tokens and presents many years before I, came in person to the Nahiganset, & therefore when I came I was Welcome to Osamaquin & that old prince Conanicus." In a deposition of June 18, 1682, Williams mentions "my great frjendship with him [Ousamequin] at Plymmouth" in the context of receiving Indian help "when the Hearts of my Countrimen & Friends & Brethrens fajled me" after the momentous flight. So far as the Indians knew, Williams's standing with the Bay and New Plymouth had not changed; part of his effectiveness with the Indians came from their never having found out that he had been banished.

Manton's Neck, where Elder Brown says Williams abode the latter part of the winter of his flight, should not be confused with the present-day town Matunuck across the bay (jutting into Point Judith Pond and known in the seventeenth century as Mattoomuc Neck) but a neck somewhere in Seekonk. Williams says that at Seekonk (*Secunk*, he spells it) "I first pitcht & begun to build & plant." He identifies it as the Rehoboth, Massachusetts, of later years rather than the site that is today the city of Seekonk, contiguous with Providence. Elder Brown's grandson, Moses Brown, told the early Williams biographer James Knowles, on the basis of one of his grandfather's papers, that Williams's Seekonk habitation on Manton's Neck stood near the cove a short distance above Central Bridge. One Leonard Bliss, Jr., in 1836 located the probable spring near which Williams settled, a few rods from the east bank of the cove, and described the spring as cool, clear, and beautiful. Bliss found no signs of Williams's temporary cottage, as one would presume he would not after two hundred years.

"The latter part of the winter" would technically mean, in the seventeenth century, up to March 25; but it would just as easily have meant up to the time wintry weather ceased, some weeks later than that. The usual planting time was mid-April. Soon after beginning to build and plant, says Williams, he received a letter from Winslow, who had been elected governor of New Plymouth on March 1, advising that, since Williams had fallen into the edge of Plymouth bounds and the Pilgrims "were loth to displease the Bay," Williams should "remove but to the other side of the water," where he "had the country free" before him, and that he and they "should be loving neighbours togeather." Williams complied and "quietly & patiently departed . . . to my Losse of a Harvest that yeare." He further says that "betweene those my Frjends of the Bay & Plymmouth I was sorely tost for one 14 weekes (in a bitter Winter Season) not knowing what Bread or Bed did meane."

He has been taken to mean by "14 weekes" the period from his flight to his planting at Seekonk, but he actually uses the words to include the tossing from Plymouth-claimed Seekonk as well as the tossing from Massachusetts; the tossing ended with his founding of Providence at the end of the fourteen weeks. Fourteen weeks from January 8 would be April 16 as the approximate date of the founding of Providence, bearing in mind that Williams uses "14 weekes" as a round number (which would imply it was actually a few days fewer) and that he could have left Salem as late as a week later than January 8. Benedict Arnold, great-grandfather of the American Revolutionary general and traitor, recalled that his father and family came to Providence to dwell on April 20 that year. Unless the large Arnold family preceded Williams to Providence—a most improbable possibility—Williams obviously founded Providence no later than April 20, 1636, and presumably three or four days before.

John Cotton said in 1647 that some of Williams's friends went to the place he had appointed beforehand to make provision for housing, etc.; Cotton, who never visited Narragansett Bay, assumes this place to be Providence, but it would obviously be Seekonk. April 20 is, of course, too late for Williams to have been preceded to Seekonk; but we shall see that the Arnolds were not among the group whom Cotton could have meant as preceding him there.

Williams refers to himself alone as fleeing Salem, pitching at Seekonk, and moving from there to Providence, in his lengthy narration to Major Mason and in his usual references to the flight. But in a reply to William Harris on November 16, 1677, addressed to the Court of Commissions, Williams said that while he desired not to be troubled with Englishmen, he nevertheless "out of Pity" gave leave to Harris, "then poor and destitute, to come along in my company." He also, he continued, relented toward the Dorchester miller John Smith, who had been sentenced to banishment just before Williams; "a poor young fellow, Francis Wicks," whom Smith had brought along; and the "lad of Richard Watermans" identifiable from other sources as Thomas Angell.

Williams's language, "to come along" and "to go with me," implies he met up with these men at some point before reaching Providence. They could have joined him after he reached Seekonk, or preceded him there, or accompanied him there from Salem or from Manton's Neck. It is likeliest that they importuned him in Salem and joined him in the spring at Seekonk, with the plausible exception of Angell; for which other of the Salem men than Williams could have brought a servant? (Angell, of course, might have come to Seekonk with the Harris party by Williams's prior arrangement.) The Harris party would have sought Williams out, whatever the time they themselves left Salem and Dorchester, because Williams had acquired some land grants when no one else except Oldham could as yet move the Narragansett sachems to grant further and when no other refugee could plausibly at that date prevail on Massasoit's magnanimity. The Harris party would hardly have preceded Williams to Seekonk, being too dependent on Williams's conversance with the Indian language—and having much less of Williams's urgent motivation to depart unseasonably.

Cotton Mather understood that Williams "with his party" went abroad on the sentence of the Court and gathered a "thing" like a church. Mather here telescoped the original decision of banishment, the January court judgment, the flight, the founding of Providence, and the gathering of the Baptist church there, into a couple of sentences; so that the "party" would not necessarily have materialized before Seekonk even if Mather's sources on this migration were reliable. Williams, on the other hand, sometimes discloses that a party accompanied him on other occasions which he elsewhere mentions only in terms of his own transit.

The Rhode Island senator and document-collector in the early years of the Republic, Theodore Foster, on the oral authority of his historian predecessor, Stephen Hopkins, governor of Rhode Island in the mid-eighteenth century, whose sister married General James Angell (Hopkins was born twenty-four years after Williams died),

deposed on June 6, 1821, that Thomas Angell alone accompanied
Williams in a canoe down Seekonk River on Williams's first visit to
the Indians living near the site of future Providence, and that when
they came opposite a cove some distance above what in later times
was called Indian Point, a Narragansett on a then-existing hill
greeted them, "What cheer, Netop?"—"what cheer" being a common English salutation of the time (it occurs in five of Shake-
speare's plays) and *netop* the Indian word for "friend." Hopkins
knew that place himself in the early eighteenth century as What
Cheer Cove. Williams made signs to the Indians that he would meet
them on the western shore of the neck where the Indians stood. He
and Angell paddled around Fox Point and met the Indians at Slate
Rock.

The usually repeated tradition refers to the actual move of the
men from Seekonk rather than a preliminary voyage, and confuses
the former with the latter. By the time they paddled as a group
across the Seekonk (later Blackstone) River, a newcomer, Joshua
Verin, had augmented the company to five, as we know from several later recollections. From the top of the bay they glided westward over their Jordan, steered around the headland and points at
the Seekonk's mouth and landed on Slate Rock, where (the com-
monest tradition goes) an Indian above them called "What cheer,
Netop?" Williams motioned to the Indians that his party would
meet them around the bend, and did. Another version says that the
place he met them, on rounding the bend, was Slate Rock; another
that he did not actually land on Slate Rock; and still another that it
was *Williams* who called out to the nearest *Indian* "What cheer,
Netop?" A now-buried rock, together with a cove and the land
adjacent, did bear the name What Cheer; so it is called in the early
property records; Williams in 1657 referred to the Indian field
whotcheare as one of the two fields he planted as his own with his
own hand "at my first coming." Thomas Hutchinson in his
eighteenth-century *History of Massachusetts-Bay* mentions the famous rock and nearby spring; they were situated a little southwest
of the old Episcopal Church. Williams would doubtless have
returned the Indian greeting even if he did not initiate it. If the
Indians called out the greeting at all, it indicates their previous experience of Englishmen, mainly Williams. Because of previous arrangements with Canonicus and the Narragansett co-grand sachem
Miantonomy, the Indians would have been expecting Williams.

Slate Rock, according to the usual tradition, was the site of the greeting but not of the meeting landing. Williams's party coasted around Indian and Fox Points, in either case, and slit up the broad Mooshassuc through the dense oak forest to a peninsula where a spring issued and a hill rose near the confluence of the Mooshassuc and Woonasquatucket. Williams established his own home a few rods east of the spring, which lay in his plot and came to be known as Williams's Spring.

He surely already knew of this spring, whether the removal voyage followed an earlier reconnoitering one or not. His deposition of June 18, 1682, speaks of his "Coming into this Narriganset-Countrey" "about fifty years since" and traveling among Canonicus, Miantonomy, and Massasoit to assure them he meant to live peaceably by them, which would refer to the time of his residence at Plymouth. He goes on to say that "being inquisitiue of what Roote the Title or denominatjon Nahiggonsit should Come" and hearing that the name came from a little island between Puttequomscut and Musquomacuk on the sea and fresh-water side, "I went on purpose to see it, & about the place Called Sugar Loafe hill I saw jt & was within a pole of jt, but Could not learne why jt was cald Nahigonset." Thus the Providence area would not have been new country to him. He probably returned there, or even made the exploring trip to Sugar Loaf, while a resident of Salem; Angell might have accompanied him then too. Williams says in his deed of December 6, 1661, that he "had several treaties with Conanicusse and Miantonome . . . in the year 1634 and in the year 1635 . . . and in the end purchased of them the lands and meadows upon the two fresh rivers called Mooshassick and Wanasquatucket," and that two years after, the sachems established and confirmed the bounds by deed, "I having made covenant of peaceable neighborhood with all the Sachems and natives round about us; and having in a sense of God's merciful providence unto me in my distress, called the place, Providence."

The deed he here refers to bore the date March 24, 1638, and itself referred to an agreement of two years before, made probably at the time of his April 1636 landing at Providence or a little earlier. But this 1636 verbal agreement confirmed a yet earlier agreement accompanied by the usual gift, "for," says Williams, "I neuer gat any thing of Counounicus but by Gift." He, however, disclaimed that the land had been purchased, or could have been purchased, in the ordinary sense, even though he sometimes used the word "purchase" in alluding to his acquisition of it, and collected £30 from his twelve first fellow householders to defray the cost. But, as he said of Aquidneck (the island of Rhode Island) on August 25, 1658, "It was not price nor money that could have purchased Rhode Island. Rhode Island was purchased by love." Williams also understood what was almost incomprehensible to Europeans that, from Canonicus's point of view, the treaty of "purchase" did not bestow ownership but only the right to settle on the sachem's land as his subjects. When Canonicus would help himself to any of Williams's trading stock he pleased in later years, Williams patiently endured the situation, knowing that the grand sachem regarded all property in the Narragansett domain as his own.

When Winslow obliged Williams to seek quarter from Canonicus across Narragansett Bay, the shift in Williams's nominal allegiance from Ousamequin (Massasoit) to Canonicus and Miantonomy roused Ousamequin's jealousy. Ousamequin protested to Plymouth that Providence actually lay in Wampanoag territory! Williams's recollection in 1682 of having to travel in these early days among Canonicus, Miantonomy, and Ousamequin to calm their fury and satisfy them and their subordinate sachems of his honest intentions to live peaceably by them, patently includes his post- as well as pre-Providence settling. He says in an affidavit of December 13, 1661, that he consulted the two Narragansett grand sachems about Ousamequin's sudden claim to Providence, and that they told him Ousamequin was still their subject! He had solemnly subjected himself and his lands to them, they said, only now he seemed to revolt from his loyalties under the shelter of the English at Plymouth. Williams then declared this to Ousamequin, who admitted he was so subjected but that he had not been subdued by *war*, which he and his father had successfully maintained against the Narragansetts; "but God," said he, "subdued me by a plague, which swept away my people, and forced me to yield."

This conviction and confession of his [Williams continues], together with gratuities to himself and brethren and followers [from Williams's trading stock], made him often profess, that he was pleased that I should here be his neighbor, and that rather because he and I had been great friends at Plymouth, and also because that his and my friends at Plymouth advised him to be at peace and friendship with me, and he hoped that our children after us would be good friends together.

All the sachems in the end consented freely to Williams's occupation of Providence and to his joint ownership with Winthrop of Prudence Island. (For Williams functioned not only as an intelligence agent for Winthrop but as a business partner.) Ousamequin had really no other choice but consent after Bradford and his Council declared that, even if what the barbarian (their word) said should prove true, Williams "should not be molested and tost up and down againe while they had breath in their bodies."

The place Williams named Providence was "The Neck," a peninsula extending from Fox Point to Pawtucket between the Mooshassuc and Seekonk rivers. (Later, The Neck designated a larger area.) Sometimes Williams referred to it as "Mooshausick," its Indian name. In his first letter from there to Winthrop he calls it New Providence. This letter is undated. The earliest letter he wrote from there that is dated is one to Governor Vane of July 26, 1636. The first entry in the Providence Records bears the date June 16. Thus about two months of staking out, clearing, building, Indian negotiating, and so on, went by before the pioneers got round to formal meetings, records, or letter writing.

Williams names the first householders with him at Providence as "my loving friends and neighbors" Stukely Westcott, William Arnold, Thomas James, Robert Cole, John Greene, John Throckmorton (who had sailed from Bristol with his wife Rebecca and their two children on the same voyage as the Williamses), William Harris (the able but gnarled and grasping opportunist, apparently with some legal training, who became Williams's worst local enemy), William Carpenter (Arnold's brother-in-law), Thomas Olney, Francis Weston, Richard Waterman, and Ezekiel Holyman (who became the first pastor of the Providence Baptist church). All of these men had families, at least a few of whom had arrived with their house heads. A servant like Angell would be regarded as belonging to the household of an unindentured family man (Angell probably rejoined Waterman's household), and there may have been (in a short time definitely were) some nonservant single men in the group who, by virtue of not having families, could not qualify as householders. Verin fell in this category or else Williams forgot he was one of the first householders. As in Massachusetts and New Plymouth, only householders could have land or a voice in government. Benedict Arnold, who was to serve three times as governor of Rhode Island, is an instance of a settler who, in 1636, was yet a boy.

Mrs. Williams with her two daughters and with other wives and children made it from Salem the next spring. Winslow, "that great and pious soule," Williams calls him, "melted" (Williams's word) and paid the Williamses a visit. Touched at their poverty, he pressed a gold piece into Mrs. Williams's hand. Winslow speaks of his former "prophesier" as "a man lovely in his carriage [deportment], and whom I trust the Lord will yet recall."

Thirteen householders in the population of thirty-two in the first year formed the first genuine democracy—also the first church-divorced and conscience-free community—in modern history. This despite its lineaments as a typical New England farm town and Williams's temporary feudal character as sole owner of the land who asked the right (evidently denied) of personal veto over future comers, and despite the simultaneous origin of the century-long plague of dissension in the settlement, as of the land arrangements which stunted the democracy in its earliest infancy.

The simple frame cottages, backed by cornfields on high ground rising to steep bluffs, faced eastward across the broad expanse of the river. At the end of 1638 the village had 85 residents; in 1640, 120. It remained small, pig- and mosquito-ridden, dirt-laned, isolated, insecure, poor, narrow, contentious, mean; but however mixed the blessing, it was for the moment the freest place, perhaps, anywhere in the world.

10 : *The General Question of Government*

FROM the first, Williams insisted that the civil government at Providence be restricted to civil affairs. It is in a letter to Winthrop of probably June 1636 that he gives us our best clues to the political system he intially set up. "Hietherto," he writes, "the Masters of ffamilies haue ordinarily mett once a fort night & Consulted about our Common peace, watch, & planting; & mutuall Consent hath finished all matters with speed & peace." Of late, he says, some young *single* men have wanted the vote. He has drawn up a compact, or civil covenant (which shows him falling back on the Mayflower Compact of the Pilgrims); this, he says, he is going to have each master of a family subscribe to. It reads as follows:

We whose names are here vnder written, late inhabitants of the Massachusetts (vpon occasion of some difference of Conscience) . . . doe with free & ioint Consent promise each vnto other, that, for our Common peace & welfare (untill we heare further of the Kings royall pleasure Concerning our selues) we will from time to time subiect our selves in Actiue or passiue obedience to such orders & Agreements, as shall be made by the greater number of the present Howsehoulders, & such as shall be hereafter admitted by their Consent into the same priviledge & Covenant in our ordinarie meeting.

The town meeting and majority rule in the meeting were features already in operation in both Massachusetts and New Plymouth. Both of the latter colonies had already taken strides toward the day when voters and householders would be synonymous. Even before Winthrop died, a *non*freeman in the Bay could serve on juries, vote in town meetings for his local selectmen and militia captain, and hold office in the militia. He had the same protection a freeman had of his property and person or his trading and farming. That church-membership stumbling block to the general franchise did not apparently mean as much to the nonfreemen as it would have meant long later. Adult church members outnumbered freemen in Massachusetts; i.e. church members showed some reluctance to enter upon their political privileges. Once that stumbling block (or *Hedge*, as Cotton Mather put it, which separated the sheep from the goats) had been removed by the Crown—the Puritans of course would never have done it on their own; they even got an excoriation of its removal included in the Declaration of Independence—householding, regardless of poverty, heresy, or lack of social rank, meant the status of a freeman or voter. But from the founding of Massachusetts, the most conservative Puritans recognized that sovereignty resided in the people, who had a right to choose and depose rulers and set the bounds of their authority. "Free consent" (Hooker), "joynte consent" (Bradford), "mutuall consent" (Winthrop), "free mutuall consent" (Jacob), are terms one encounters over and over in Puritan writings. "The people," said Winthrop in 1637, "may not be subjected to any lawe or power amonge themselves without their consent; whatsoever is more than this, is neither lawfull nor durable, and instead of liberties may prove bondage or licentiousnesse."

To debase ourselves "to a meere Democratie" from the Bay's stable mixture of aristocracy and democracy would be a manifest breach of the Fifth Commandment, Winthrop went on (in a written debate with Vane), "for a Democratie is, among most Civill nations, accounted the meanest and worst of all formes of Government." The people choose but the rulers rule—according to their inner-restrained discretion within constitutional authorization. Winthrop reminded Vane that a magistrate was bound by the church covenant, by his freeman's oath, and by his very office, which required his seeking the public welfare in all things. "Where the people have Libertye to admitt, or reiect their Gouernors; and to require the Rule, by which they shalbe governed and Judged, this is not an Arbitrarye Gouerment," Winthrop reiterated to Hooker. He even concluded to Vane that the ultimate authority for Bay government was not its charter but the social compact of the people.

Williams had no serious quarrel with Winthrop on any of these points. His quarrel came over the proper domain of government. On the *Arbella* Winthrop had projected "a due forme of Government both ciuill and ecclesiasticall." Whether this made technically for a theocracy or not is an academic question, since the civil and church leaders had the identical, pre-agreed aim. "The Common weale and the Church is yet but one," as Williams says, for "hee that is banished from the one, must necessarily bee banished from the other also." Cotton's strict disciple and successor, John Davenport, preferred in *A Discourse about Civil Government in a New Plantation whose Design is Religion* to refer to the ecclesiastical and civil as "co-ordinate States . . . reaching forth help mutually each to other, for the welfare of both, according to God." Winthrop himself defined the purpose of this dual government on the *Arbella:*

> The end is to improve our lives to doe more service to the Lord the comforte and encrease of the body of christe whereof wee are members that our selves and posterity may be the better preserved from the Common corrupcions of this evill world to serve the Lord and worke out our Salvacion vnder the power and purity of his holy Ordinances.

(Compare Calvin:

> Civil government is designed, as long as we live in this world, to cherish and support the external worship of God, to preserve the pure doctrine of religion, to defend the constitution of the Church . . . and to establish general peace and tranquility.)

The chief end of civil government as Winthrop understood it was to insure the primacy of religious aims in the society—to make the world safe for Puritanism. So the government should govern in the interests of the church. As Cotton "anatomized" in *The Keyes of the Kingdom*, civil government is concerned with the civil peace, which entails two categories, of which the first includes disposing of men's goods, lands, lives, liberties, tributes, worldly honors, inheritances, etc.

> The second sort of things which concern civill peace, is, the *establishment of pure Religion, in doctrine, worship, and government*, according to the word of God: as also the reformation of all corruptions in any of these.

Williams quoted Luther in *The Blovdy Tenent:* "The *Government* of the *Civill Magistrate* extendeth no further then over the Bodies and Goods of their Subjects, not over their *Soules*."

If that were true, Cotton replied, it would still justify the government's "watchfulnesse against such pollutions of Religion as tend to Apostacy."

> For if the Church and People of God, fall away from God, God will visit the City and Countrey with publicke calamity, if not captivity for the Churches sake.

In pledging acceptance of God's graciously proffered New Covenant, church members assumed a stewardship over the whole community; to suffer doctrinal aberration anywhere in the community would amount to a breach of contract which would invite divine retribution upon all the inhabitants. Massachusetts was different in being a *covenanted* commonwealth. As Winthrop said on the *Arbella:*

That which the most in theire Churches maineteine as a truthe in profession onely, wee must bring into familiar and constant practise . . . neither must wee think that the lord will beare with such faileings at our hands as hee dothe from those among whome wee haue liued. . . . When God giues a speciall Commission he lookes to haue it strictly obserued in every Artickle . . . wee must Consider that wee shall be as a Citty vpon a Hill, the eies of all people are vppon vs; soe that if wee shall deale falsely with our god in this worke wee haue vndertaken and soe cause him to withdrawe his present help from vs, wee shall be made a story and a by-word through the world.

With the covenant doctrine the keystone of the Bay dual system, Winthrop and Cotton could not even listen to such observations of Williams as that pagan and antichristian kingdoms have been known to prosper and that, if magistrates in all parts of the world have the duty of judging in spiritual cases, they must judge according to their consciences, "whether *Pagan, Turkish* or *Antichristian.*"

. . . Notwithstanding their confidence of the *truth* of their owne way, yet the experience of our *Fathers errours,* our owne *mistakes* and *ignorance,* the sense of our own *weaknesses* and *blindnesse* in the depths of the *prophesies* & *mysteries* of the Kingdom of *Christ,* and the great professed *expectation* of *light* to come which we are not now able to comprehend, may abate the *edge,* yea sheath up the *sword* of persecution toward any, especially such as differ not from them in *doctrines* of *repentance,* or *faith,* or *holinesse* of *heart* and *life,* and hope of glorious and *eternall union* to come, but only in the way and manner of *administrations* of *Jesus Christ.*

The Bay Puritans hated to be called persecutors; they very much wished to regard themselves as mild and reasonable. Cotton insisted that the Bay did not compel a rigid uniformity, that it in fact allowed quite a degree of loving latitude. Cotton said explicitly that the Bay insisted on obedience only in *fundamentals* and itemized these under two heads—foundation of the Christian religion (like doctrines of salvation) and foundation of the Church ("as the matter and forme of it"). Without "right beliefe" in both, Cotton told

Williams, a man cannot be saved, so he cannot be permitted to err herein.

Cotton saw no inconsistency between this position and the one he stated in *An Exposition upon the Thirteenth Chapter of the Revelation* that all power fundamentally lies in the people, who must learn to set limits on both civil and church government; rather, he was really saying that the people should seek to ascertain what limits God has set in His Word. In the same sermon Cotton ringingly approved of the full liberty granted by God; "there is never peace where full liberty is not given, nor never stable peace where more than full liberty is granted." But he did not mean freedom of speech, exactly. Our tongues are our own and we have liberty to speak, he conceded, but we do not have liberty to speak blasphemies. "There is not the least blasphemy, but it is a great Sinne." We also have the liberty to enter church fellowship, liberty to choose and call gifted men to church office, and liberty to partake of the sacraments. Winthrop, Hooker, William Penn, *et al.*, agreed with him that the political liberty of the people, in church or civil government, is the liberty to carry out God's will. Winthrop likened the liberty of the people under the magistrates' autocratic rule to that of a woman's free choice in making a man her husband, which choice made him her lord, she subject to him. But this is not bondage for her; it is liberty.

If Williams had lived just four years longer than his allotted eighty, he would scarcely have believed his ears at hearing that the principal Bay minister of that time was calling for gratitude at James II's decree of religious liberty. Did Increase Mather really want religious liberty for all consciences in Massachusetts? Little if any more than his own father, or posthumous father-in-law Cotton. But he did want freedom for Congregationalists to worship in their own way, even if that meant everybody else would have the same freedom. He was salvaging what he could. The question by then, however, had turned to whether the Puritans could possibly realize their religious aims without external coercion by the civil government.

Cotton had not thought so. Puritanism required men to go against the natural bent of their nature, which the Puritans said is slothful, lecherous, and otherwise hopelessly depraved, at best deserving eternal perdition; the saints are overwhelmingly outnumbered. Williams had little faith in "naturall, sinfull, and inconstant man" either; he, furthermore, put the same priority on saving of souls that Cotton did. But only by free consent, he said, could the soul decide; and man was no less depraved when given the power of government. What if the governors decided to coerce *false* religion? Williams saw falseness in Bay orthodoxy. He scoffed at the Bay's "fig-leaf" pretensions to being Israel when, in his view, all Christian believers collectively constituted the new Israel. He went so far as to regale Winthrop from Providence on October 24, 1636,

> that amongst all the People of God wheresoeuer scattered about Babells Bancks either in Rome or England etc. your case is the worst by farr, because while others of Gods Israell tenderly respect such as desire to feare the Lord your very Judgment and Conscience leads you to smite and beate your fellow Servants.

Williams said that government is the natural way provided by God to cope with the corrupt nature of man. But since government cannot be trusted to know which religion is true—in all probability will single out the true for crushing—the best hope for true religion lies in protecting the freedom of all religion, along with nonreligion, from the state.

So long as no denomination could disturb the peace, free permission of conscience and of assembly would not hurt the civil government, Williams said, while it would be one of the most expedient ways of propagating the Gospel. Cotton said that if civil weapons were thus debarred from defending religion, "then let all Seducers to Apostacy, Idolaters, & Heretiks . . . rejoyce in an open doore of liberty, & safety," which Williams "hath set wide open before them." If civil states cannot help the Lord, "shall the curse of *Meroz* be so avoided, because the Lord wanteth not the power to help himselfe?"

"The civill Sword may make a Nation of Hypocrites & Antichristians, but not one Christian," says Williams in a marginal note citing Isaiah 10. "If it did so," said Cotton in a letter of about 1651 to Sir Richard Saltonstall, "yet better to be hypocrites than prophane persons. Hypocrites give God part of his due, the outward man, but the prophane person giveth God neither outward nor inward man."

"The Sword hardneth," Williams protested. "If any be hardned by the just faithfull severity of Magistrates in this case, it is meerely accidental," Cotton replied. "It is but *Humanity*, it is but *Christianity* to exercise *meeknesse* and *moderation* to all men," Williams further protested. "The punishments executed upon false Prophets, and seducing Teachers, doe bring downe showers of Gods blessings upon the civill State, 1 Kings 18:40, 41," said Cotton.

"The blood of so many hundred thousand souls of *Protestants* and *Papists*, spilt in the *Wars* of *present* and *former Ages*, for their respective *Consciences*, is not *required* nor *accepted* by *Iesus Christ* the *Prince* of *Peace*."

"But to say that Christ delighteth not in the bloud of men, who after the acknowledgement of his Truth doe tread the bloud of his Covenant under foote, and wittingly and willingly reject him from reigning over them . . . and joyn with his enemy Antichrist, in blaspheming and persecuting Christ, and his Saints, This the *Discusser* can never make good to the word of Christ."

"I observe the *unmercifulnesse* of such *doctrines* and *hearts*," said Williams, "as if they had forgotten the *Blessednesse, Blessed* are the mercifull, for they shall obtaine mercy, Math. 5." To which Cotton countered with Luke 19:27: "Those mine enemies, that would not that I should reigne over them, bring them hither and slay them before my face."

"But [Christ] chargeth straitly that his Disciples should be so far from persecuting those that would not bee of their Religion, that when they were *persecuted* they should *pray* (Matth. 5.) when they were *cursed* they should *blesse*, &c." Cotton came up with another Scripture, Deuteronomy 13:10: "Thou shalt put him to death, because he sought to thrust thee away from the Lord thy God."

Cotton thanked God, he wrote Williams, that God never left him to fall into any fundamental error, let alone persist therein after conviction and admonition. Williams was being obstinate and self-willed; he had been punished, not "*for his conscience*, but for sinning *against his conscience*." Williams notes that the substitution of "punish" for "persecute" attempted to clothe Bay action in a term more proper to justice. "But is not this the *guise* and *profession* of all that ever *persecuted* or *hunted* men for their *Religion* and *conscience?*"

When Saltonstall wrote from England in alarm at the Bay Puritans' tendency to persecution so soon after fleeing persecution themselves, Cotton replied in effect that the Bay was actually tolerant in disposition and continuing as tolerant as possible under the circumstances. But

Doe you thinke the Lord hath crowned the state with so many victoryes that they should suffer so many miscreants to pluck the crown of soveraignty from Christs head?

What the Bay Puritans fled from was "mens inventions, to which wee else should have been compelled; wee compel none to mens inventions." What we compel to is "God's institutions." "Wee believe there is a vast difference betweene mens inventions and God's institutions."

Williams reaffirmed an old Puritan (and Jesuit) point of view, one that Cotton, Winthrop, and Hooker already subscribed to, when he declared in 1644 that "Kings and Magistrates must be considered (as formerly [i.e. back into the Middle Ages]) invested with no more *power* then the *people* betrust them with." A civil government "is an *Ordinance* of *God*, to conserve the *civill peace* of a people, so farre as concernes their *Bodies* and *Goods*."

> But from this *Grant* I infer . . . that the *Soveraigne, originall,* and *foundation* of *civill power* lies in the *people*, (whom they must needs meane by the *civill power* distinct from the *Government* set up.) And if so, that a People may erect and establish what *forme* of *Government* seemes to them most meete for their *civill condition:* It is evident that such *Governments* as are by them erected and established, have no more *power*, nor for no longer time, then the *civill power* or people consenting and agreeing shall betrust them with. This is cleare not only in *Reason*, but in the experience of all *common-weales*, where the people are not deprived of their *naturall freedome* by the power of *Tyrants*.

If, however, the magistrates get their power to govern the *church* from the people, Williams continues, that is a different story altogether, for then

> undeniably it followes, that a *people* . . . have fundamentally and originally . . . a power to governe the *Church*, to see her doe her *duty*, to correct her, to redresse, reforme, establish, &c. And if this be not to pull *God* and *Christ*, and *Spirit* out of *Heaven*, and subject them unto *naturall*, sinfull, and inconstant men, and so consequently to *Sathan* himself, by whom all *people* naturally are guided, let *Heaven* and *Earth* judge.

Whereas the Puritan axiom of popular sovereignty, when applied to church government, reached the extreme expressed by Increase Mather that the only way he knew to find the will of God was by a vote of the congregation, Williams held civil democracy inapplicable in church. For him, the church remained an inviolable monarchy under Jesus, and holiness a sphere in which popular judgment would be incompetent or irrelevant. A congregation might erect its material interests or way of life as the Truth; it is not qualified or trustworthy to make decisions about the Truth to be taught. The difference between church and state government is fundamental: the state seeks to establish peace, not Truth; the church, unhindered —in fact, *freed* by the civil peace established by the state—seeks Truth but bears no responsibility for keeping the civil peace.

Williams never deceived himself that a democratic state should be weak or decentralized or merely presided over by its executive. Strength was necessary for freedom as well as for peace. But dearly bought freedom got an admixture of ashes when Williams found that other men did not share his moral self-discipline, self-denial, or concern for the general welfare. "We enjoy liberties of soule & body," he said to Winthrop Jr. on February 15, 1654, "but it is licence we desire, except the Most Holy helpe vs." He had a hard time trying to persuade his fellow colonists that he never meant freedom of conscience to be construed as freedom from law or government. Establishing authority proved even harder than maintaining liberty. He worked constantly for a strong government, on the model of New Plymouth and Massachusetts, and wrote the town clerk of Providence on January 15, 1681, that "it is the duty of every man to maintain, encourage, and strengthen the hand of authority." "That ever I should speak or write a tittle," he had said to the town of Providence in January 1655, "that tends to . . . an infinite liberty of conscience, is a mistake, and which I have ever disclaimed and abhorred"; he went on to compare the elected office holder to the captain of a ship at sea, who should permit every kind of worship aboard without compelling any to come to the ship's worship; but

notwithstanding this liberty, the commander of this ship ought to command the ship's course, yea, and also command that justice, peace and sobriety, be kept and practiced, both among the seamen and all the passengers.

Williams was entirely aware of both the precedence and degree of the liberty of the democracy he established: "the first of our spirits which neither Old nor New England knowes the like, nor no part of the World a greater," he said a little archaically in his impressive letter to the nearby town of Warwick on January 1, 1666, on the meaning and responsibilities of liberty. What he meant by the term "liberty" is substantially what we mean today, not some special obsolete construction. He spells out his meaning:

> Libertie of our persons: No Life no Limbe taken from us: No Corporall punishment no Restraint, but by knowne Lawes and Agreements of our owne making.

> Libertie of our Estates, Howses Catle, Lands, Goods, and not a peny to be taken by any rate [tax] from us, without euery mans free debate by his Deputies, chosen by himselfe and sent to the General Assembly.

> Libertie of Societie or Corporacion: of sending or being sent to the General Assembly, of choosing and being chosen to all offices, and of making or repealing all Lawes and Constitutions among us.

Since Williams remained a Puritan, it is evident that Puritanism did not have to be overthrown for democracy to arise. The first American democrat was not the last Puritan preacher to espouse the cause of democracy while remaining a Puritan preacher. John Wise, for instance, formulated and advocated Jeffersonian democracy in all its essentials more than a quarter of a century before Jefferson was born. Wise, a Puritan preacher at Ipswich, could be highhanded but had gained fame about thirty years before writing his two little books which extol democracy when he chose jail in the Andros regime in protest against the suppression of free discussion and against taxation without representation. His 1717 book not only defines and commends democracy but speaks as though it happily prevailed in the Bay at the time. The tendency of Massachusetts toward the same end result as Williams's fledgling democracy of 1636 had become so marked in Cotton Mather's time that the British government looked on the Bay just as the Bay had looked on her "back door," Rhode Island. "Disorderly"—the same word—expressed the reaction of each. The lords commissioners of the Board of Trade reporting to the king in 1721 deplored the democracy and independence, thus disorderliness, of Bay government:

> . . . The unequal Balance of their Constitution having lodg'd too great a Power in the Assembly; This Province is, and is always likely to continue in great Disorder. . . . the Assembly is generally fill'd with People of small Fortunes, and mean Capacities, who are easily led into any Measures that seem to enlarge their Liberties, & Privileges, how detrimental soever the Same may be to Great Britain, or to Your Majesty's Royal Prerogative.

Despite Williams's liberal private tutoring of servants, children, and others, he did not manage to do much for universal literacy or higher education, on which democracy must fundamentally depend; nor did he bring about much material progress, measures for which he worked in vain against his parochial fellow townsmen. Frontier circumstances proved too great a barrier also; he can hardly be blamed. Most dismaying, he could not so much as say his experiment had achieved that harmony and affection without which Jefferson says liberty and even life itself are but dreary things. Williams felt as Jefferson on this score: "For all Experience tells us," he tried to reason with the town of Providence in an undated document, "that Publike Peace and Loue is better than abundance of Corne and Cattell." But the history of Rhode Island and Providence Plantations in Williams's time is shot through with dreary discord and hate. The wonder may be that he could hold the weak and divided colony together at all—which he sometimes did almost single-handed, resisting its foes within and without, in America and England, by an uncanny resourcefulness. The commonwealth became permanent.

WILLIAMS proved equal to a consistent systematization of democratic principles, but he made no effort to hide what an amateur he found himself to be in the mechanics of implementing them. He repeatedly sent to Winthrop for advice, and got gracious answers. In an undated letter, probably May 1637, for instance, Williams wrote Winthrop:

Dear Sir, (notwithstanding our differences concerning the worship of God and the ordinances ministred by Antichrist's power) you have been always pleased lovingly to answer my boldness in civil things.

Now, on this occasion Williams has a new problem: what to do about

one unruly person who openly in town meeting more then once, professeth to hope for and long for a better government then the country hath yet, and lets not to particularize, by a general Governor, &c. The white [i.e. the target] which such a speech or person levels at can be no other then the raising of the fundamental liberties of the country.

Whatever advice Winthrop gave, he did not likely smile about anyone's difficulties with a malcontent who wished to give up Puritan autonomy to royal authority.

He surely smiled at the dilemma of Providence democracy of late summer 1638. Williams and his first companions had made an order that no man should be molested for his conscience. But by midsummer 1638 Joshua Verin, one of Williams's original company, got tired of his wife's being frequently gone to Willaims's private religious meetings on weekdays and forbade her to attend any more. Williams with his fellow communicants (who, within a few months, became sprinkle Baptists) therefore prosecuted Verin in town meeting "for a breach of a covenant for restraining liberty of conscience." William Arnold stood up to object that when he consented to that order he never intended it should extend to the breach of any ordinance of God, such as the subjection of wives to their husbands. John Greene (whom Winthrop delightedly exposes as a bigamist) countered that if they should restrain their wives, all the women in the country would cry out on them. Arnold answered him: "Did you pretend to leave the Massachusetts, because you would not offend God to please men, and would you now break an ordinance and commandment of God to please women?" Some thought that if Verin would not suffer his wife to have her liberty, the *church* should dispose her to some other man who would use her better. Arnold argued that it was not the woman's desire to go so oft from home but only Williams's and his fellow religionists'. The Assembly proceeded to censure Verin anyway—over Arnold's protest that it was against their own order; for Verin did what he did out of conscience, whereas their order had been that no man should be censured for his conscience. Verin removed temporarily back to Salem in disgust, but Winthrop, who relates the story, more probably got it from Arnold, whom Williams in a letter to Winthrop in September 1638 charges with plotting many odious accusations in writing and asks Winthrop for a chance to see what Arnold has written. Thus the wrangling patriarchs at Providence revealed a widening rift that soon divided the little democracy against itself when the Arnold faction appallingly seceded with their lands and subjected themselves to Massachusetts. (American democracy, incidentally, did not finally grant suffrage to women until 1920, the Presbyterian President reluctantly supporting it as a war measure.)

"NOT ONLY I but the many millions of millions of our Father Adams children (which are as sand upon the Sea Shoare) are not of your perswasion," Williams lectured the Massachusetts General Court in the same letter that he requested free passage into the Bay in October 1651. Both he and the Bay leadership put true religion first;

the Bay leaders sought to ensure it by state enforcement, Williams by freeing it from the state. Williams also grew more and more doubtful as to what true religion was, while Massachusetts grew even more certain (though this defensive certainty implies over-compensation for the same doubt). Williams's civil democracy fol-lowed logically from the Puritanism he and the Bay held in common, once the principle of separation of church and state had been wedged through the ancient dualism (which dualism, in fact, was no more Puritan than it was Anglican, Lutheran, Roman Catho-lic, or Roman Pagan, etc.). Separatism from the established church and from the Bay churches (which the Bay claimed to remain part of the Anglican establishment and which Williams claimed to be but another establishment) stemmed from some basic disgust with official orthodoxy, and separation of church and state continued and confirmed that basic disgust. It hurt Williams to have to disagree, especially with Winthrop, but friendship could no more keep him from rushing to religion's rescue than it could Winthrop, who voted for Williams's banishment for the same reason, differently in-terpreted. Williams wrote Winthrop on April 16, 1638, that he would rest in his appeal to the Most High in what they differed; "it is no small griefe that I am other wise persuaded"; but, he warned, "the fire will try your workes and mine."

Winthrop could not understand why Williams would have delib-erately deserted the Bay cause, deliberately incurred exile, and, we may guess, deliberately failed to support Winthrop's moderate "party" with his clergical prestige in the practical power struggle which was deciding the Bay's destiny. It could hardly have escaped Winthrop's mind that he and Williams had, in a sense, gone down together, and that Williams's forcing of issues had put an added strain on Winthrop's partisan struggle when he found himself caught between the popular movement to reject authority and the "reactionary" movement among the magistrates and clergy which exploited the popular movement for repression and rigid conform-ity. When changes in the scheme of things toward humaneness and flexibility depended on Winthrop's retaining power, both the popu-lace and Williams deserted their best hope. Winthrop adjusted to the turn of realities by reversing his natural moderate bent. His re-grets over this course began to emerge about two years after Wil-liams's flight, though it was too late then to alter the course, which he however managed to justify to himself. He felt sure by October 1636 that Williams must have regrets. He asked Williams what he thought he had gained by his course. Williams replied:

I Confess my Gaines Cast vp in mans Exchange are Loss of Friends, Esteeme, Maintenances, &c but what was Gaine in that respect I desire to count losse for the Excellencie of the Knowledge of Christ Jesus my Lord[.]

To His all glorious Name I know I haue gained the honour of one of his poore Witnesses, though in Sackcloth[.]

Is your spirit as even as it was seven years since?

I will not follow the Fashion either in Commending or Condemning my Selfe. You & I stand at one dreadfull Dreadfull Tribunall: Yet what is past I desire to Forget & to press forward towards the marke for the price of the High Calling of God in Christ[.]

And for the Euennes of my spirit . . . I hope . . . to mourne dayly, heavily, vncessantly till the Lord looke downe from Heaven & bring all his precious living stones into one New Jerusalem[.]

Are you not grieved that you have grieved so many?

. . . I vehemently Sorrow, for the Sorrow of any of Zions Daughters, who should euer reioice in her King &c[.] Yet I must (& o that I had not cause) grieue because so many of Zions daughters See not & grieue not for their Soules Defilements, & that so few beare John Companie in weeping after the vnfoulding of the Seales which only Weepers are acquainted with.

Do you think the Lord hath utterly forsaken us?

I answer Jehovah will not forsake His People for His great names Sake. . . . & if it proue as I know assuredly it shall that though you haue Come farr yet you never Came out of the wildernes to this Day . . . & this Sir I beseech you doe more Seriously then euer & abstract your selfe with a holy Violence from the Dungheape of this Earth, the Credit & Comfort of it.

From what spirit and to what end do you drive?

Whether the Spirit of Christ Jesus, for whose visible Kingdome & Ordinances I witnes &c or the Spirit of Antichrist (1 John 4) against whome only I Contest: doe driue me let the Father of Spirits be pleased to Search & (worthy Sir) be you allso pleased by the word to Search: & I hope you will find that as you Say you doe, I allso Seeke Jesus who was nayled to the Gallowes, I aske the way to lost Zion, I witness what I believe I See patiently . . . in Sackcloth I long for the bright appearance of the Lord Jesus to Consume the man of Sinn. . . . I reioice in the hopes that . . . within a few yeares (Through I feare though many tribulacions) the way of the Lord Jesus the first & most ancient path shall be more plainely discovered to you & me.

Whether your former condition would not have stood with a gracious heart?

Who then can wonder (& yet indeede who Can not but wonder) how a Gracious Heart before the Lords awakening & Calling & drawing out may lie in many Abominations?

11 : *The Pequot War and Antinomian*

Insurrection

JOHN OLDHAM, the logical choice, became the Bay agent who effected peaceful trade with the Pequots in accordance with the Newtown treaty of November 7, 1634. He did this during the year 1635 in the course of his tireless trading rounds. Returning to the Connecticut from Boston in April 1636, about the time Williams was founding Providence, he delivered a letter to Winthrop Jr. at Saybrook from the latter's foster-mother Margaret. She warned that Winthrop's pregnant wife, in Margaret's care, seemed farther along than their estimate allowed for when the young governor left Boston in March.

"Sayebrook" is the name as given the plantation at the Connecticut's mouth by Lord Saye and his obstinate but tolerant colleague, Lord Brooke (Robert Greville). Baron Brooke, at twenty-seven in 1632 (a couple of years younger than Winthrop Jr.) was hardly more than half Viscount Saye's age. As two of the few Puritans in the House of Lords, Saye and Brooke had constant reminders that they might soon need a haven abroad. The Earl of Warwick, president of the fairly defunct Council for New England, had issued a patent to them and ten of their friends in March 1632. Saye and Brooke never got to New England, which they in fact wound up subverting for purer aristocracy elsewhere. Most men miscalled their settlement "Seabrooke" in the seventeenth century, but it eventually came to be known officially as "Saybrook."

On November 24, 1635, after Winthrop Jr. had reached Boston with his commission, he sent a bark under Edward Gibbons (a long-reformed Old Planter of Morton's Merrymount crew) and another officer with twenty workmen to take possession of the mouth of the Connecticut before the Dutch could. Four days later, Winthrop's engineer Lion Gardener landed in Boston in a twenty-five-ton Norsey bark with his Dutch wife. They wintered with the Winthrop Jrs. in or near Boston.

Gardener had been discovered and engaged in Rotterdam, where he had stayed as engineer and master of fortifications to the Prince of Orange after voyaging to the Low Countries under General Thomas Fairfax. The pastor of the English church at Rotterdam was none other than Winthrop Jr.'s new stepfather-in-law Hugh Peter (Peter had entered into a marriage of convenience with a rich old Essex widow) and the teacher none other than Cotton's disciple John Davenport, who had succeeded the great Ames as Peter's colleague and who in time became a founder of New Haven. These two clergymen, together with gentlemen unidentified, persuaded Gardener to pioneer on the Connecticut. Their £30 advance enabled him to marry a Dutch girl before he left and to take two servants along.

In March 1636 Winthrop Jr. and the Gardeners (Mrs. Gardener eight months pregnant) proceeded, apparently overland, to meet the company boat at Narragansett, the Indian capital where the co-grand sachems dwelt. It must have stood somewhere near the modern town of Narragansett, far down the west side of the bay below and opposite later Newport. Winthrop does not mention seeing Williams in his report to his father of April 7 but likely located his unusual acquaintance in the vicinity and got him to conduct Gardener and himself to Canonicus's "great Citty," where he says he conferred with the old sachem. The governor and the lieutenant sailed from Narragansett the afternoon of April 1 and made Saybrook at about six o'clock the same evening.

Peter and Vane, whom the proprietors had commissioned as agents in association with Winthrop Jr., remained in the Bay to forward supplies expected from Europe, as well as supplies Peter arranged for on the proprietors' credit. In May, Sir Arthur Hazelrigg reached Boston with news of the proprietors' discouragement with their Connecticut design; he took immediate offense at Peter's part and refused to pay the bills contracted in the proprietors' name.

Vane shortly resigned his Connecticut commission because, on May 25, 1636, the General Court elected him governor of Massachusetts. The guns of the ships in Boston Harbor echoed and re-echoed against the Trimountain. The Court elected Sir Henry, though he was only twenty-three, partly out of deference to his social rank and to his father, a Privy Councillor (albeit incompetent); partly for the well-being his influence seemed to promise the economically depressed and partly dispersing colony; but perhaps most of all because of himself. This last suggestion might have mystified a stranger who saw this medium-height man for the first time. If Vane were not actually cross-eyed, his lopsided face made him appear so; his overlarge chin, accentuated by his plumpness, made him seem like a petulant child about to break into a tantrum; and he wore a habitual harried expression as though evil spirits were pursuing him. But anyone forgot all this the moment Vane's countenance lit up as he conversed in his animated, deeply sincere way. Since his little busybody father was the king's chamberlain, Vane had been brought up at court; his gracious manners and impeccable grooming therefore came as naturally as his seriousness. A youthful religious crisis disconcerted his parents and made him available to the Puritan cause in England; the Puritan party accepted him as a gift from above in a desperate hour. Everybody liked him; he was grave, pleasing, accomplished. Winthrop Sr. describes him as "a wise and godly gentleman." His gravity, piety, and youth probably reminded old-timers in Massachusetts of the lamented young Sir Isaac Johnson. Like Johnson, Vane had real ability for leadership, though in 1636 it had not approached that subtle refinement which he employed so adroitly a few years later as a leader of the revolutionary Long Parliament. The Bay fathers had no suspicion at the time of this May election that Vane brought into power with him the set of attitudes called "antinomian," and they could not remotely have foreseen the intimate friendship which eventually developed between him and Williams.

The English ship captains in Boston Harbor did not salute the election of Winthrop Sr. as deputy-governor on May 25; they did not deem him in any way identified with the king. (Charles I was not the King who symbolized Winthrop's allegiance.) Winthrop's return to favor within the colony should not go unnoticed; but for Vane's unanticipated presence, he would probably have returned to the governor's chair that May. It was from his position as deputy-governor that Winthrop later marshaled the counterattack against antinomianism and virtually directed the Bay's "foreign" policy in the Indian war crisis (Vane having to defer to unsubstitutable experience in Indian affairs). Winthrop civilly bore with his young superior, who was less than half his age, both in the Council and in the Boston congregation, where they also sat together on the bench of highest honor.

One of the first acts of the new administration was to call at last for the delivery of the Indians involved in Captain Stone's murder. The reply Oldham brought back in late June was that the old men of the Pequot tribe had not consented to that part of the treaty which required delivery on demand. "They haue broken the very condition of the peace betwixt vs," Vane and Winthrop reacted in their joint statement of July 4, the day the Court of Assistants decided to wait no longer in taking steps to avenge Stone. Vane and Winthrop wrote Winthrop Jr., charging him to confer with the Pequots, hardly fifteen miles eastward from Saybrook. This commission instructed him to call the Pequot grand sachem, Sassacus (who had succeeded his murdered father, Wopigwooit), to account for the Pequots' part in the murder of three Englishmen on Long Island (in 1635, when a bark bound from the Bay for Virginia was cast away there in a tempest; two, rather than the three the governors thought, may have fallen; the rest of the crew managed to escape) and for efforts to seize a Plymouth bark anchored at Pequot for trade, as well as for the murder of Stone and party; and "if they shall not giue you satisfaction according to these our instructions, or shall bee found guilty of any of the sayd murthers, and will not deliuer the actours in them into our hands, that then . . . we . . . shall reuenge the blood of our countrimen as occasion shall serue."

Vane entrusted this document to Peter, who despite bad health, insisted on traveling overland to Connecticut at this time. He undoubtedly wanted Winthrop Jr. to hear his side of the supply story, and he intended to scout commercial possibilities at Long Island and New Amsterdam with George Fenwick before returning. Fenwick, the one Warwick patentee who ever actually settled at Saybrook, accompanied Peter on this journey with a servant lad.

Vane and Winthrop sent the heavy Pequot present of otterskin coats, beaver, and skeins of wampum, which had sealed the 1634 treaty, to Winthrop Jr. by Oldham, to be returned to Sassacus in case the sachem refused to come to terms.

Winthrop Jr. and Gardener were expecting three hundred men from England for building and tilling at Saybrook when Oldham hove in instead around July 8 with the Pequot present. Peter and Fenwick arrived soon after, having engaged a shallop at Hartford belonging to the young Indian interpreter Thomas Stanton, who brought them on down the river. Besides the commission and news of the falling through of the patentees' immediate plans, Peter brought word from Elizabeth Winthrop that her time was now very imminent.

Already disappointed at the failure of large reinforcements to arrive, Gardener blanched both at Winthrop Jr.'s decision to depart from Connecticut "temporarily" and at the emissaries' flat statement that the Bay would have the Pequots' lives, not their presents. Over the Lieutenant's strenuous objections, Winthrop Jr. forthwith summoned "the malignant furius Pequot," Sassacus, to Saybrook and spoke with him through Stanton. Not even Gardener tells us what they said, but the governor returned the present—a virtual declaration of war. Winthrop Jr., Peter, and Fenwick left the Fort for Boston, via New Netherland, apparently in Stanton's pinnace, for Oldham proceeded upriver.

Two or three days later, an Indian named Cocommithus who had lived at Plymouth and learned to speak good English, came to the Fort from Pequot to invite Pynchon's agent there, Stephen Winthrop (Winthrop Sr.'s fourth son), to trade for furs at Pequot and receive two horses (stolen from a man named Eltow) which had been there a long while. Gardener appreciated that this invitation, coming right after the ceremonial cancellation of the treaty, might be a trap but nevertheless allowed young Winthrop to take the Fort shallop and five men provided they observe strict precautions. In spite of finding little of the trade that had lured them, the traders ignored Gardener's warnings. Two men even waded ashore to boil a kettle. One of them, Richard Hurlbut, stepped into Mononoto's wigwam, not far from the landing, to inquire about the promised horses. (Mononoto was second only to Sassacus among the Pequots.) As the men inside moved out, Mononoto's squaw, Wincumbone, made desperate signs to Hurlbut, who drew his sword and ran for the boat, shouting. His companion, Sergeant Tilly, clapped the kettle over his head, and the two clambered aboard just as a crowd of Pequots appeared at the waterside. The shallop raced back to Saybrook, where Gardener realized that the Pequots now "plotted our destruction."

When Oldham came back down the Connecticut on July 19 or 20, Gardener purchased a few items from him that cost five pieces and noticed that Oldham tied them in a clout together with £50 in gold he had collected elsewhere. Oldham bade Gardener good-bye and shoved off from Saybrook for Block Island, his next stop. He had with him two Narragansetts and two English servant boys.

That trusty but callous sailor, John Gallop (a West Country man who had come over on the *Mary and John* and settled at Dorchester), happened to be returning from the then-regular Connecticut run with another man and two little boys in a twenty-ton bark on July 20, making for Long Island, when at the very mouth of the destined harbor, a sudden shift of wind forced them to bear up instead for Block Island. There they saw a small pinnace anchored two miles from shore and, drawing closer, recognized it as Oldham's.

Gallop hailed Oldham but got no answer. Fourteen Indians scurried on the pinnace deck, and a canoe was making away full of Indians and goods. Gallop suspected they had killed Oldham; he felt certain of it as the scurriers let slip and clumsily set up sail, going with the off-shore wind and tide for the Narragansett main. Gallop darted his boat ahead of them and let fly with duck shot, which is all the ammunition he and his little crew had, and nothing but two muskets and two pistols all around. The opposing Indians stood ready with guns, pikes, and swords. But the duck shot galled them enough to send them all under hatches. Gallop then stood off, returned with a good gale, and rammed the pinnace on her quarter— almost oversetting her. Six of the Indians incredibly jumped overboard and drowned.

Still too outnumbered to dare boarding the pinnace, Gallop and his fellows stood off again, this time fitting their anchor to their stem, and bored into the pinnace's bow. The anchor held them fast to the pinnace while they fired away through the inch boarding and raked her fore and aft, sure to have killed or hurt some of the concealed Indians. Seeing none show, Gallop pried loose to stand off again. Four or five Indians then leaped into the sea and drowned. With only four left on the pinnace, Gallop and his crew boarded her. One Indian immediately came up and surrendered. Gallop had him bound and thrown in the hold. A second came up, who also got bound. But, knowing the Indians' skill at untying each other when left together, and having no other place to keep them separately (Gallop reported), he threw the second bound prisoner overboard. He could not get to the other two Indians, who held a little room below decks with their swords.

The Gallop company looked about and found Oldham under an old seine, stark naked, his head cleft to the brain and his legs and one hand cut as if the Indians had been trying to amputate them, yet still warm. They slid him into the sea. Then they took the goods left aboard, also the sails, and towed the pinnace away. As night approached, the wind rose, forcing Gallop to turn the empty boat loose, which carried to the Narragansett shore.

Whether it was Gallop or the Narragansett grand sachems who notified Williams of this incident, he immediately went to work on the case. From this moment, his career and status underwent a radical redefinition. He found out later that summer that one Audsah had done the actual braining of Oldham and that Wequashcuck, a petty sachem of Niantic married to the mother of Sassacus, was sheltering him. Miantonomy managed to have Block Islanders execute Audsah at a cost of six fathom of wampum. Williams's certification of what had befallen Oldham, together with news of the grand sachems' reaction of grief and of Miantonomy's setting forth with two hundred men in seventeen canoes to take revenge, arrived in Boston on July 26 in a letter to Governor Vane, carried by none other than the two Indians whom Gallop had been unable to extricate from Oldham's pinnace, plus a third Narragansett, all three emissaries of old Canonicus.

The Assistants, or several of them, summoned the Indian prisoner whom Gallop had brought back from the pinnace. The prisoner divulged that all the petty sachems of the Narragansetts had contrived Oldham's death without the privity of the grand sachems and that the two escaped Indians who at this moment faced him had been acquainted with the plot. Since, however, the escapees came as official messengers, the Assistants would not imprison them or, at any rate, not both of them. Vane wrote Williams to let the Narragansetts know that the Bay expected them to return the two boys who had worked with Oldham and to take revenge on their Block Island subjects. Vane ominously added that Williams should take precautions for himself in case Massachusetts took occasion to make war on the Narragansetts.

The next day, the twenty-seventh, Vane wrote Canonicus via one of Canonicus's messengers (knowing Williams would do the translating) to explain that the magistrates suspected this messenger of complicity in Oldham's murder and were sending him back only because he was a messenger, but that they had decided to keep the other suspected messenger, together with the earlier prisoner. If Canonicus should send for them, he could have them but should return them again to clear themselves. Williams, meanwhile, had got Miantonomy to order the sachem of Niantic to send to Block Island for Oldham's two servants. A man of Miantonomy's escorted the boys home to the Bay.

The sachem of Niantic would have been either Wepiteamock or Ninigret. Wepiteamock, a fairly obedient brother-in-law of Miantonomy's, ruled at Wekapaug (later Westerly)—interchangeably called Niantic (or Nyantaquit) after the tribe—on the east bank of the Niantic, or Pawcatuck. The more notorious Ninigret—a cousin of Miantonomy—known at this time by his name Janemo, ruled at the site of later Charlestown, Rhode Island, between Wekapaug and the seat of the grand sachems on the bay. "Niantic" seems to have referred to the seat of either of the two petty sachems or to their country as a whole. Their country was that of the East Niantics.

Williams found out that Ninigret, whom in 1654 he characterized as "proud & fierce," had hired two of the petty sachems who boarded Oldham's pinnace, and that one of these was dead. Three of the seven Indians who drowned, said Williams, were sachems, in addition to the subordinate of Ninigret's who evidently died of duck-shot wounds. Williams learned in July 1640 from Stanton that some of Oldham's goods and gold were even then kept at Niantic. Gardener says he saw several Dutchmen with some of Oldham's gold coins which the Narragansetts had punched and made into necklaces to sell.

But toward the end of July 1636 Miantonomy had already recovered a large part of Oldham's goods and nearly a hundred fathom of wampum, which he turned over to Williams, who in turn told Vane he was holding it for the Bay. Vane and Winthrop wrote back to Williams to have the rest of the accessories to Oldham's death sent to Boston, also the rest of the goods, and that he should inform Canonicus and Miantonomy that Massachusetts held them innocent but six under-sachems guilty. These latter, or several of them, took refuge with the Pequots.

Winthrop Jr. probably did not make it back to Boston in time for the birth of his daughter Elizabeth on July 24 (Ann Hutchinson undoubtedly in attendance). When he did arrive in a few days with his report on the parley with Sassacus, the Council's hatching plan to attack Block Island enlarged to include Pequot as well. But they did not dare attack Block Island without first making sure of the Narragansetts. On August 8 Vane sent Lieutenants Edward Gibbons and John Higginson (nineteen-year-old son of Francis) with the Massachusetts sachem Cutshamekin, to treat with Canonicus about revenge upon the sullen Block Islanders. Canonicus received the deputation well and greatly impressed them with his wisdom, authority, and dignity. He offered assistance to the avengers, "yet upon very safe and wary conditions," says Winthrop.

On August 22 or 23, almost as an afterthought, the Bay Council notified Plymouth of the imminent undertaking and on August 25 called in the clergy to bless the endeavor. That very day, the Court of Assistants sent forth the expedition of ninety volunteers with two Indian interpreters in three pinnaces and two shallops, under Endecott, now forty-eight, as "general." The Court charged Endecott to *exterminate* the men of Block Island but to spare the women and children, whom he should bring away, and to take possession of the island. Thence he was to proceed to the Pequots and demand the murderers of Stone and Stone's company, together with a thousand fathom of wampum for damages and some of their children as hostages, to be taken by force if refused.

A STIFF WIND out of the northeast kicked up a handicapping surf against Block Island, but as soon as the wading invaders could get firm footing, their muskets dissipated the brief resistance of fifty to sixty tall bowmen. Thereafter the natives lay low in swamps. The invaders got only glimpses of a few of them in the next two days of ranging the oak-brushwood-covered small hills, burning the sixty wigwams of the two villages, located three miles apart, and great heaps of shelled corn, cutting down over two hundred acres of growing corn, killing some dogs left in the wigwams, and carrying away "well-wrought mats" and "delightful baskets." Endecott's "extermination" amounted to one Block Islander, whom the Narragansetts later learned had died of his wounds.

The little Bay navy proceeded to Saybrook. After four wind-bound days, Endecott coasted with a task force of twenty men in two shallops the fifteen miles back to Pequot Harbor (later New London). Gardener, unable to dissuade Endecott, hired a Dutch shallop then anchored at Saybrook and detailed twelve of his own men in the Fort shallop to go with Endecott to plunder corn. Multitudes of Indians came running along the waterside calling "What cheer, Englishmen," and grew alarmed at the answer of stony silence. As the invaders tried to sleep aboard in the middle of the river that night, the Pequots and West Niantics built fires on either bank in fear of a night raid and wailed eerily till dawn.

Pequot means "Gray Fox." Variously spelled, it seems usually to have been pronounced "PEE-cwaht." Both Indians and whites agreed to the greater vigor, valor, and viciousness of the Pequots compared with other Indians in southern New England. The Pequots had invaded New England from the northwestward fairly recently (perhaps about 1575 but no later than 1614, when Adriaen Block found them precisely where the Puritans found them two decades later). They had wedged through the Niantic nation, occupying a strip of approximately eighteen miles on the southern coast which divided the Niantics in two. They maintained large forts across the Mistick to the east, from which they attempted to bring the East Niantics (on across the Pawcatuck) under their sway. They already had thoroughly amalgamated the West Niantics. The principal West Niantic stronghold lay less than two miles up the Connecticut from Saybrook, on the opposite bank, at the site of later Old Lyme. The Pequots themselves used this stronghold as a western base of operations constantly enough that no one could say at a given time whether Indians issuing from it were Pequots, Niantics, or both.

Early in the morning after the all-night anchorage in Pequot River, a portly elder statesman went out to Endecott's shallop by canoe. When Endecott bluntly demanded the heads of the murderers of Stone and company, the ambassador recounted the revenge murder by way of justifying it and disclaimed any ability to distinguish English from Dutch. Endecott gave him short shrift and disembarked his troops before the ambassador could give a clear cue to cut them off at the high, rugged rocks on shore. Endecott marched his men in formation all the way to the top of the hill, the ambassador trying to keep up. Endecott allowed the ambassador and messengers to put him off for more than two hours because he thought that if he bore with them he would get the chance to land a greater blow. Great numbers of unarmed Pequots flocked up the hill and talked with the Saybrook men they knew, pointing out the places the English armor did not cover. A messenger arrived at length to say that if the English would lay down their arms and approach to within about thirty paces of the Pequot main body,

Mononoto would cause his men to do the like and there should be a parley. Endecott saw the purpose of this was to get the English arms and ordered the drum to beat.

With a great shout the fleet Indians vanished behind a hill some way off as the Bay volunteers and Saybrook allies, weighed down by their armor, marched in formation into a "champaign field" displaying their colors and daring the Pequots to a pitched battle. But the Pequots stood on their distant hilltop and laughed at the troops for being duped into waiting so long. Endecott would not let his men fire upon the scattering Indians until they had got out of musket range. As at Block Island, he kept expecting a concerted resistance to form that would enable him to break their power in one decisive clash. Again, however, he found himself reduced to an exasperating hunt for fractional bands who took occasional potshots from rocks and thickets. The Bay men's return fire did kill a total of twelve and wounded forty more, as the Narragansetts later found out.

To about midafternoon, apparently, the troops burned wigwams and mats, spoiled corn, and raked up the possessions they had watched the natives bury during the delay. Gardener's men did not forget to fill their bags. But they had to work without cover from the main force, for Endecott peremptorily departed, leaving the Saybrookers with their eight Dutch mercenaries to fend for themselves. Each of the abandoned twenty men took a full sack to the shallops, then suddenly the wind changed, condemning them to remain the rest of the afternoon where they were. Each man had filled his sack a second time when the Indians opened up on them from a covert across the clearing about a musket shot away. Half the corn-looters fired periodically while the other half stood ready to intercept a rush. The Indians would flash in sight about ten at a time and discharge a flight of arrows in a very high arc. They got one Englishman in the leg, perhaps while he was gathering up fallen arrows; the musketeers thought they killed and wounded a number of their foes. The Indians gave chase and wounded another man as the looters retreated empty-sacked. Their shallops made adequate forts until the evening breeze wafted them safely to Saybrook. "I was glad of the corn," says Gardener, who was glad of nothing else.

Next morning, Endecott's reunited expeditionaries landed on the Niantic shore across the Connecticut, where the Indians ran as deer from dogs, says Underhill. (John Underhill, the smart-dressing, antinomian-inclining captain of the Boston militia, one of four commanders under Endecott, described himself as "a rude soldier"; he had been bred to arms in Holland as a son of a military adventurer in the service of the House of Orange.) The invaders burned and spoiled whatever they could light on and sailed for home. On the way, they stopped off in the Narragansett country, where Cutshamekin crept into a swamp and scalped a Pequot, then sent the scalp to Canonicus. Canonicus presently sent it to all the sachems about him, tendered his thanks to the English, and transmitted four fathom of wampum to Cutshamekin.

The expeditionaries reached Boston on September 14. The public reaction was jubilant, largely out of relief that every boy came back, none sick. Endecott basked in a decidedly lifted popular prestige, and Winthrop's correspondence shows approval of his conduct of the campaign—immediately after it. In time Winthrop and other magistrates took a second look; General Endecott did not get command of the big expedition Massachusetts sent against the Pequots the following June. Edward Johnson, whose mid-century history takes the official position, admits that Endecott's demonstration had been a "bootlesse voyage" which "incouraged the Indians very much."

The Bay magistrates obtusely failed to grasp for some time how dreadfully they had exposed their kinsmen on the Connecticut to Pequot retribution, much less that they had opened at least the possibility of a united tribal effort to carry out against all the white colonies of New England the policy Massachusetts had designed in vain for Block Island. The Pilgrims had a trading house not only on the Connecticut but also at Sowams and various other points in Indian country and quickly perceived the ultimate threat to their colony proper. They also rankled that Endecott's blundering tactics had made the English look ridiculous in Indian eyes. Winslow wrote Winthrop on about October 20 flatly charging the Bay with fomenting a war, unilaterally. The letter irritated Winthrop, as Winthrop admits of himself: "The deputy took it ill." He replied somewhat heatedly that "We went not to make war upon them, but to do justice, etc., and having killed thirteen and destroyed sixty wigwams, etc., we were not much behind with them. . . . They had no cause to glory over us, when they saw that they could not save themselves nor their houses and corn from so few of ours." But he avoided the main charge: that Massachusetts had provoked a war.

Before this accusation—on October 8 as exactly as we can ascertain—Winthrop received the chilling intelligence from Williams that the Pequots (Mohegans, he first heard) had killed some English at Saybrook, that the Pequots and Narragansetts had concluded a peace after four years of hostilities, and that Pequot ambassadors were already on Narragansett Bay urging Miantonomy to ally the Narragansetts with the Pequots and so form a numerically superior force with which to annihilate the barely four thousand English in all of New England.

INSTANTLY grasping the possible doom of Massachusetts in an alliance of the Pequots and Narragansetts, Vane and Council rushed a frantic appeal to Williams to use his "vtmost & speediest Endeavours to breake & hinder the Leauge laboured for by the Pequts" and work for a league between the Narragansetts and English instead, excusing their not sending company and supplies by "the hast of the Busines."

Williams did not hesitate. "The Lord," he says, "helped me jmmediatly to put my Life into my hand, & (scarce acquainting my wife) to ship my selfe all alone in a poore Canow, & to Cut through (a stormie Wind & with great seas, euery minute in hazard of Life) to the Sachims howse." It was about a thirty-mile voyage down the west side of the bay. Winthrop Jr. had said after first seeing Canonicus's "great Citty" that "there be many wigwams but they stand not together as I have heard reported." Williams got there before a pact with the Pequots could be concluded, and recalls the nick-of-time mission in his petition to the Massachusetts General Court October 1651 but more circumstantially in his great letter to Mason of June 1670:

> There dayes & nights my Busines forced me to lodge & mix with the bloudie Pequt Embassadours, whose Hands & Arms (me thought) reaked with the bloud of my Countrimen murther'd & massacred by them on Conecticut Riuer, & from whome I could not but nightly looke for thejr bloudy Kniues at my owne throate allso.

Grave old Canonicus and his co-sachem nephew, the touchy, haughty giant Miantonomy, carefully weighed Williams's arguments and at length decided in his favor. "God wondrously praeserued me, & helpt me to breake to pieces the Pequts Negociatjon & Designe, & to make & promote & finish (by many Travells & Charges) the English League with the Nahiggonsiks & Monhiggins against the Pequts." He not only broke the Narragansett-Pequot alliance but set up and largely effected a counter Narragansett-Mohegan-Massachusetts alliance—surely one of the greatest feats of diplomacy in American history.

Within a few days an embassy hurried from Boston to Canonicus's court, fourscore miles away by their own estimate. Edward Johnson, recently returned from England, must have been a member of the embassy which capitalized on Williams's achievement; his account sounds like that of an eyewitness. Stoughton probably headed the delegation.

Williams entertained the embassy at his house in Providence, sent word to Canonicus, then escorted the delegation as interpreter. An imposing assembly received them at Narragansett, where proceedings opened with a feast of white chestnuts and cornmeal mush (hasty pudding) with blackberries mixed in. The parley took place afterward in a "State-house" about fifty feet wide covered with mats except for a small hole in the middle of the roof to let light in and smoke out. Canonicus, "well stricken in yeares," lay on his side on a mat, his *pinesses* sitting on the ground with their knees doubled up to their chins as they listened intently to Williams's translations. Again Canonicus amazed the English by his wisdom and discreet answers. Miantonomy, though more forward in siding with the English, struck Johnson as "a very sterne man, and of a great stature, of a cruell nature, causing all his Nobility and such as were his attendance to tremble at his speech." The Bay emissaries actually believed at that time that the two Narragansett grand sachems could field thirty thousand fighting men. Though the number was nearer four thousand, that would still have been formidable for Massachusetts.

At the time of this embassy Williams had already won Canonicus to pro-Bay neutrality but quickly transformed this neutrality to active alliance. He did it by working on Miantonomy more than Canonicus. Canonicus, Williams points out, was always shy of the English. While, as Williams says, he was a "Prudent & Peaceable Prince," he never cared to court the English, never feared them, and never acknowledged any precedence of their government over his own. Williams, furthermore, had to recall him from time to time to a friendship with the English that the old sachem always felt leery of. In May 1637, for instance, when Williams went to notify him of the Bay preparations against the Pequots,

Caunounicus (morosus aeque ac barbarus senex) was very sour, & accused the English & myself for sending the plague amongst them, & threatening to kill him especially.

Such tidings (it seems) were lately brought to his ears by some of his flatterers & our ill-willers. I discerned cause of bestirring myself, and staid the longer, & at last (through the mercy of the Most High) I not only sweetened his spirit, but possess him, that the plague & other sicknesses were alone in the hand of the one God, who made him & us, who being displeased with the English for lying, stealing, idleness & uncleanness, (the natives epidemical sins,) smote many thousands of us ourselves with general & late mortalities.

Thus Williams wrote Winthrop on Monday, May 15, 1637. Another way Williams sweetened Canonicus's spirit was by gifts of sugar, for which the sachem had a great fondness; frequently he importuned Williams to ask Winthrop to send more. Canonicus must have been around seventy years old at this time, and he lived to be past eighty, as nearly as we can judge. Already, in 1636, he had turned over the active administration of his government to Miantonomy, who had exercised equal authority since 1632. Not that Canonicus did not have able sons to inherit his scepter, but the nephew Miantonomy appeared far more impressive; the arrangement seemed to be best for the tribe and entirely acceptable to the sons.

"Miantunnómu kept his barbarous court lately at my house, & with him I have far better dealing," Williams told Winthrop and Vane on May 15, 1637. "He takes some pleasure to visit me." The English never got straight whether this sachem's name ended in *y, e, u, uh,* or *o;* but he became a familiar and cooperative personage to them, while Canonicus always remained aloof and remote. Miantonomy craved English approval. He would go to Boston (or Hartford) if Williams gave sufficient assurances and even held court in Williams's house. "All the Cords that euer bound the Barbarous to Forreiners were made of Selfe & Covetousnes," Williams wrote Winthrop July 15, 1637. "Yet if I mistake not I obserue in Miantunnómu some sparkes of true Friendshipp." Years later, Winthrop said the Commissioners of the United Colonies had observed the sachem's "proud and treacherous disposition"; Winthrop also recorded the sachem's rude departure from a parley at Boston in 1640. Winthrop, however, observed that, in all Miantonomy's answers at a 1642 Boston parley, "he was very deliberate and showed good understanding in the principles of justice and equity, and ingenuity withal." If often temperamental and scowling, he sometimes behaved magnanimously. Williams probably put his finger on the nub of Miantonomy's incongruity when he wrote Winthrop July 15, 1637, that the sachem would attend the Bay with five hundred men "could it be deeply imprinted into him that the English never intended to despoile him of the Countrey."

The crowning of Williams's diplomatic success came when Miantonomy hiked to Boston with two of Canonicus's sons, another sachem, and close to twenty sannups. A day ahead of time Cutshamekin gave notice they were coming; Governor Vane sent twenty musketeers to meet them at Roxbury on October 21, 1636. Vane called together most of the magistrates and ministers at Boston "to give countenance to our proceedings," says Winthrop, and the Indians with musketeer escort reached Boston about noon. Vane had the sachems and their council dine by themselves in the same room with him (a few years later Miantonomy would insist on eating at the same table as the governor), and sent the sannups to dine at the inn.

After dinner Miantonomy propounded that the Narragansetts had always loved the English and desired firm peace with them; that they would continue in war with the Pequots and their confederates until they were subdued, and desired that the English do the same; that they would deliver up enemies of the English or kill them; that if any Narragansetts should kill English cattle, the English would not kill them but cause them to make satisfaction; and that they would now make a firm peace, to be sealed by a present they would send two months hence. Young Vane, no doubt suppressing a feeling of exultation, told Miantonomy he should have his answer next morning.

In the morning, Vane and the sachems, also Cutshamekin (who had been serving as interpreter) signed the articles of alliance, the Indians by their marks. Miantonomy's mark was a single arrow pointing straight up. "But because we could not well make them understand the articles perfectly [like returning fugitive servants], we agreed to send a copy of them to Mr. Williams, who could best interpret them to them," reports Winthrop. After dinner the second day, the Indians took leave. Some musketeers escorted them out of town and dismissed them with a volley of shot.

IMMEDIATELY after Gardener's men returned to Saybrook from abetting Endecott's destruction at Pequot, Gardener took some of them to gather corn at their two-mile-distant field, diagonally back of the Fort on the Sound. He sent others there by shallop to pick up the corn that should be gathered and stationed "five lusty men" with long guns in the blockhouse at the seaside edge of this field to guard the corn already stored.

Three of the five guards, when left on their own, went fowling a mile away. A host of Pequots let them pass, waited until they had loaded themselves with birds and started back, then ambushed them in an Indian cornfield less than a bowshot from the blockhouse. One fowler, who got an arrow through a leg, cut his way through the Indians with his sword and made it to the blockhouse. He said he urged his fellows to follow but that they stood paralyzed until overpowered, though another account says one of them killed two Indians first. The men at Saybrook learned in time that the fun-loving Pequots slowly tortured the captives to death.

Gardener meanwhile returned to the Fort with his laden shallop and the next day sent the boat back to fetch the five guards and the corn they were guarding. Finding only three men, including the wounded fowler, the crew hurriedly loaded just the corn that had been shelled. Shortly after shoving off, they saw the blockhouse ablaze.

No sooner did they return to the Fort and report than Matthew Mitchell, a visiting trader from Wethersfield, pressed Gardener to lend him the Saybrook shallop so he could send his four men to gather hay upriver at Six-Mile Island. Gardener represents Mitchell as an old man and takes him for a minister. Mitchell must have been one of the substantial Watertown laymen who organized the wrangly Wethersfield church in May 1636; he probably had been elected a ruling elder. Before he and the four employees now with him at Saybrook had started down from Wethersfield, Mitchell had sent three other employees downriver in a shallop and lost them and the boat to Indians on the way. Visions of lucrative grass ripe for harvest must have tantalized him to recoup his recent loss at any risk. Gardener at length relented as usual; he even allowed a couple of his own men to assist Mitchell's—one to stay with the boat. But he cautioned them to be sure to scour the whole meadow, marching abreast with their three dogs, before they carried a single cock of hay.

Instead, when the five-man detail got ashore on the island, they fell immediately to gathering. Indians rose out of the high grass, slew three of the hay-cutters outright, and overpowered a fourth who was bearing a load of hay on his back. The fifth man made it back to the boat with five arrows in him; one account says he died in fourteen weeks, another that he eventually recovered. The captured hay-cutter, "a godly young man," says Winthrop, was a brother-in-law of Mitchell's named Butterfield. The Indians roasted him alive.

Gardener knew what the burning at Cornfield Point portended. When he had seen the shallop off to Six-Mile Island, he had the warehouses beyond the pale broken into and their goods transferred to the Fort. The largest of these warehouses belonged to Captain John Tilly, a Bay trader who had built upriver from the site of the Fort before Gardener ever came into the country.

Late that day the shallop returned from Six-Mile Island with its two survivors, one a bloody mess. Toward sundown the day after, Tilly's warehouse, the other outhouses, and all the haystacks, up to a bowshot of the Fort, burst into flame in an instant. A cow was killed; many other cows came home with arrows in them. For the rest of the fall and almost all winter the Pequots desisted from further hostilities as the Saybrook men holed up inside their palisade.

On October 30, 1636, came the first public test of the antinomian party's strength, with the attempt to install John Wheelwright as a third associate minister of the Boston church. Wheelwright, a member of the church who had spoken at a recent exercise, was a brother-in-law of Ann Hutchinson. Winthrop's lone objection defeated the move, since such a decision had to be unanimous. He found particularly distasteful Wheelwright's and Vane's holding to the doctrine of an individual's union with the indwelling *person* of the Holy Ghost. He could not get these two men to leave out that word "person"; otherwise, the union of spirit and Spirit he quite approved. Winthrop also instanced Wheelwright's doctrine that a believer was more than a creature. Governor Vane "marvelled" at Winthrop's objection, "seeing Mr. Cotton had lately approved his doctrine." Cotton (all innocence as usual) said he had not caught the point about the creature and asked Wheelwright to explain his meaning. Wheelwright did some gallant explaining. Winthrop said he thought highly of Wheelwright's godliness and abilities, but saw that "he was apt to raise doubtful disputations." To prevent public disturbance, Governor Vane and Deputy-Governor Winthrop carried on the debate about the indwelling of the person in writing. Little did Winthrop realize that the Boston public was already well

on its way to a general conversion to the dubious antinomian doctrines. Vane's open championing of them this October 30 may in
fact mark the moment when antinomianism decisively captured Boston hearts.

Winthrop and Wilson, besides not noticing that the capital of the
New Israel had turned virtually antinomian under their very noses,
failed to comprehend that it was not merely a few misguided doctrines they confronted but the juggernaut of authority-rejecting,
standard-relaxing modern individualism. Strange-sounding doctrines
like indwelling of the person and sanctification before justification
really mean an assertion of self-esteem, of one's inner feeling as
more trustworthy than logic or convention, of the individual's right
to decide religious questions for himself (and in his interests), of a
need for relief from the strain of rectitude and otherworldliness, and
a rebellion against the restraints and assumed injustices of the traditional, largely medieval system—its confusion of church and state,
its community-centeredness, its "priesthood" ("hireling ministry" is
Williams's and the Quakers' later term), its status-quo-freezing
magistracy, its enmeshing legal inhibitions, its artificially rigged
gradations of privilege, its sources of authority, and authority itself.
When analyzed, the sentiments of this movement expressed in theological gobbledygook in England, both before and after the controversy in New England, confirm their tendency, compared to
orthodox forms of Puritanism, toward a more indulgent view of
human nature (i.e. as less innately depraved), a less rigorous standard of behavior, the bounding of a larger area of life as belonging
beyond the reach of either church or state, a stronger distaste for
sanctimoniousness or other outward show of superior piety (or sham
or implied privileged status from any cause), and a relaxation of individual effort or responsibility in seeking salvation.

The anti-antinomians reacted in a way to confirm their fight as
partly to maintain the old high standard. They insisted that assurance of election must in some measure be furnished by a self-
examined holy life visible to others (by their fruits ye shall know
them) when the antinomians opened a more casual road by holding
that assurance was invisible, a matter of one's soul with God, a
mystic union unaffected by action or institutions, and that the only
authority which could attest it was one's personal inward witness.
To the orthodox, antinomianism widened the strait gate. Yea, said
Winthrop, many profane persons became of Mrs. Hutchinson's

opinion, "for it was a very easie, and acceptable way to heaven, to see nothing, to have nothing, but waite for Christ to do all. . . . And indeed most of her new tenents tended to slothfulnesse, and quench all indeavour in the creature." But the old Puritanism was too demanding; the prize remained too remote from ordinary mortals, who were beginning to care shockingly less about the prize anyway. The tension of Puritan ideals could not stay so unrelieved or so in conflict with normal human nature in an imperceptibly easing environment and expanding opportunity.

The antinomian disposition overlapped much of orthodox Puritanism and also some of Williams's disagreement with orthodox Puritanism. There was a leveling element in Williams's view, for instance, inclining to regard the poor as closer to God than the rich. But Williams refused to put his personal intuition above reason or Scripture, and he insisted on the necessity of rigorous scholarship for getting at Truth. In some ways antinomianism overlapped the whole Reformation; had not Luther struck a blow for the right of private judgment? Although Puritanism inclined to interpret this right as conservatively as Lutheranism, the Puritanism of the Bay founders actually included antinomianism insofar as that meant mysticism and religious feeling, even intuition. But orthodox Bay Puritanism equally included the counterbalance of Arminianism, in that it insisted on rationality, intellectual discipline, and outward works. Either strand at the expense of the other amounted to half truth, or heresy. With respect to this equilibrium, Williams was wholly orthodox. The beauty of Bay theology, as of Augustine's from which it basically derived, was a complex integration of opposites which any simplistic or monomanic line would wreck; which made it antinomial in the true sense. Cotton retained its essential delicate balance, holding, both before and after the controversy of 1636–38, to tenets unacceptable to either side yet maintaining the subtle theological balance which was intrinsically nonantinomian (in the partisan sense). The antinomians wanted to do away with subtlety and complexity. They *used* Cotton, possibly with his permission; for *politically* he may have wavered from Winthrop to his duplex neighbor Vane and his dear family friends the Hutchinsons and the Coddingtons.

The issue of 1636–38 took this form: Is preparation for salvation a matter of chance divine visitation or a course of conscious effort—in short, by grace or works? Without going through the process at

the moment of showing that this apprehension about salvation, together with this raising of the question of the need for works, means
a deep doubt of traditional belief and a deep resentment—even
rejection—of traditional institutions, we can quickly perceive that
the orthodox Bay Puritans held both positions at once, as when their
Cambridge mentor Richard Sibbs said: "Though God's grace do all,
yet we must give our consent." Such a haughty enemy of antinomianism as Hooker said in *A Survey of the Summe*: ". . . its
certain, you can neither see, nor know, for truth of grace is invisible
to men"—as the antinomians kept contending. But antinomian sub-
jectivity must not be at the expense of the exalted old-Puritan moral
and intellectual standard, in Hooker's orthodox dualism. The antinomians' experience of a restive new age struggling to displace the
old left them unappreciative of the complex symmetry of a Puritan
theology which did not any longer correspond to the reality they
knew or wanted. They wished to force a split of the Puritan polari-
ties and discard the Arminian pole—as the later counterpart movement within Puritanism wished to discard the antinomian. The
antinomians wished to discredit the old-fashioned, over-rationalized
view of the world and enthrone their own. By such action they
could enthrone more than a simplified view; they could enthrone
themselves. Their movement represents an insistent but largely unconscious response to little-understood forces for change. It, in
short, symptomized a basic cultural change.

Antinomianism is better understood when we realize that it
tended to develop into Quakerism; many of the Bay antinomians,
among them the Scots (Mrs. Scot was Ann Hutchinson's sister), the
Dyers, and the Coddingtons, in fifteen or twenty years became
avowed Quakers. Change of itself does not necessarily occur in the
direction of tolerance or democracy; it may and may not. Antinomianism had a direct bearing on both, but as by-products rather
than as objectives. Whatever may be said *after* 1638, neither Vane
nor Mrs. Hutchinson was more tolerant or more democratic than
Winthrop in the course of the controversy proper. The English
civil war and the New English-Pequot War catalyzed the forces for
change heralded in antinomianism, and men changed too. Vane became a devoted manipulator for toleration back in England later.
Even so inflexible a type as Hugh Peter later embraced Williams in
England and apologized for his former narrowness. Neither Peter
nor Williams, however, turned antinomian or Quaker, and Williams

had been a conscious and deliberate democrat at least since 1636.

Ralph Waldo Emerson admitted that the nineteenth-century transcendentalist, such as he, "easily incurs the charge of anti-nomianism by his avowal that he, who has the Lawgiver [indwelling of the Person of the Holy Ghost, the Bay antinomians in the seventeenth century would have said] may with safety not only neglect, but even contravene every written commandment." Which precisely puts the finger on the presumed threat to the Bay system; for the practical implication of antinomianism for Massachusetts was that an antinomian, claiming, unverifiably, to have received the grace that united his soul directly with God, could—if he carried his doctrine to its logical conclusion—short-circuit clergy, church, magistrates, the Bible, education, experience, manners, morals, law, and government itself. For the clergyman's daughter Ann Hutchinson we should probably have to add a revolt against men and, possibly, an unconscious revolt against the bondage of religion itself. Most of the Bay magistrates and clergy branded antinomians as subversives and used the word "antinomian" as implying the anarchy, especially sexual anarchy, of extreme Anabaptist groups during the Reformation. Cotton saw Mrs. Hutchinson's denial of the resurrection of believers' bodies as adding up to the same result. He incredibly told her at her church trial that "though I have not herd, nayther doe I thinke, yow have bine unfaythfull to your Husband in his Marriage Covenant, *yet that will follow upon it.*" The civil Court expressly held of her "bottomlesse revelations" that, "being above reason and Scripture, they are not subject to controll." If subject to no authority but his own professed revelation, the antinomian would be a self-proclaimed, specially privileged outlaw in the holy commonwealth, perverting the very source of the colony's commission from God to carry out His will. Orthodox Puritans also regarded antinomians as "enthusiasts" (i.e. hysterics). So the usage of "antinomian" in 1636-38 in the Bay had no reference to the ancient Gnostic or to the literal meaning of the word. Rather it connoted the priority of personal intuition and the hysteria and libertarianism which were thought to follow from such a priority.

How long the antinomian conspiracy had been premeditated and at what point Mrs. Hutchinson initiated it (perhaps many months before Vane's arrival, let alone before his election) remain obscure because the anti-antinomians did not become aware of it until it was far advanced. Welde, in his preface to Winthrop's official account of the court proceedings, reconstructs the antinomians' public-relations conquest:

1. They laboured much to acquaint themselves with as many, as possibly they could, that so they might have the better opportunity to communicate their new light unto them.

2. Being once acquainted with them, they would strangely labour to insinuate themselves into their affections, by loving salutes, humble carriage, kind invitements, friendly visits, and so they would winne upon men, and steale into their bosomes before they were aware. Yea, assoone as any new-commers (especially, men of note, worth, and activity, fit instruments to advance their designe) were landed, they would be sure to welcome them, shew them all courtesie, and offer them roome in their owne houses, or of some of their owne Sect, and so having gotten them into their Web, they could easily poyson them by degrees; It was rare for any man thus hooked in, to escape their Leaven.

3. (Because such men as would seduce others, had need be some way eminent) they would appear very humble, holy, and spirituall Christians, and full of Christ; they would deny themselves farre, speake excellently, pray with such soule-ravishing expressions and affections, that a stranger that loved goodnesse, could not but love and admire them, and so be the more easily drawne after them. . . .

Those thus cultivated would tell others, Welde continues, that not since the Apostles' times, they were persuaded, had anybody received so much light from God. The antinomians commonly sought to work first upon women, says Welde, whereby to catch their husbands by them. They would seize every opportunity to counsel people who were full of doubt and fears, pointing out that they had been taking the wrong (i.e. legal) course for comfort. And then they would undermine the good opinion of the ministers. They were careful to divulge their views only gradually, with Mrs. Hutchinson's weekly "lecture" a principal means of conveyance.

At first five or six persons, according to her, and in time fifty to eighty (from other towns as well as Boston), according to Welde, met twice weekly in her home—ironically just across the street from the Winthrops—to hear Mrs. Hutchinson recapitulate Cotton's latest sermon, elaborate on it, and answer questions. Thus she organized her party and disseminated her own intepretation of Scripture for a long time with the highest social sanction; although Cotton noticed that she grew more and more independent of him and in time ceased to consult him at all (as if she might learn something she preferred not to know, he thought). Both he and Wilson testified that they had heard of her strange opinions shortly after her landing, but that she had quite satisfied them of her orthodoxy when they examined her for admission to the Boston church. Only with the greatest reluctance did she admit at her court trial that one of her twice-weekly meetings was for a mixed audience, not just women. She hoped to conceal this fact because of the patriarchal injunction against women teaching men. (If women have any questions, says Paul in First Corinthians 14:35, let them go home and ask their husbands.) Vane's election brought her activity more into the open, although she continued to disavow publicly what she pressed privately.

Everyone appreciated her charity and expert advice in the field of childbirth and pre- and post-natal care. This proved to be another avenue she exploited for building her party. When numbers of women, pretending indisposition, followed her out of the meeting-house as Wilson preached, they worked a studied insult to the pastor and to the system of a kind that confounded disciplinary measures. To Mrs. Hutchinson Wilson evidently seemed insidiously overbearing and a little stupid. Perhaps his slight build or the "thick utterance" of his preaching roused her contempt; or possibly she transferred to him the contempt she felt for her husband, whom Winthrop describes as a mild man, honest, peaceable, and of good estate, but weak in ability "and wholly guided by his wife." (Wilson had not been notable for command of his wife.)

Aged forty-five in 1636 and the mother of fourteen children (the youngest, Susanna, was four), Mistris Hutchinson had grown up in the semi-rural setting of Alford, near the east coast in Lincolnshire. Her father ruled as a Dissenting vicar there. He moved his family to London in 1605; so that from the age of fourteen to her marriage at 21 Ann underwent the metropolitan conditioning that her later friend Williams experienced from the cradle (which he was just about out of at the time she reached London). She married a home-town boy, William Hutchinson, son of a well-to-do merchant, and of course went back to Alford to live on his estate. From there she conceived her adoration of the vicar at Boston, not forty miles west. She seems to have been a headstrong, high-strung, domineering, dissatisfied woman, whose remarks in court in 1637 betray she had something of a persecution complex before she ever sailed for America—and *she* made the decision to sail, not her husband. She was charitable, industrious, courageous, and articulate, though not above dissimulation, intrigue, or arrogance. She attracted many friends, high and low, who demonstrated a strong loyalty even when loyalty to her was socially and politically dangerous. To her husband, to the end, she was "a dear Saint."

She must have had great personal magnetism and consuming ambition. She could not have been the crushed violet of modern romance, or hardly the "Jezebel" Welde called her in 1644. Winthrop referred to her in the fall of 1636 as "a woman of ready wit and bold spirit"; after her court trial he modified that to a "woman of haughty and fierce carriage, of a nimble wit and active spirit, and a very voluble tongue, more bold then a man, though in understanding and judgement, inferior to many women." Later still, in January 1639, he spoke of a Mrs. Oliver, who had been jailed for disturbing the peace of the church, as being in "ability of speech, and appearance of zeal and devotion . . . far before Mrs. Hutchinson, and so the fitter instrument to have done hurt, but that she was poor and had little acquaintance." Shepard, the intense, tuberculous pastor of Newtown, characterized her in a speech at her church trial to her own congregation: ". . . she is of a most dayngerous Spirit, & likely with her fluent Towinge & forwardness in Expressions to seduce & draw away many, Espetially simple Weomen of her owne sex." Hooker thought her "a self-deluding and deluded creature" and spoke scornfully of her "heap of hideous errors." Edward Johnson, a champion of orthodoxy if not an outright bigot, called her "this Master-piece of Womens wit." Cotton recognized attractive and unattractive elements in her personality, before as well as after her church trial. While admonishing her during the latter, he acknowledged her superior gifts when he said the Lord "hath given yow a sharpe apprehension, a ready utterance & abilitie to represe yourselfe in the Cawse of God." Baillie said Williams, who came to know her after her banishment, "spake much good" of her to him while Williams was in England in 1644.

She could not bear to be humble or repentant; she was saddest in quietly bowing to authority. She was happiest in defiance. In her defiance she was asserting her own natural superiority of mind and supernatural preferment. As Wilson pointed out, she herself usurped God's room, which she charged the ministers had. She expected people to follow her with the devotion they owed a prophetess specially favored of God—specially favored according to the authority of her own intuition.

Was she right about Wilson? "His low opinion of himself, was the *top* of all his other excellencies," says Cotton Mather, whom, by the way, Wilson baptized. He refused to have his portrait painted, which tends to bear out some absence of vainglory. Mrs. Hutchinson proved no match for him in explicating Scripture. If he seemed slow-witted to her, he had been a brilliant student at Eton, King's College, and Emmanuel. He had been born in Windsor in 1588, the third son of an influential, non-Dissenting clergyman and of a niece of the Archbishop of Canterbury. Thus he knew a more privileged and sheltered upbringing than most Puritan preachers; he had a reputation, also, of remaining aloof from the dissipations of his fellow students. His "proper" behavior may have irritated Mrs. Hutchinson, as it had Lord Scudamore when Wilson served as a young chaplain in the Scudamore household and forbade talk about hawks and hounds at Sunday dinner. Winthrop admired Wilson especially for his sincerity, as no doubt also for his sober, studious life. Everyone had to indulge his incorrigible versifying; he sent pious poems to anybody on any occasion. Like Mrs. Hutchinson, he prided himself on being psychic—predicting who would live and who die, and so on. One time his son John fell on his head from a loft four stories high. Wilson prayed confidently, and John Jr. lived to preach at Medfield to old age. (Which confirms that Puritan preachers were *born* hardheaded.) Another time, he received news on the road that his house had burned down again. "Blessed be God," was his reaction; "He has burnt this house, because He intends to give me a better." After the third or fourth house-burning the pastor acquired a virtual mansion. The first child, a daughter, born to Mrs. Wilson after she finally reached New England, fell sick of a fever. Only Wilson himself did not despair of her life. Instead, he called in a godly group for a fast. "While I heard Mr. Cotton at prayer," says Wilson, "I was confident the child should live!" Sure enough, the daughter was still alive when Cotton Mather recorded this toward the last of the century.

Mrs. Hutchinson might have recognized her own trait of arrogance in Wilson which remained mostly concealed to others. After her banishment, he displayed a supersensitivity to deviationism of any stripe (which could be another way of saying any affront to his authority or his interpretation of absolute truth). He, for instance, rushed up and struck a Baptist preacher, Obadiah Holmes, who had just been sentenced by the Court on July 31,

1651, and said "The Curse of God goe with thee." Eight years later he railed unbecomingly at a couple of Quaker preachers about to be hanged. On his deathbed he told the visiting Bay ministers who came in a body: "I have long feared several sins" as provoking the displeasure of God against the country, in particular Corahism, i.e., "when people rise up as Corah against their ministers."

But the crucial alienation of Mrs. Hutchinson from Wilson must have come over the keystone covenant. The orthodox insistence on the covenant doctrine actually played into antinomian hands. If the New Covenant, personified in Jesus, was accepted, then faith in His saving grace, regardless of deserts for goodness or works or lack of either, superseded the old conformity to law of the violated and lapsed first dispensation. The antinomian could claim more genuine orthodoxy in coming out of an Old Testament orientation and relying on undeserved grace through Jesus's loving sacrifice.

THE FACTIONALISM which Mrs. Hutchinson's inflated sense of power or power-to-be furthered in Boston and increasingly between the metropolis and the smaller, slower-changing rest of the colony upset Vane as much as anybody and apparently wore him down faster. He believed in harmony the way Winthrop did, and it was *his* administration which was failing to achieve it. Since all had seemed well at the time he took office, he naturally wondered if he had not brought about the discord—or felt keenly such wonderings of others.

By December he had had enough. Early that month he turned over to the Council and some others a batch of letters he had received from friends in England urging his return to preserve his estate, and declared his resolution to go. Calling a full General Court, he asked the deputies to give him leave.

Next morning, one of the Assistants intoned some pathetical passages, Winthrop says, on the loss of such a governor in a time of such danger to the country, at which Vane broke down sobbing. He confessed he would rather hazard the utter ruin of his estate than go at this time, "if something else had not pressed him more, viz., the inevitable danger he saw of God's judgments to come upon us for these scandalous imputations brought upon himself, as if he should be the cause of all." When the Court concluded it would not be fit to allow his departure on this ground, he "recalled himself," as Winthrop continues, and asked to go solely on the sufficient ground of his estate. The Court silently consented.

They decided to adjourn four days and reconvene for an election of both governor and deputy-governor. During this adjournment, "divers" of the Boston church sent a delegation to declare their objection to the Governor's departure upon the reasons alleged. At this, Vane about-faced. He said he was an obedient child to the church, that "without the leave of the church, he durst not go away." The adjourned magistrates and deputies, giving in to demands of "divers" of the Boston church, had already generally agreed, in order to avoid trouble, to postpone the election to the regular time, i.e., the following May.

But the December Court went ahead to call in the clergy for advice about discovering and pacifying the differences among the churches in point of opinion. Vane announced the occasion from the chair. Dudley desired everybody to be free and open. The clergy fully intended to be, having already met and drawn up points of doctrine on which they suspected Cotton of differing from them and obliging him to write his answers, and having been rebuked in court the day before by Vane for having so met without his privity. The redoubtable Peter, perhaps on edge anyway from battling the Separatist majority Williams had bequeathed him in Salem, told Vane plainly, professing all due reverence, how it "sadded the ministers' spirits, that he should be jealous of their meetings, or seem to restrain their liberty." Vane excused his speech of the day before as sudden and mistaken. But Peter bore on. Before Vane came, he told the governor to his face what Vane must most have hated to hear, "within less than two years since, the churches were in peace." Vane answered that "the light of the gospel brings a sword, and the children of the bondwoman would persecute those of the freewoman." Peter refused to consider why anybody in the Bay might regard himself in bondage. With no tact at all, he "besought him humbly to consider his youth, and short experience in the things of God, and to beware of peremptory conclusions, which he [Peter] perceived him to be very apt unto." Whereupon he preached Vane a little sermon on having observed in the Low Countries and here that new opinions and divisions stemmed from three principal causes: pride, idleness, and something else which Winthrop could not remember when penning this account.

Cotton had preached the formal sermon that opened this Court session, showing that evident sanctification was an evidence of justification. In the discussion period of the service, he and Vane had sided together in denying that evident sanctification could be evidence to a man without a concurrent sight of his justification. (It is certain no one smiled.) Later in the day of Peter's plain dealing with Vane, Wilson chose to deliver his "very sad speech" on the condition of the churches and the inevitable danger of separation if these differences and alienations among the brethren were not speedily remedied. All the magistrates except Vane and two others (one would have been Coddington), and all the ministers but two (doubtless Cotton and Wheelwright) agreed with Wilson that "these new opinions risen up amongst us" had caused the dissensions.

Cotton took sufficient offense at this speech to instigate a prosecution against Wilson in the Boston church. Vane there pressed violently for admonition, says Winthrop, "and all the congregation, except the deputy [Winthrop] and one or two more, and many of them with much bitterness and reproaches." Winthrop took the position that the state was not accountable to the church, though he had concurred in Wilson's holding Boston Church accountable to the state. Wilson tried to maintain that he had not necessarily meant Boston Church, but that was the only one perceptibly infected with "these new opinions." Because there were some members who opposed all-out admonition, Cotton restrained his execution to a "grave exhortation." Wilson managed to preach splendidly the next day, and Winthrop, now a decidedly unhonored prophet in his own hometown, publicly lauded his performance. He also wrote Cotton a letter which "dealt very plainly with him" about his diverse failings. Cotton made "a very loving and gentle answer" which, however, reneged nothing. The clergy of the other towns, Peter in the forefront, also took Cotton to task in a running written dispute, to no better avail.

But the whole antinomian heresy, including tenets Winthrop had never heard before, erupted into open discussion in the Boston church. The winter's climax, which everyone remembered afterward as a determinative milestone of the controversy, occurred in the form of Wheelwright's guest fast-day sermon of Thursday afternoon January 19, 1637, to "a great Assembly" in the Boston meetinghouse. Wheelwright's calling on his hearers in this sermon to bear themselves so that "we give not others to say we are libertines or Antinomians" probably started the currency of the term "antinomian" in the Bay as applied to his persuasion.

Aged about forty-five and evidently a burly person who had distinguished himself as a soccer player, John Wheelwright had arrived from England the day before Vane's election. His career had gone well so far. After working his way through Sidney College, Cambridge, to an M.A., he had inherited property in Lincolnshire and became well-to-do for a clergyman when he married the vicar's daughter at Bilsby and, not long after, inherited the vicarage. By the time he came to America he was the father of five children, three by his first wife Marie and two by his second, Mary, a sister of Ann Hutchinson. When Winthrop foiled his bid to infiltrate the ministry of Boston Church, Wheelwright took the pulpit at Mt. Wollaston (old Merrymount, later Braintree), where many Bostonians, including Coddington and William Hutchinson, kept farms. "The Mount" served as a principal hatching nest for the antinomian intrigue. Wheelwright, who probably spent more time scheming than preparing sermons at Mt. Wollaston, plainly had ability and ambition for bigger things than this rural pulpit. Shepard called him "a man of a bold and stiff conceit of his own worth and light," but he was also a man with the courage of his convictions, for which, like Shepard, he had suffered silencing in England.

Nineteenth-century authorities like James Savage (a descendant of Mrs. Hutchinson) and Charles Francis Adams, Jr. (an anti-Puritan), found Wheelwright's celebrated line-drawing sermon of January 19 colorful but not seditious or inflammatory. Their supporting quotations, however, omit the climax passages:

When the enymies to the truth oppose the way of God . . . we must kille them with the worde of the Lorde, Hos. 6:5, the Lorde hath giuen true beleuers power ouer the nations, & they shal breake them apeces, as shiuered with a rod of Iron; & what rodde of Iron is this, but the worde of the Lorde. . . . the Lord hath maide vs of thrushing instruments, with teeth, & we must beate the hils into chafe, Isa. 41:15. . . . I must confes & acknowlege the saints of God are few, they are but a littel flocke, & those that are enymies to the Lorde, not onely Pagonish, but Antechristian, & those that runne vnder a couenant of workes are very strong: but be not afraide the battel is not yours, but Gods. . . .

Ob[jection]: . . . It wil be obiected that diuers of those who are opposite to the waies of grace, & free covenant of grace, they are wonderous holy people, therefore it should seeme to be a very vncharitable thing in the seruants of God to condemne such. . . .

A[nswer]: Brethren, those vnder a couenant of workes, the more holy they are, the greater enymies they are to Ch[rist], Paule . . . sath . . . the more he founde in a legal way, the more he persecuted the waies of grace, 13 & 14 Act. where al deuout people were such as did expel Paule. . . . It maketh noe matter how seemingly holy men be, according to the law, if they doe not know the worke of grace & waies of God. . . . they shal dye, sath the Lorde, Exek. 33:13. . . . Seest thou a man wise in his owne conceite, more hope there is of a foole then of him. Pro. 26:12. . . .

Ob. . . . It wil be obiected this wil cause a combustean in Church & comanwealth.

A: I must confesse & acknowlege it wil doe soe, but what then, did not Ch[rist] come to sende fier vpon the earth? Luke 12:49. . . . Bretheren, we know that the whore must be burnt, Reu. 18, it is not shaueing of her heade, & paireing her nails, & changeing her rayment, that wil serue the turne, but this whore must be burnt. . . . why should we not further this fier . . . after the burneing of the whore follows Alleluia . . . the conuirtion of the Jues . . . must come by the downefal of Antech[rist], & if we take him away, we must burne him, therefore neuer feare combusions & burneings.

The next General Court was forty-nine days away, but the war within, which would shake the Bay to its foundations, had been openly declared. On February 3 came the infighting of Cotton and Wilson in their clashing sermons to the passengers of a departing ship. Cotton, in his turn, says Winthrop, "willed them to tell our countrymen that all the strife amongst them was about magnifying the grace of God: one person seeking to advance [it] within us, the other . . . toward us (meaning by the one justification, by the other sanctification)." Three days later, perhaps reflecting the incipient religious hysteria, a man of Weymouth (but a nonchurch member, Winthrop hastens to add) cried out in the night, "Art thou come, Lord Jesus?" and bounded from bed, broke away from his wife, leaped out a high window into the snow, and ran in his nightshirt about seven miles before succumbing.

ABOUT FEBRUARY 21 Lion Gardener ventured forth with a work crew to a neck of land half a mile from Saybrook Fort and felled twenty trees, doubtless to make lumber for rebuilding the burned structures. Next day, he returned to the neck with ten men and three dogs to burn the weeds, reeds, leaves, and small bushes which obstructed rolling of the logs to the waterside to float to the Fort. He stationed two sentinels, Robert Chapman and Thomas Hurlbut, on the small of the neck and set the rest to burning. With dried-weed fires going here and there over the neck, Gardener circled back to its small and called to the men firing the reeds to come away. They would not come until they had used all their match.

Suddenly the flames flushed three Indians from the reeds, who streaked for the woods. Gardener and some others raced to cut them off, but Chapman and Hurlbut yelled that other Indians were coming out of the woods on the opposite side of the marsh. They were "a great Company," says Gardener, and they rushed from two different directions. Gardener motioned the men near him to follow as he strode to intercept, but these Indians were not trying to slip away. Gardener heard the sentinels shouting that some of his men had hung back. Thomas Rumble and Arthur Branch, in fact, threw down their guns and tore for the Fort. The Indians shot two of the reed-burners who remained engrossed in their task and closed in on a third who did not fall even with an arrow stuck in his neck. He drew his sword; the Indians wrested it from him. He tried to kill himself with his own knife rather than be captured (some Indians later related), but they forced it from him first.

The main body of the ambushers sought to edge between the remaining Saybrook men and the Fort. In usual Indian fashion, they tried to avoid presenting direct targets, but they also, for the first time in New England history, crowded right into the muzzles of the muskets. Gardener, who had fought Spaniards in the Low Countries when Spain boasted the greatest army in the world, contended (as Winslow quoted him to Winthrop May 22) that the Pequots were more formidable fighters than the Spaniards. About to be surrounded by a hundred Pequots, according to one estimate, seventy according to another, Gardener and his company retreated in a half-moon, desperately firing and trying to reload. Gardener got an arrow in the thigh (and many in his buff coat); Hurlbut got one almost clear through a thigh, and John Spencer one through his back into a kidney. Gardener kept Hurlbut and Spencer slowly moving in agony ahead of himself and the other four linemen, who resorted to their swords when expecting to be taken alive altogether. "Sometime shouttinge and sometime retraightinge," says Gardener, "we recovered a bayre place of the ground which this winter I had cleared for the same vse," where the Indians dared not venture because the big guns of the Fort had it in range.

Inside the Fort, Gardener ordered the two cowards who had fled to draw lots to see which should be hanged, "for the articles did hang up in the hall for them to read." But the three resident gentlemen, Mitchell, Higginson, and Pell interceded, and the Lieutenant finally forbore. Spencer died within fourteen hours. Hurlbut lived to behead the very Indian who had pierced him. The captured man with a neck wound, the Saybrookers found out in time, got his nose and hands cut off in the course of a slow death.

In a few days, when Gardener's own wounds had sufficiently healed, he went out with eight men to bag some fowl and found the guns that had been thrown away. They also came across the body of one of their men, who had died by an arrow that entered his right side and stuck half through a rib on the left. Gardener cut the piece of rib out to send to the Bay, "because they had said that the arrows of the Indians were of no force." A Massachusetts mariner, Anthony Dike, had recently pulled in in his bark bearing a letter from Vane asking Gardener's advice about how to quell the Pequots. Gardener sent the rib along with his reply appealing for help.

The increasingly insolent Indians, in truth, had Saybrook under constant siege. They would stand outside the Fort, some of them carrying arms and wearing clothes of dead Englishmen, and taunt the men inside as squaws and their God as a fly. Gardener and his men got a good laugh one day when they discovered blood all over the nails they had driven through planks and placed spikes-up just outside the pale. Thomas Stanton, the 21-year-old linguist from London who had emigrated first to Virginia and come up to Connecticut in 1635, put in at Saybrook to wait for a fair wind to Long Island. He was luckily on hand, then, March 9, when Gardener spotted a band of Indians scooting prone behind a little rising hill and two great trees within musket range. He called the carpenter to load the two big saker guns with musket cartridges and arranged for him to fire them both at the Indian hiding place when Gardener should wave his hat over his head.

Presently three Indians crept out and called to come parley. Gardener advanced with Stanton ten or twelve rods beyond the gate to a big tree stump, having ordered six musketeers to the corner of the garden pales, where they headed off a crowd of sannups sneaking behind the fort. At first the parleying Indians could not believe Gardener's claim to be himself, having last seen him full of arrows; but one of the Indians had lived at Saybrook until Endecott came there, and he recognized the Lieutenant's voice.

In a while the Indian spokesmen grew brazen, admitted they were Pequots who had killed Englishmen, and announced they were going to Connecticut to kill men, women, and children. Gardener would not allow Stanton to shoot, because it was a parley, but told the Indians through Stanton's interpreting that it would do them no good to go upriver—English women were lazy and wouldn't work much; the Indians had better fight here, where the blockhouse held twenty pieces of Mr. Pynchon's trucking cloth, also hoes, hatchets, and all manner of trade; "and then go up the river after they had killed us." Hearing this, says Gardener, they were as mad as dogs and ran away. When they rejoined their fellows at the place they had emerged from, Gardener whirled his hat around his head. The two guns erupted, and "there was a great hubbub amongst them."

By a Dutch ship that had put in at Saybrook on its way to Fort Good Hope, Gardener sent letters up to the Connecticut villages telling how to prevent the catastrophe the Indians had threatened. Though the village magistrates felt real concern for the river's mouth, they scoffingly received Gardener's warning about their danger at home.

THIS SAME March 9 the General Court convened at Boston and brought in the clergy for joint deliberation, then summoned Stephen Greensmith, a person of some consequence, for saying that all the ministers except Cotton, Wheelwright, "and, as he thought," Hooker taught a covenant of works. The Court sentenced him to acknowledge his fault in every church and pay a fine of £40. The disposition of the majority of magistrates, deputies, and ministers thus demonstrated, the Court solemnly summoned Wheelwright and produced a transcript of his fast-day sermon, which he acknowledged. The Court found him guilty of sedition and contempt but deferred his sentence to the May term.

"Much heat of contention was this [March] court between the opposite parties," writes Winthrop; "so it was moved, that the next court might be kept at Newtown." The slow little community of Newtown would provide a far more favorable setting for unseating the Vane administration than the antinomian stronghold Boston. The ride or walk from Boston to Newtown, which involved a leisurely fording of the Charles, took a good chunk of a day and would effectively minimize the presence of Bostonians at a Newtown session. Vane refused to put the motion for change-of-venue to a vote. Winthrop, next in authority, professed himself loath to bypass the Governor to put it, since he dwelt in Boston. The Court took the hint and delegated Endecott who, nothing daunted, took charge. Vane must have sat incredulous as Winthrop thus out-maneuvered him. The motion carried.

On April 6, in the interim, Winthrop and Wilson joined in the day of humiliation observed at Newtown for the gathering there of the church of Concord, the Bay's newest incorporated town. It was on this auspicious occasion that the Concord congregation formally chose Peter Bulkley their teacher, but no one of note of the Boston church, save Winthrop and Wilson, attended. "The reason was conceived to be," Winthrop frankly states, "because they [of Boston] accounted these [officers who were being installed] as legal preachers, and therefore would not give approbation to their ordination." It is very damaging to Cotton's later pose of having been caught asleep and not knowing what the antinomians were up to, that he stayed home this April 6 with Vane, Coddington, the two other antinomian magistrates of Boston, as well as Wheelwright and the lay elders of Boston Church.

OLD MITCHELL, whose employees had had terrible luck with his own and the Fort's shallop, inopportunely sent for his other shallop from Wethersfield this early April. When it descended, its crew of two made the fatal mistake of stopping at Six-Mile Island. The two men went after geese in a canoe they had carried along in the shallop, and the report of their guns led a party of Indians to them, also in a canoe. The Englishmen paddled away fast at first sight of their pursuers, who, however, sent an arrow into the head of one of the pair, who fell overboard. The other, wounded and wearied, was overtaken. He cleft one of the Indians' heads with his paddle before they swarmed him, and of course he later died by torture. The body of his friend washed down to the Fort with the arrow stuck in his head through an eye.

On Mitchell's initial loss of a shallop and three armed men before he himself first came down, Gardener had nailed up a notice over the gate of the Fort prohibiting any boat from passing until it had been inspected as to arms and men and been given order not to land anywhere between Saybrook and Wethersfield. John Tilly, the strong-willed sea captain from the Bay (not the gentler Pilgrim of the same name), came ashore at Saybrook this early April with a permit to go up to Hartford. On reading the notice at the gate, he swore. When Gardener showed him his burned-down warehouse, he swore more. Gardener then gave him all his rescued goods and admonished him to heed the notice at the gate. Tilly, unimpressed, reboarded his pink and proceeded upriver.

When he came back down again, about April 11, he anchored at the point he had purchased on Saybrook side within sight of the Fort and went ashore with one of his men. The garrison at the Fort heard his gun discharge. Indians fell on him, killed his companion and, within plain view of the garrison, carried Tilly alive across the river before the Saybrook shallop could intercept. Gardener hurriedly despatched seven men afoot to fetch the pink, which otherwise would have been taken with the remaining three of its crew. Tilly did not favor the admiring Pequots with so much as a groan, although he lived three days after they amputated his hands and feet and thrust red-hot coals in the stumps. The squaws made hatbands of his fingers and toes.

Two days after the ambush at Tilly's Point, Captain Underhill reached Saybrook with twenty "lusty" men, sent out April 10 by Vane and the Assistants in response to Gardener's appeal after the narrow escape at the neck. Winthrop says they had been sent more to keep the Fort from the Dutch than from the Indians.

While Underhill waited out the warming days, Captain John Mason, who had made an earlier scouting trip to the mouth, returned with several aides and some volunteers. Twenty soldiers at a time would scour the neighborhood looking for the enemy, who decided to let them through their ambushes in view of the arms and numbers in action. The Pequots' belief that they had lost their advantage at the Fort turned out to be the immediate cause of their going through with their northern assault. Another cause was the quarrel which the Wethersfield settlers had stupidly picked with the sachem Sowheag, who had granted them their land on condition he be allowed to dwell near them. They drove him out, and he took his grievance to Pequot. That had been shortly before the Pequots appeared defiantly at Saybrook and parleyed with Gardener and Stanton. (Within another couple of years, the once-powerful Sowheag had completely resettled his tribe, usually called the Sequins, at Mattabesett (later Middletown), whence he constantly feuded with the Mohegans.)

In the late afternoon of April 27, Underhill, Mason, Gardener, and others of the garrison stood on the roof of the Fort and made out about a hundred Pequots in three canoes far across from the Fort. Many of the Indians were wearing white shirts and, on improvised masts, had hung English shirts and smocks. Their bravado filled the garrison with dread. Gardener, at the fraction of a second that he calculated the biggest canoe, a mile distant, would meet the bullets of the leveled big guns, commanded his carpenter to fire. The beakhead of that canoe blew off or, at least, the men in the garrison thought so. It happened to be the canoe carrying two captive English girls. Mason recalls that the Indians speeded up, drew their canoes over a narrow beach quickly, and so got away. Underhill says the garrison could not pursue because of being "destitute" of boats, "etc."

It took two weeks for the full story to filter down to the Fort accurately. The Pequot band had camped the night before their foray on a small tributary of the Connecticut close to their objective. They struck at daybreak and killed six men who were at work sawing, three women, twenty cows, and a mare. The girls taken captive seem to have been accompanying an "elder" woman some distance from their home when a man on horseback charged up and said he had just seen Indians stealing toward the town. The old lady did not believe him and minutes later lost her life. Along with the girls, the Indians carried off some horses.

Mason went back upriver with his staff to find the cluster of villages unnerved by the Wethersfield incident. A rumor that Indians had slain sixty men at Pynchon's post proved false but intensified the agitation at Hartford, where six magistrates and nine committeemen (among them Mitchell) representing the three towns convened in General Court in the primitive little meetinghouse Monday, May 1, Ludlow presiding. Their situation looked very sad, says Mason; "for those Pequots were a great People, being strongly fortified, cruel . . . and the English but an handful in comparison." The three towns, plus the Springfield post, boasted a grand total population of 250; 24 more, including two women and two children, resided permanently at Saybrook Fort. (Saybrook, strangely, did not become legally integrated with the rest of Connecticut until 1644.) One of the Court's first acts that May 1 was to write the Bay seconding New Plymouth's accusation of provoking a needless war. Even now, the Connecticut leaders held to their line that this was the Bay's war. The Court levied ninety men from the three villages, requisitioned provisions, expropriated Pynchon's shallop, and named Captain John Mason commander-in-chief. Mason was thirty-seven (a year younger than Underhill), a very tall, portly, but agile veteran of Netherlands combat under General Fairfax; Fairfax tried to get him to resume their earlier association a few years later against Charles I. Probably a relative of the Captain John Mason who nearly became governor-general of New England the year before, our Connecticut Captain had migrated from England to Dorchester in 1630 and from Dorchester to Windsor in 1635.

Hooker apprized Winthrop of the Court's measures some days later. He rejoiced, he said, that the Lord had kept Winthrop "from any taynt of those new-coyned conceits" in the "heavy distractions" unexpectedly risen in the Bay. He hoped Winthrop would "hasten execution" against the Pequots "& not to do this work of the Lords revenge slackly." He divulged one of the strongest pressures operating on the Court to go to war immediately as the importunity of "the Indians here, our frends"; Connecticut would have appeared cowardly and turned them into enemies by failing to act any longer.

Hooker here alluded to the Mohegans, who had splintered off from the Pequots and resumed their separate tribal identity only that spring—sometime between March 25 and April 25—and come to live in the environs of Hartford as a colony large enough to field seventy sannups. Underhill understood that Sassacus had driven them from their hunting grounds neighboring the Pequots', rather than that they had voluntarily withdrawn. Those grounds would have lain directly above the West Niantics off an eastern branch of the lower Connecticut. Two branches of the Pequot River formed a V, which the Nipmuks directly east of Hartford occupied and so wedged between the Mohegans and Pequots. The huge Mohegan grand sachem, Uncas, had been in some degree of rebellion against Sassacus since the time that young prince succeeded his murdered father. Uncas may have had ambitions of running the Pequots or may merely have been loath to give his allegiance to a younger and smaller man. He was also a wily politician with an enormous talent for staying alive; he may have parted company with Sassacus over the latter's risky policy of belligerence with the whites, whom he possibly foresaw as a power the Indians must adjust to to survive. His wife was the daughter of the petty sachem and friend of the Dutch, Tatobam, whom Uncas watched powerless to dislodge a conquered enemy (Attawanyut) when the Pilgrims reestablished said enemy at Windsor. Uncas, in any event, made common cause with the English at Hartford just in time to avoid the Bay and Connecticut Englishmen's avenging wrath ever after.

"Mohegan" refers to the Hudson River that Uncas's people had formerly lived along. The Mohegans or Mohicans—or Maikans, as the Dutch usually called them—occupied the country where the Dutch founded Fort Orange (later Albany) in 1624. The Mohegans' traditional enemies, the Mohawks, decisively defeated them early in 1628, with "cruel murders on both sides," says the clergyman Jonas Michaëlius. It was the remnant of the Hudson Mohegans which fled to the lower Connecticut and confederated with the nearby Pequots, who were still in process of subduing that valley. Michaëlius wrote August 11, 1628, from Manhattan that the Mohegans by then had gone, their pleasant and fertile lands lay vacant, and the fur trade stood dull. The Mohegans had some kind of earlier kinship with the Pequots; they, for instance, spoke the same Algonquin dialect, which was very close, also, to the dialect of the Massachusetts and Narragansett Indians. The language of the Mohawks, on the other hand, differed as much from that of the Mohegans as Dutch from Latin, according to Domine Johannes Megapolensis in 1644. The Mohawks had the same reputation for dominance and tyranny in New Netherland as the Pequots in New England, only more so; their very name, as Williams points out, signifies "Man-eater."

Haynes did not leave the Bay for Hartford with his family and servants until May 3. It was his report of the Wethersfield incident, written while he stopped over at Saybrook, that reached the Council in Boston May 12, the first reliable word they received.

About Saturday, May 13, Hooker preached a send-off sermon to the expeditionaries, assuring them "you need not question your authority to execute those whom God, the righteous Judge of all the world, hath condemned for blaspheming his sacred Majesty, and murthering his Servants. . . . and your feet shall soon be set on their proud necks." Thus fortified, Mason started down the river with his ninety conscripts and Uncas with seventy sannups, in a pink, a pinnace, and a shallop. What with the extreme lowness of the water just then, plus crosswinds, the boats kept going aground. The Mohegans grew so impatient they asked to be put ashore, promising to meet Mason at Saybrook. Mason agreed, though the Connecticut people had known the Mohegans too short a time to be sure of their loyalty. As Mason later tried to explain to Gardener, the Connecticut forces had to trust Uncas because they did not know the country.

Gardener must have gasped to see seventy-one Mohegans walk right up to the Saybrook gate and announce that Mason had sent them ahead. Underhill admitted them, but Gardener told Uncas he would have to prove he meant to help Mason by sending twenty men to Bass River to fetch six Indians, dead or alive, who had gone there in a canoe "yesternight." It was Sunday, however, and Underhill would not allow a foray until early Monday morning. Uncas then (May 15) sent a detail which surrounded a party of seven Pequots not far from the Fort, killed four outright, mortally wounded a fifth, and took two captive, of whom one got away. A single Mohegan was wounded; Underhill sent him back home in a skiff. Gardener gratefully gave Uncas fifteen yards of trading cloth to portion out to his men according to their desert. Kiwas, the Pequot prisoner brought in, had lived at Saybrook as a professed friend of the English and spoke English well. He turned out to have been a continuous spy at the Fort for Sassacus, had instigated a number of English deaths, and had been present at the death spectacle of all the Englishmen who died by torture in that vicinity. He had deserted the Fort at the time of the Endecott expedition and thenceforth served as a guide for his own people. Underhill turned his execution over to Uncas, whose men pulled his limbs apart and burned them, then sang as they ate his flesh about the fire. Gardener, Mason, and Underhill all omit mentioning this festival, as well as that they set all six Indian heads up on the Fort. Williams's intelligence report of these events reached Boston May 24 and was confirmed next day by eyewitnesses arriving from Saybrook.

Underhill rowed up May 17 to meet Mason's forces and came alongside the big boat while the Connecticut men were gathered funereally about Samuel Stone in prayer. Stone, whom the Court had sent as chaplain, was voicing anxiety about the fidelity of the Mohegans. Underhill stepped up and told Stone that God had already answered his prayer. At the news of the Mohegan foray, the Connecticut men became different persons and reached Saybrook rejoicing. They may have arrived in time to witness the execution-festival, which likely took place that very night.

Both Gardener and Underhill registered disappointment at the Connecticut troops. Mason said they were all the Court could send.

Gardener hated to supplement them with his own men for another Endecott type of goose chase. Underhill offered himself and nineteen Bay men. But Mason's orders allowed him but a short radius from Saybrook. The three ex-officers of the war in Holland had plenty of time to argue out their course before the wind came fair on Friday (Mason had arrived on a Wednesday). During this period of indecision a Dutch ship came in with the Wethersfield prisoner-girls. Its crew had lured seven Indian men aboard at Pequot (more came aboard but jumped in the river), then yelled ashore that the maids must be brought if the sannups were not to be drowned. As the boat weighed anchor, Indians ashore grew alarmed enough to fetch and deliver the girls. The seven sannups walked off, and the pinnace sailed to Saybrook. Underhill's first concern in interrogating the girls was whether they had managed to keep their virtue (which Hooker had leaped to the conclusion had been lost). It became clear that no Indian solicitor had been a match for the older girl's constant praying. She was about sixteen and her sister evidently half her age. The sixteen-year-old said that the Pequots had taken them from place to place, showed them their forts and curious wigwams, and encouraged them to be merry. They remained merely terrified. The squaw Wincumbone interceded to save their lives. They learned, among other things, that the Pequots had sixteen guns, with powder and shot, as well as an overwhelming superiority in population. Their total population must have come to about a thousand. The sentimental Dutch governor at Manhattan, when he first heard of the girls' abduction, had outfitted a pinnace to redeem them at all costs and had ordered any other Dutch ship which might redeem them to bring them to him. Thus the skipper of the ship that had just brought the girls to Saybrook had not let the girls go ashore there until Underhill promised to give them back up. After their interrogation, accordingly, the girls, who were then forty-six miles from home, had a sixty-league round trip to New Amsterdam before finally arriving safe at Wethersfield.

Mason accepted Underhill's offer and sent twenty of his own worst men back upriver; Underhill and his nineteen replaced them. The captains decided it would be best to sail to the Narragansett country and attack the Pequots from the rear, since it was going to do no good to remain in Saybrook Fort, which the Pequots kept under surveillance day and night, and since the Pequots' large numbers and swiftness of foot might frustrate a direct landing in the

Pequot River. But newly dispatched letters from Hartford expressly instructed a landing in the Pequot, and Mason felt anxious anyway about an expedition into the unknown eastern country beyond Pequot. He had Stone pray about the question.

Early next morning Stone, who spent his nights aboard the pink, came ashore to Mason's chamber and informed the Captain he "was fully satisfied to sail for Narragansett." The next morning after that—Friday, May 19—the joint expedition embarked, with a clear conscience.

THOMAS SHEPARD, the pale, thirty-two-year-old scholar who ironically had spent his first three days in America in the home of Coddington, preached the election sermon the hot morning of May 17 at Newtown. He endeavored to conciliate the factions, suggesting, for instance, that justification and sanctification came *simultaneously*. But only his fellow anti-antinomians appreciated his efforts. Back in Boston, where the town meeting had insolently declined to hold its local election for deputies until after the Court election, Margaret Winthrop wrote her husband across the river: "Sad thoughts posses my sperits, and I cannot repulce them which makes me unfit for any thinge wondringe what the Lord meanes by all these troubles amonge us."

The General Court duly convened at about 1 P.M. near a great oak tree on the north side of the Newtown common. The antinomian magistrates from Boston (not yet out of office) preferred a petition to revoke the Wheelwright verdict. Vane started to have the petition read. Winthrop properly protested that no business took precedence over elections. Vane still refused to put the customary call for voting until the petition had been considered. Winthrop called for the delegations to divide. They did, disclosing a majority in favor of proceeding immediately to the elections. But the Governor and his party refused to budge. "There was great danger of a tumult that day," says Winthrop; "for those of that side grew into fierce speeches, and some laid hands on others; but seeing themselves too weak, they grew quiet." Wilson got up in the bough of a tree and exhorted the deputies to look to their charter and consider the present work of the day; the cry, "Election, election!" went up from the deputies. Winthrop informed Vane he would go ahead and hold the elections without the minority; Vane gave in and conducted them himself.

Winthrop won back the governorship, with Dudley as deputy. Vane lost out altogether, as did Coddington and the other two Boston antinomians (Dummer and Hoffe) who had held seats in the magistracy. These defeated Bostonians went home the same evening. The next morning the Boston town meeting returned Vane, Coddington, and Hoffe as deputies, "and the court not finding how they might reject them," says Winthrop, "they were admitted." Isolated by the vote of the day before, they flailed about as an opposition of three out of forty-three. Two of the men who replaced antinomians on the Board of Assistants were Saltonstall Jr. (who had come over with Winthrop on the *Arbella* at the age of twenty, helped found Watertown, gone to England and back, and now resided at Ipswich) and the one-time deputy from Dorchester, Stoughton, whose about-face in favor of Winthrop had cut short his three-year disbarment from office.

The newly constituted Court summoned Wheelwright. Because a general day of humiliation had been appointed when all the churches were going to choose representatives to confer about the doctrinal differences a-raging, the Court gave Wheelwright respite to the next session, set for the first Tuesday in August. It hinted leniency if he retracted and reformed; otherwise, he must expect no consideration. He answered that if he had committed sedition, he ought to be put to death; if the Court meant to proceed against him, he meant to appeal to the king's court, for he would retract nothing.

The Court passed an alien law that prohibited newcomers to remain in the province longer than three weeks without a magistrate's permission. (All the magistrates were now anti-antinomian.) This embittered the antinomians more than anything so far, because their friends and relatives began arriving about this time in large numbers and had to be denied homes in Massachusetts. Winthrop said this preventive hardship was better than forcible ejection after they had taken root.

The four antinomian sergeants who had constantly attended Governor Vane with halberds (one of the four was Edward Hutchinson, a brother-in-law of Ann) refused to perform the same office for Winthrop. Although it had been customary for the governor to appoint his own honor guard, Winthrop dramatized the insult to his authority by having two of his own servants attend him. Towns all over the colony offered to send him halberdsmen. Boston offered to send him four men other than Vane's former four, but Winthrop grandly declined them all. Vane and Coddington sulked publicly. They refused to sit in the magistrates' seats in the Boston meeting-house, although Winthrop—glorying in his condescendency—sent to desire their presence with him. They sat with the deacons. On the general fast day, they went to the Mount to keep it with Wheel-wright.

Soon after Vane had despatched Underhill to Saybrook, he wrote Governor Bradford urging New Plymouth to join Massachusetts in a large-scale operation to chastise the Pequots. On May 12, the same day the authentic news of the Wethersfield raid reached Boston from Haynes, Winslow sailed into the harbor to confer on behalf of Bradford and the Pilgrim Council. To a closed session of magistrates he declared, first, the Plymouth Council's willingness to aid Massachusetts but that they could do nothing until their General Court convened the first Tuesday in June. After that unpromising intro-duction, he made some objections, says Winthrop, such as

1. Our refusal to aid them against the French [in Maine]. 2. Our people's trading [in competition with them] at Kenebeck. 3. The injury offered them at Connecticut by those of Windsor, in taking away their land there. 4. Their own poverty, and our ability, which needed not any help from them.

The magistrates granted that they had not been blameless in the French matter but that it had been the Pilgrims' private quarrel, "and we thought it no wisdom for us to engage ourselves in a war with the king of France." They said they "gave no allowance" to Bay people's trading at Kennebec (but Vane had licensed a couple of vessels to carry mail, and they had taken occasion to offer trade competition); and had dealt with the Dorchester people at Connecti-cut to give satisfaction for the injury they had done the Pilgrims; "but it was not in our power to do them justice in it."

Winslow went on to suggest that this war did not concern the Pil-grims, seeing the Pequots had killed none of their number. "We an-swered," says Winthrop, who probably did most of the answering this afternoon, "that Capt. Stone, etc., for whom this war was begun, were none of ours neither." Winslow also brought up the Pilgrim displeasure that they had not been acquainted with the Endecott expedition until two or three days before it set forth. The answer to that played down the impetuousness with which Endecott had been loosed and the war-provoking vengefulness of his orders:

"we intended at the first to send only to Block Island, and for that we thought it not needful to trouble them, and our sending them thence to the Pequods was with hope to draw them to parley, and so to some quiet end." Winslow knew only too well what had actually happened at Block Island and Pequot. But he left Bradford's letters which set forth the Pilgrim views in full, and the magistrates concluded to write a further answer to them from the next Court.

The following day, Williams wrote a letter for either Vane or Winthrop to be sent "with speede," reporting that Miantonomy with a great retinue had arrived at Providence a day or two before—the day Anthony Dike put in at Providence on his way to Boston with Haynes's letter from Saybrook. (Dike's custom was to anchor his bark at Providence and proceed to the Bay overland, so avoiding the shoals of the Cape.)

"The Nanihiggonsicks are at present doubtfull of Realitie in all our promises," Williams wrote; "I haue alleadged the best Arguments I haue heard or Could invent to perswade Realitie of purpose & speedie performance, as allso reasons of delay." In an undated letter of sometime this May Williams reported: "The Pequts heare of your preparations Et & Comfort themselues in this that a witch amongst them will sinck the pinnaces by diving vnder water & making holes Et as allso that they shall now enrich themselues with store of guns." Already, at the time Williams wrote on the thirteenth, the Pequots were making new fields of corn in the vicinity of Montauk Point on the easternmost tip of Long Island about fifteen miles southwest of Block Island, and especially on Plum Island, just off the northeastern prong of Long Island about fifteen miles south-southwest of Pequot, "in Case the English should destroy their fields at home." The Pequots were "scarce of provision" anyway and had gone to the seaside between the Pequot and the Pawcatuck and to the nearby islands in greater numbers than usual to take sturgeon and other fish. The women, of course, did the planting and fishing. Most of the Pequot men, it developed, stayed close to their inland forts.

Miantonomy with his council was still at Williams's house as Williams broached the sachem's proposal in this letter of the thirteenth: that Miantonomy, with forty or fifty of his men and Wequash, a renegade Pequot sachem living with Canonicus, take Dike's boat and land in the night at Plum Island to despoil the Pequot canoes, spoil their fields, slay such men as might be found, and most of the

women and children. Miantonomy proposed to do this without
landing an Englishman and would remain on board himself in English clothes with the English crew of two or three. Williams says he
will wedge the eager planners in "from any starting aside vntill your
forces should follow." But if these forces speed, Miantonomy's plan
will not only weaken and distress the enemy, it will "allso much en-
rage the Pequts for euer against them [the Narragansetts], a thing
much desirable." Even Williams here temporarily reflects the cor-
rosive coarsening the holy experiment had gradually undergone.
While he was writing, a messenger came to Miantonomy from the
northernmost Nipnets (who lived beyond the Nipmucks, apparently in Connecticut) reporting a far greater slaughter than Dike
had brought word of. This referred to the panic-rumor of a massacre at Springfield. Williams could not bring himself to mention his
friend Pynchon's name in such a connection yet; knowing the falli-
bility of Indian reports, he said he hoped and longed to hear the
news countermanded. Winthrop alludes to this letter and to another
of near the same time when he enters in his *Journal* that the Court
—about May 18—ordered forty men by land to the Narragansett
country, there to take in Miantonomy and the sixteen sannups Winthrop says the sachem offered (the number kept changing), "and so,
in the night, to set upon them." The forty Bay men marched under
Captain Daniel Patrick, an intrepid, intractable, and quite un-Puritan
blade.

On May 15, having received an account of the Bay's precise intentions, Williams wrote Vane and Winthrop that the Narragansett
sachems "were glad of your preparations." Not a week passes, he
went on to say, without some skirmishings between the Narragansetts and Pequots, "though hitherto little loss on either side."
Miantonomy's plan continued to modify. From long conferences
with him, Canonicus, and others, Williams had extracted these significant items as of the fifteenth:

1. Miantonomy no longer believes that the two-or-three-day job
would accomplish enough but that the night raid must be followed
up three weeks or a month later. The Massachusetts troops should
retreat as if departing and reattack within three or four days when
the Pequots had returned to their houses and thought themselves
secure.

2. The Pequots are prepared, on the first sight of a pinnace, to
hurry their women, children, and old men to a swamp some three of

four miles behind them, "a marvellous great & secure swamp, which they called Ohomowauke, which signifies owls nest"—the place later called Pine or Mast Swamp, on the Mystic within the later township of Groton, Connecticut.

3. The eastern division of the Niantics, the division nominally subject to the Narragansetts (and practically always referred to as Narragansetts), are at present definitely within the Narragansett fold and at enmity with the Pequots. Miantonomy, in fact, designates Wekapaug as the place of rendezvous for all vessels.

4. The sachems believe it will be most convenient for the English if provisions and munitions first be brought to Aquidneck, whence messengers could be sent to Boston and Providence to signal the dispatch of infantry to the vessels; otherwise, the soldiers might eat up their supplies in the long passage of the Cape shoals.

5. Yes, the assault should be by night. The English could then "enter the howses & do what execution they please."

6. Williams warns that before the assault commences, an ambush should be laid between the Indian houses and the swamp to prevent a flight.

7. He recommends that two renegade Pequots, Wequash (whose name meant "Swan") and Wuttackquiackommin, "valiant men, especially the latter," go along as guides. They have lived these three or four years with the Narragansetts, "and know every pass & passage amongst them."

8. "That it would be pleasing to all natives, that women & children be spared, &c."

9. In case of any more land travel to Connecticut, some course should be taken with the Wunhowatuckóogs, inland confederates of the Pequots and a refuge to them, despite having been apparently pushed back from the coast by them at an earlier date. The Wunhowatuckóogs lay athwart the path of anybody who walked from Massachusetts to the Connecticut.

Williams also noted that Canonicus "would gladly accept of a box of eight or ten pounds of sugar" and at the end of the letter drew a "rude view" of the Indian dispositions:

On the east bank of the Connecticut, somewhat upstream and opposite Saybrook, he located the fort of the West Niantics. He skipped the Pequot capital on the west bank of what he called the Mohigadic, but came on east across that river to locate Sassacus at Weimshauks, a fort in the environs of the later town of Groton. Two miles on east of this fort, high on the rugged, rocky west bank of the Mystic, Williams located the Number-Two Pequot, Mononoto (whom he called Mamoho), at Fort Mistick. This stronghold became the immediate objective of the English attack from the east. It stood on a commanding but not steep hill less than half a mile back of the river and about three miles from the river mouth in what is today Old Mystic. About two miles upstream from the fort, a place identifiable by two boulders, later named Porter's Rocks, provided "lodging" in the rough ravine for Mason's surprise attackers. Another mile or two above Porter's Rocks, between the Pequot and the Mystic, Williams located Ohomowauke Swamp. On eastward across the Pawcatuck, which he knew as the Niantic, he located Wepiteamock "and our friends" at Niantic.

Winthrop would not have had to relay this intelligence to Captain Patrick, who arrived in Providence around May 20 and got it direct from Williams; Patrick refers to Williams's outline of strategy for the westward expedition in a letter to Winthrop from Providence May 23. But Patrick had no influence on the campaign that presently materialized. On the twentieth Winthrop wrote the Bay's full reply to Bradford's exceptions. He said the Bay did not expect the Pilgrims to act other than in their own forms at their own pace, but this statement strained his forbearance, since he urgently felt that time was of the essence; the preliminaries were over; and "it concernes us much to hasten this warr to an end before the end of this sommer, otherwise the newes of it will discourage both your and our friends from coming to us next year; with what further hazard and losse it may expose us unto, your selves may judge." He insisted that it was not just the Bay's war; he presumed that New Plymouth looked on the Pequots "and all other Indeans" as a common enemy

who, though he may take occasion of the begining of his rage, from some one parte of the English, yet if he prevaile, will surly pursue his advantage, to the rooting out of the whole nation.

MASON AND UNDERHILL, with seventy-five Englishmen and fifty Mohegans, reached a Narragansett harbor toward evening on Saturday, May 20, and remained aboard keeping the Sabbath until Monday, when an offshore wind whipped too violently against them to permit a landing all that day and until sunset Tuesday. On Monday Winslow wrote Winthrop the latest news: Captain Underhill and his men were in good health at the Fort and expecting Captain

Mason down with ninety men! But the seaside Pequots had observed the troopships passing east, Mason later learned. Reprieved of the expected attack in Pequot River, they took this movement for a cowardly abandonment of the fight.

Tuesday evening, after the sunset landing, Mason and Underhill marched to Narragansett and got an audience with Miantonomy, who had been expecting Patrick. Though Miantonomy thought the captains' task force insufficient to assault the mighty Pequots, he answered their close questioning and so passed on directly the intelligence Williams had forwarded to Winthrop. The captains found themselves seeing eye to eye with him. Wequash, who had figured in the planning of Miantonomy and Williams all along, probably served as interpreter for this parley (there is only an outside possibility that Williams had been notified and had come down); Miantonomy gave Wequash up as a guide for Mason and Underhill, as he had intended for Patrick.

Wednesday morning Mason ordered the skippers of the ships to set sail Thursday for a rendezvous at Pequot Harbor, for he would attack Fort Mistick at dawn Friday. He marched the eighteen or twenty miles to Wekapaug, the Mohegans with him in the van; Underhill brought up the rear. The East Niantics took a high tone and would not permit any of the expeditionaries inside their fort. Mason thereupon forbade any of his "hosts" to come out, fearing informers to the Pequots. Not a Niantic stirred all night. Many stirred elsewhere. Miantonomy's messengers notifying Williams of the Tuesday-night parley roused Williams to urge assistance, so that perhaps fifty Narragansetts arrived at Wekapaug early Wednesday morning. This encouraged about four hundred Niantics to join the expedition also. At Weimshauks Fort, meanwhile, Sassacus learned of the English beach camp on Narragansett Bay. Assuming the "cowards" to be awaiting a fair wind to proceed home, he sent perhaps 150 sannups on Thursday to reinforce those residing at Fort Mistick, for a descent on the beach camp Friday. In anticipation of a war feast Thursday night, the women of Fort Mistick went fishing in Pawcatuck River the Wednesday Mason was marching to Wekapaug.

Faint from the heat and overly limited rations and disturbed at the numerous Niantics turning back in fright, the expeditionaries reached the Pawcatuck ford after about a twelve-mile march Thursday morning where they saw the ominous signs of fish dressing, had a scanty meal, constructed a raft, and resumed their march for the rest of the day and after nightfall, finally halting in the rugged country where their sentinels heard the feasting Pequots singing until midnight from the fort high above the river. The burden of their song, the English afterward found out, was the cowardice of the voyagers who had passed the Pequots by.

Shortly after 1 A.M. the march commenced along the path Wequash and Uncas pointed out which led directly to the Fort. At a newly planted cornfield at the foot of the hill the Fort crowned, Mason and Underhill agreed to divide in order to storm both entrances at once. Mason told the guides to tell the Indians to ring the Fort at whatever distance they pleased and see whether Englishmen would fight or not. His final order was not to resort to fire—so the plunder could be saved.

The Fort covered about an acre, by Underhill's estimate. Its encircling palisade consisted of trees and half-trees set three feet deep in the ground. Underhill marched his company around to the southwest entrance and strung them around the wall clockwise, as the now three hundred Indian confederates deployed in a circle well beyond. Mason made for the northeastern, or main entrance. Within a rod of it, his company heard a dog bark and a shout *"Owanux! Owanux!"* ("Englishmen! Englishmen!"). Mason called to rush close, and both companies fired a simultaneous volley through the pales—low, because Indians slept on the ground. This clap of doom at break of day roused the village from a dead sleep and set it into such a doleful cry that the soldiers had to remind themselves of the thirty English deaths to keep from commiseration. Some of the old Pequot men grabbed their kinsmen who started to flee; "As we have lived together, so let us die together," they said.

Mason's hulking figure bounded over the waist-high brakes and branches that blocked the doorway, but the less agile men immediately behind him furiously pulled out branches before they broke through. Mason saw no Indians, so battered into a wigwam, where quite a few jumped him. He ran one of them through; when William Heydon crashed in, stumbling over the dead Pequot, the grapplers fled out or slithered under mats. Mason chased a number of Indians down to the end of a lane; several of his men intercepted and slew seven sannups. Mason wheeled about and walked slowly back toward the entrance, badly out of breath.

Underhill had not been able to dislodge the tightly packed

branches in the opposite doorway, so he ordered a powerful young
gentleman from Northamptonshire named Hedge, with some
others, to try his hand. Hedge heaved out enough wood to leap
through and got an arrow clean through his right arm, but slashed
his assailant in the upper arm, ran another bowman through, and
slew two or three more defenders before getting an arrow through
his other arm. Underhill, gun in left hand, sword in right, lunged
through and got arrows stuck in his buff coat and headpiece. He and
Mason each lost a man, one apparently killed by a fellow musketeer
by mistake. Mason, bleeding from various cuts, pulled an arrowhead
out of his lieutenant's eyebrow. A total of twenty Englishmen sustained incapacitating wounds as perhaps half the attacking force
streamed inside the palisade. There they found the wigwams cramp-
ing their movement and providing abundant cover for the defenders. They also quickly perceived that as soon as the first shock of
surprise wore off they would be the defenders against overwhelming numbers.

As Mason, huffing, returned up the lane, he purpled to see two of
his soldiers standing near the gateway with their swords pointed
groundward. Hoarsely yelling "We should never kill them after
that manner," he suddenly added, *"We must burn them!"* Grabbing
a firebrand from the wigwam he had just scuffled in, he thrust it to
the mats covering the wigwams in that neighborhood, the windward
side of town. Underhill, at the first sight of flames from the opposite
side, followed suit, using a train of powder. Both fires converged
with a roar at the center of the town of tinderbox wigwams. The
smoke and heat drove Underhill and his men outside the wall;
Mason ordered his men on the windward side to fall off and surround the Fort without. One man who could not move because of
his wounds got pulled out in time.

From three hundred to seven hundred men, women, and children
found themselves instantly trapped in the great oven; the wind carried everything before it. Several Pequot men climbed to the tip of
the pointed pales; several went mad and ran straight into the flames;
some coolly refused to break out but fired through the wall from
the windward side until their very bowstrings burned. Others and
their families, in bunches of twenty or thirty at a time, burst out
onto the swords of the soldiers. A few who sieved past the soldiers
fell, eighteen of them, into the hands of the Mohegans and Narragansetts forming the second ring. Only another five or seven es-

caped; only seven of the hundreds of inmates were taken alive. "It was a fearfull sight to see them thus frying in the fyer," Bradford repeats certain unidentified eyewitnesses, "and the streams of blood quenching the same, and horrible was the stinck and sente ther of." People lay gasping on the ground so thick around the edge of the palisade that the swordsmen could hardly pass in some places. "Sometimes the Scripture declareth women and children must perish with their parents," said Underhill. "We had sufficient light from the word of God for our proceedings."

The fire raged with such intensity as to consume the fortress in half an hour. The sun had been up just one hour when all was quiet and Mason reassembled his troops. They felt weak and desperately thirsty. Many, surprisingly, suffered from the sharp coolness of the morning. It took twenty able-bodied men to carry the five badly wounded (one of whom died some weeks later); not more than forty Englishmen remained both able-bodied and free to fight. Forty of the second-ring Mohegans and Narragansetts (this term including Niantics) had been hurt, mainly because the soldiers had been unable to distinguish them from Pequots.

Suddenly, three hundred or more Pequots from the Weimshauks fort appeared on the southern slope and advanced uphill toward the expeditionaries, letting fly as they came. Twelve or fourteen men (two files) under Underhill headed directly toward them; their outreaching bullets intimidated the Pequot host into a temporary retreat. This enabled the expeditionaries to gain the small brook at the foot of the hill, where they refreshed themselves. When they had resumed their march about a quarter of a mile, the Pequot host mounted the hill. At the appalling spectacle on top they stamped and tore their hair and, with one accord, charged downhill to overrun the victors. Underhill, commanding the rearguard, faced about and dropped enough runners that the rest grew wary and kept their distance. They, however, hung on the English rear and flanks, infesting thickets, rocks, and swamps, until the English, slowed down by their wounded, were ready to throw up their hands in frustration. Fifty Niantics struck eastward in a body, and the rest of the Niantics and Narragansetts intended to follow, on learning that the English meant to continue westward if the ships showed up. Concealed Pequots emerged and headed the first fifty off. Their kinsmen who had not yet departed pleaded with the captains to rescue the Niantics. The captains felt disgusted at the "deserters," but

Underhill with thirty men brought back the trapped Niantics in an hour, killing and wounding over a hundred Pequots in his retreat back to the main body.

The wind suddenly changed directions about noon, giving the guerrillas an assist, though their arrows remained largely ineffectual. As the troops neared a swamp or thicket they would clear it with a volley, and the Mohegans with a bloodthirsty shout would fetch the heads of the fallen. Some Indians later estimated that more Pequots died while ambushing during the march away from the Fort than in it. When a Sergeant Davis somersaulted a Pequot backward with a carbine shot, hitting just the top of the head showing above a rock, the stalkers lost heart. By the time the column had crossed to within two miles of the mouth of Pequot River, they had dispelled.

Seeing no sign of the ships, the Englishmen made for a seaside neck to quarter for the night. The ships had been held up by cross-winds until the sudden noontime change and passed in full view of the expeditionaries shortly before 10 P.M. The expeditionaries had left their drum back at Porter's Rocks but, with colors flying, marched up the hill adjoining Pequot Harbor instead of proceeding to the neck. They descended to the riverbank where the ships had come to anchor and quietly sat down.

To their consternation, they found that Captain Patrick with his forty men had arrived in one of the Connecticut shallops—to rescue Mason, Patrick said, from supposed pursuers. Mason pleaded for this shallop to transport the twenty-three wounded to Saybrook. At last Underhill, who also argued hotly, took them in the other shallop when Patrick agreed to stay with the Niantic allies until it could return to ferry them home. Patrick then decided he must go on and await the Bay vessels at Saybrook. Mason could not cram all the Indians in the remaining pink with his men, and could not march them back home through hostile country with so few men; so he ordered his troops ashore to walk, with the Indian allies, to Saybrook. Patrick thereupon quit the precious shallop and went ashore with his men! Mason plainly told him the Fort fighters did not desire or delight in his company; but Patrick, pathetically eager for adventure, marched with them regardless.

About halfway to Saybrook, the combined group fell upon a large party of West Niantics, who fled to a swamp. As long as this prey stayed together in a single body, the Englishmen tracked them, but the inevitable dispersion threw them off around 2 or 3 P.M.

Saturday. The Sabbath approaching and the men exceedingly weary, Mason decided to make straight for Saybrook. He reached the Connecticut at sunset, and Gardener shot off the big guns in welcome. But the troops had to quarter on the east bank for the night. Gardener fetched them across next morning to his generous entertainment. He also feasted the East Niantics and Narragansetts for three days at Saybrook. After arranging their return, Mason led his men back upstream to an exultant welcome June 9 and services of thankgiving a few days following.

NOT KNOWING that Mason and Underhill were bound for Narragansett Bay to effect just such a surprise attack as Williams had persuaded the Council at Boston (and Newtown) to undertake, the Massachusetts General Court ratified the Council's program to send another 160 men after Patrick. When the towns produced their quotas of troops, it grieved Winthrop that, whereas Boston had been as forward as any other town to send their choice men out during the antinomian administration of Vane, now that he, Winthrop, had taken over again, Boston "sent not a [church] member, but one or two whom they cared not to be rid of, and but a few others, and those of the most refuse sort, and that in such a carelesse manner, as gave great disappointment to the service." In open Court the Council proposed three nominees for commander of the big expedition; the clergy proposed two for the chaplain of it. Solemnly invoking God, Winthrop bade the three and the two draw lots. Stoughton and Wilson received the "divine" appointments. Not a single antinomian would consent to go under Wilson's chaplaincy. The Stoughton expedition could not be assembled and victualed nor the antinomian subversion stifled, for another month. Even then, the troops argued about the new doctrines while abroad. Wilson gradually grew popular in the field.

Williams heard the tidings of the Mistick Fort fight from his incoming neighbor Throckmorton within two days of it, but along with them the Niantic allegation that the English expeditionaries and three hundred Indian allies had been killed in their retreat for want of powder and provisions. Williams immediately relayed this word to Winthrop, then jumped in his canoe to check with Miantonomy. On May 28 a letter reached Boston from Plymouth confirming the cut-off retreat, so that, as Winthrop says, it was generally believed in the Bay. The Narragansetts, when Williams reached the sachems' village, confirmed, too, the "truth" of the rumor. Williams tried to persuade them that the troops had either gone to Connecticut for supplies or assaulted the second Pequot fort. Even if they had all been cut off, Williams assured the sachems in Winthrop's name, fresh forces of English would come who would never sheathe their swords. Williams's problem of the moment was to prevent a Narragansett bolt to the victors in case of an English disaster. He left at noon June 1 to paddle back to Providence. That same evening, the Niantics and Narragansetts whom Mason had arranged to return in a Saybrook pinnace, arrived home, and Miantonomy shortly dispatched the correct news to Providence. On June 2, therefore, Williams passed it on to Winthrop.

This included the new development that the day after returning to Saybrook, meaning Monday, Underhill and Patrick and their men went to take the second Pequot fort and found it deserted. Sassacus, according to hearsay, had said he would flee to Long Island and had either already gone or was hidden in the swamps, "but not a Pequt is to be found."

From reports of five pathetic Pequot women and an old Pequot man who came and submitted to the Narragansetts, Williams was able to sharpen this account in a letter of July 10. All the surviving Pequots had assembled at Weimshauks about June 1 with Sassacus. (The exact day would have been May 27 or the evening of May 26; the expeditionaries' observance of the Sabbath from nightfall Saturday to daybreak Monday is what gave the Pequots time to convene and depart unmolested.) Some wanted to counterattack and fall first on the Narragansetts (which Williams had heard before), but the majority preferred immediate removal. Sassacus and about fourscore more resolved for the Mohawk country, a hundred others for Long Island, and a smaller company for some part of Connecticut. Still another group of seventy men, women, and children (between twenty and thirty men) intended to go to the Narragansetts and beg for their lives. Sassacus and his company fell to skirmishing with these latter, but they made their getaway with casualties.

Mason had access to information through the Mohegans similar to Williams's through the Narragansetts and East Niantics. He said later that the whole body of surviving Pequots had descended on Sassacus at Weimshauks right after the Mistick disaster, charging him as the sole cause of all their troubles, and would have killed him, together with all his relations, had the *pinesses* not interceded.

Underhill understood that the *chief* Pequots came together at Weimshauks May 27 to deliberate whether to set upon sudden revenge against the Narragansetts or attempt an enterprise against the English or fly. Sassacus was all for blood, according to this version, but the rest for flight: "let us rather save some than lose all." Suddenly after, says Underhill, they destroyed everything of theirs they could not carry and flew, Sassacus towards the Connecticut towns. Another contemporary account (by the visitor in Boston, Philip Vincent) adds that, before breaking up at Weimshauks, the Pequots put to death all the Mohegans present—those who had remained loyal to the Pequots when Uncas defected—except seven, who escaped to the English to tell the tale.

By June 2 Williams saw no need for the big expedition under Stoughton, "considering the worck is Effected." This letter, written around midnight, reached Winthrop June 3 by two servants. Winthrop and the Assistants thereupon issued warrants for only half the troops then preparing to go. But a delegation "of the people" pressed the Council to send them all, with no less than three ministers. The Council authorized another forty men, merely to satisfy the public.

On June 3 also came the Pilgrims' formal agreement to send a pinnace with forty or fifty men to assist the Bay against the Pequots. They got ready as soon as possible, says Bradford, but just when they were set to march, "had word to stay, for the enimy was as good as vanquished."

On June 15 all the Bay churches observed a day of thanksgiving for the victory over the Pequots of late May "and for other mercies."

Patrick received orders at Saybrook on June 17 to get back to Narragansett—possibly to be reprimanded, probably to be given instructions for cooperating with Stoughton. In two or three days he rejoined his company at Saybrook, where a detail of his took "some Cannoes laden with all sorts of Indean howsell stuff" while passing the mouth of the Connecticut. He thought this but a preliminary party and sought the main body of refugees eastward to Pequot with ten men. It happened in fact to be the tag end of the main body. Thus an anonymous contemporary account could say that "Captain Kilpatrick" (i.e. Daniel Patrick) could have stopped the principal group's passage of the Connecticut's mouth but delayed till the opportunity had passed. Underhill, still based at the Fort at this time, should share the responsibility of letting them slip.

A band of about one hundred Pequots hit the Connecticut farther north and intercepted a shallop six miles above Saybrook that was on its way down to the Fort for clay. The wind did not favor it, because Cobbine Beets and the two other employees of a Mr. Michaels (Mitchell?) were rowing, which explains why canoes could impede so large a craft. The Englishmen fought stoutly even after full of arrows, some Indians later recounted. An arrow pierced one man through the nose and came out at the crown of his head; he fell overboard and drifted. The Indians, prominently including a sannup named Pametesick, swarmed the other two crewmen, ripped them from the bottom of their bellies to their throats, split their backs also, and hung them by the neck on a riverside tree for passing boatmen to view, then burned the shallop. The skipper of the Dutch yacht which was just returning downriver from delivering the captive Wethersfield girls happened to be the first to see the displayed corpses. At the Fort next day, Patrick and Underhill were among the witnesses of the corpse that washed past stuck with three or four arrows, his bandoliers about him and his drawn sword clamped under one arm. The Pequot band, instead of crossing the Connecticut, reversed their course back east-northeastward. Doubtless desperate for food, they could think of nothing better than to return to the seaside via a wide arc to dig for clams.

GALLOP brought Williams the news on June 21 that "our loving friends mr Stoughton mr [William] Traske &c are on their way" to Providence with 160 men. Williams now felt that a large expedition would be practicable after all, because the Wunnashowatuckoogs and Monashackotoogs about 200 strong had gone forth to avenge their Pequot allies upon the East Niantics, though they returned when a great mist obscured their vision.

Within a few days Williams hospitably received Stoughton and Wilson, together with what proved to be some 120 men, and escorted them to Miantonomy and Canonicus, bringing the sachems and captains "to a mutuall Confidence & Complacencie each in other," as he long later related to Mason.

Though I was ready to haue marcht further, Yet vpon Agreement, that I should keepe at Providence as an Agent between the Bay and the Armie, I returned, & was Interpreter and Intelligencer, constantly receaving & sending Letters to the Governour and Councell at Boston &c.

It was at this juncture that Winthrop and "some other" of the Council moved that Williams be recalled from banishment and honored. The motion did not pass.

Stoughton presumably marched west from Narragansett to meet the pinnaces at Wekapaug, then sailed for Pequot. Underhill and his company passed them sailing the other way for home. Underhill stopped off to negotiate for an interest in the Pequot country from the Narragansett grand sachems, who, however, referred him to Massachusetts. Patrick reported from Narragansett on the twenty-ninth that forty or fifty Pequots then remained on Long Island and another three hundred fit for fight had reached Quinnipiack (later New Haven).

By the time of this letter, Stoughton had already landed at Pequot and fallen on the doubling-back band of refugees as they camped some distance up the Pequot River at night. Following the policy originally designed for Block Island, he executed twenty-two men and youths (some of the latter of whom vainly cried "I squaw, I squaw"), sparing only two sachems on their promise to lead the English to Sassacus. He gave the Narragansett allies thirty of the captured women and children, the Massachusetts Indians three, and sent the remaining forty-eight by one Giggle's pinnace to Boston, where they arrived with Stoughton's covering letter July 6. In this letter Stoughton asked Winthrop if he could have the largest and fairest captive woman for himself. Lieutenant Davenport spoke for the tall one with three marks on her stomach. The Council distributed the boatload to various persons of quality in the country, presumably honoring Stoughton's and Davenport's requests. Some of the distributees ran away. When neighboring Indians brought them back, the magistrates ordered them branded on the shoulder. Peter, at Salem, had urged that the English soldiers refrain from taking Indian corn, "for we fear it will prove a snare thus to hunt after their goods whilest we come forth pretending only the doing of justice." But Peter had no scruples about taking the Indians themselves. He put in a request for a share of the captives on behalf of Endecott and himself and received a "servant" he named Hope, who in 1639 kept running away and getting drunk. (Peter proved to have no scruples about wholesale plunder as a fighting chaplain in the Parliamentary army in England a few years later.)

The Connecticut commissioners, hearing that Stoughton had

headquartered at the mouth of the Pequot, sent Mason down with forty men (according to Mason, thirty according to Stoughton). Ludlow and Haynes, with Stanton, accompanied them. The junction of the Connecticut and Massachusetts forces must have occurred about July 1 at Pequot, where Stoughton's unfinished fort lay convenient to two or even three hundred acres of ripe corn. The Bay hosts had no beef to offer their newly arrived friends from Connecticut but substituted the comfort of a rundlet (eighteen-gallon barrel) of sack; "and we shall the next weeke joyne in seeing what we can do against Sasacos, and an other great Sagamore: Momomattuck [Mononoto]," said Stoughton in the letter Winthrop received July 6. Patrick wrote from Pequot on the sixth alluding to difficulties between the Mohegans and Narrangansetts and doubting that the East Niantics would willingly stay under Narragansett subjection. Stoughton elaborated in another of his letters, about the same day, on the jealousy that had developed between the Narragansetts and Mohegans over jurisdiction of Pequot lands and over their respective privileges with the English. Cutshamekin wanted to go home with his men because of the Narragansetts' doings. Stoughton readily consented, so the Indians would not be able to say that the English depended on them; but he thereby lost his interpreters. Nevertheless, as Patrick said on the sixth, "wee goe the first winde for longe Ilande to sallute Sassecous."

Sassacus must have been spinning out a desperate illusion by his consultations on Long Island to have delayed an entire month after vacating Weimshauks to clear out westward. His negotiations on Long Island had serious competition. From the time the Mason-Underhill expedition terminated at Saybrook, Wequash had been operating out of the latter place as a scavenger for Pequot stragglers, whose heads he sold to Gardener. Three days after the Fort fight, Waiandance, ranking brother of the old sachem of Long Island, came to Gardener to inquire if the English were angry at all Indians. "No, but only with such as had killed Englishmen." Gardener told him he would pay him for Pequot heads just as he did Wequash, and that as soon as the heads of Pequots dwelling on Long Island had been sent, the English would resume trade. Waiandance, it seems, wanted to repay Gardener anyway for Gardener's ransoming his daughter from the raiding Ninigret sometime before. He began to send heads back—five, three, four—and Gardener kept his end of the bargain. When Stanton dropped over to Long Island later in July to ferret out Pequots, none were there.

ON JUNE 26 the *Hector* and another ship arrived from London bringing John Davenport, the *"princely preacher"* (Cotton Mather), who became John Cotton's house guest this summer and did probably more than anyone else to reclaim him from the antinomian party. Forty in 1637, Davenport had traced a career from Coventry to Brasen-Nose College, Oxford (Richard Mather's alma mater), to a pulpit in Dissent-riotous Coleman Street, London, to an association with Peter in Holland, before his flight to New England. With him on the boat came Theophilus Eaton, who the following year became the first and perennial governor of New Haven Colony, which he and Davenport closely modeled upon the principles of Cotton as Cotton had abstracted them from Mosaic Law. Eaton's son-in-law Edward Hopkins also came in the *Hector*. He and Haynes alternated annually beginning in 1639 as governor of Connecticut.

Among other eminent passengers on the *Hector* was the nineteen-year-old James, Lord Ley, son and heir of the Earl of Marlborough (young Ley became the third Earl of Marlborough the next year); he had come for a short visit. Early in July Winthrop formally invited Vane to accompany Lord Ley to dinner. Vane declined by letter, saying his conscience withheld him, and went that evening to dine with the Presbyterian Old Planter, Samuel Maverick, on Noddle's Island, taking Ley with him. On July 12 Mrs. Hutchinson's brother-in-law Samuel Hutchinson arrived, along with some friends of Wheelwright. Winthrop immediately invoked the new exclusion law and allowed them only four months in the colony.

ON SATURDAY July 8 the Stoughton-Mason mop-up expedition slipped from Pequot Harbor down to Long Island and sent an Indian ashore in a shallop at a village known to be subject to Sassacus, to spy him out. A sachem named Luz returned with the Indian spy and said Sassacus had gone to Quinnipiack, but offered to guide the English to him.

The expedition proceeded toward Quinnipiack. It either put in temporarily at Saybrook, or Gardener soon learned that it had shifted destination, because he sent Wequash to Stoughton.

Sunday the ships reached a harbor three leagues short of Quinnipiack and anchored the rest of the day in observance of the Sabbath. Early the next morning four Indians went ashore as spies. One of these was Wequash, another a powerful Mohegan called Jack Eatow. Eatow met up with three Pequot men and singlehandedly brought two of them back to the barks alive. That evening a total of four Pequots were put to death after interrogation, at least two of them—one a sachem—by beheading. The council thereupon named the promontory where they were, Sachem Head.

Coasting through the mist Tuesday morning, the voyagers saw smoke emerging from the woods near shore, swiftly landed, and broke in on some peaceful Connecticut Indians. That evening the council set Luz ashore alone and ordered Lieutenant Richard Davenport to take twenty men out at dawn. In a drenching rain just before daybreak, Davenport's detail commenced canvassing the east bank of the Quinnipiack. After wading to the west bank and traipsing nearly two hours, they sighted some Pequot scouts through the downpour and caught seven of them in a hard chase: five men, including a sachem, who were quickly slain, and two women, who were taken back aboard. It was now about noon. The council delayed until Luz should reappear; he shortly did, reporting he had found Sassacus. Coming upon the grand sachem somewhere in the woods not very far from the boats, Luz apparently greeted him as though still a loyal subject. Sassacus suspected him, however, said Luz, and intended to do away with him. But Luz escaped in the dark by presumably a wide swing northeastward. It is, of course, equally probable that he tipped Sassacus off and delayed until noon to return in order to give him a good head start. In either case, Sassacus and Mononoto with about twenty more fled on ahead of the other refugees to the Mohawks.

The barks crossed the estuary and landed their total force to pursue these sachems, dividing into half a dozen groups who ranged over the coastal country all afternoon Wednesday and most of Thursday. Nearly all the Indian guides gave up and left, saying they knew not longer whither to look. The soldiers grew so exasperated at the "base Cowardliness" (Davenport's words) of the Pequots who would not suffer themselves to be found that they fell to cutting down all the corn they could find. Eventually they uncovered a "very poore and weake" Pequot man hiding among the stalks, who told the cutters that some squaws were not far off. At the same instant came a distant sound of wood-chopping. Mason headed with half the troops for the indicated whereabouts of the squaws, and Underhill with the other half for the wood-choppers. Patrick and Davenport, taking their turn this day (June 13) to lead Mason's vanguard, caught the first view, after two miles, of the temporary settlement of twenty wigwams hard by "a most hideous swamp," Winthrop quotes Stoughton's report, "so thick with bushes and so quagmiry, as men could hardly crowd into it." This was the site of later Fairfield, Connecticut. Here eighty of the Pequots' "stoutest men" with two hundred women and children had halted. When Mason and Ludlow reached the hilltop which Davenport had already left and noted that the swamp was divided in two, they ordered Sergeant Palmer to surround the smaller section with about twelve men. Davenport, not knowing of this order, entered the swamp with his twelve men, going for the wigwams.

Several of his men stuck in the bog and became stationary targets; Davenport himself received a dangerous wound at the armhole of his armor, and one of his men was fainting from a head wound. Patrick and his twenty or more started firing from a distance, which brought Trask with his fifty onto the scene. Two of Davenport's sergeants, with two or three men, rescued the trapped van by lethal swordplay. (Davenport recovered after an agonizing removal of the arrowhead from his left armpit; Increase Mather heard him in later life telling how, with only two or three cohorts, he engaged no less than thirty Indians on this occasion and got seventeen arrows in his coat of mail.)

By about 3 P.M. the entire expeditionary force had come up and surrounded the swamp's full compass of about a mile. After disagreement on every proposed plan of action, Mason ordered Sergeant Davis to cut through the narrow in the swamp, which Davis did and thereby greatly contracted the beleaguers' circumference. Haynes, Williams rejoiced to learn, insisted on saving the women and children. Haynes's real reason for coming may have been to prevent another Mistick massacre. At last, the council allowed Stanton to go in and parley. He returned from within in a short time, and nearly two hundred women, children, and old men emerged in small groups after him. When he called in to the warriors, they said they would sell their lives there and shot at him thickly. Armored troops instantly rescued him.

The English stood all night about twelve feet apart. They got arrows through hat brims, sleeves, and stockings, but not flesh. When it grew black dark about half an hour before dawn, the Indians raised a clamor as was their custom before attack. Patrick's men beat back several attempts to break through his sector. With a deafening din, the Indians charged to the opposite side, forcing a concentration of defense there, whereby they broke past Patrick's position in a violent reverse. Some fell when pursued, but about sixty or seventy, including those who had slipped unnoticed through the cordon, made good their escape. The musketeers found a few escapees at a distance dead of their wounds. They found nine dead in the swamp. Mason says the captives came to about 180, who were equally divided between Massachusetts and Connecticut. A sachem who had surrendered with the women was spared. Certain of the captive women disclosed that, in all, thirteen of their sachems had been killed up to that time and thirteen remained yet alive. This swamp lay within what came to be called Pine Creek Point. There Gallop made a timely appearance with his shallop to carry the wounded expeditionaries to the pinnace where the surgeon and Wilson awaited.

Stoughton ordered Patrick with sixteen or eighteen men to carry Massachusetts' captives to Boston. Winthrop says the Bay sent fifteen captive boys and two squaws to Bermuda—which would undoubtedly have been the suggestion of Peter, who was corresponding with Patrick Copeland, the English minister in Bermuda, a place in which Peter's patrons, the Warwick patentees, were showing keen interest. Captain Peirse missed Bermuda and carried the slaves to Providence Isle in the West Indies, where Warwick, Saye, Brooke, and the great John Pym, *et al.*, had established a Puritan colony which easily adapted itself to piracy and slave-trafficking. Winthrop's government disposed the other women and female children "aboute in the towns" as though they were indentured servants (with no terminal date of bondage). Among the prisoners from the swamp was Wincumbone, who struck Winthrop as "a womon of a very modest countenance and behavior." He probably honored her request to keep her children with her. Mason observes that few of the Pequots lived long in servitude.

WHEN WINTHROP reported to Bradford on July 28, Sassacus and Mononoto were still alive, but an estimated seven hundred Pequots had been slain or captured. "The rest are dispersed, and the Indeans in all quarters so terrified as all their friends are affraid to receive them." In a kind of hysteria, the Indians started preying on the sur- viving Pequots, bringing their heads into Hartford and Windsor al- most daily. When at last only about 180 to 200 Pequots remained alive, they voluntarily gave themselves up and were formally di- vided at Hartford in March 1638, eighty to Uncas and twenty to Ninigret (when he should reimburse one Edward Pomroye for a mare killed by his men).

The Pequots were charged never more to inhabit their former country or ever call themselves Pequots again but Mohegans or Narragansetts. Groups of them nevertheless shortly drifted away and settled at Pawcatuck, also at a place on the Mystic in Pequot country, and at Long Island. The harrying expedition of Mason and Uncas against these remnants was entirely unnecessary to complete the breaking of the once-proud tribe. Ezra Stiles found out around 1755 that the Pequot tribe then consisted of about seventy-two souls over fourteen years of age and that the Mohegans had no communi- cation with them. The last Pequot sachem, Schuddaub, died about 1740 although Sassacus, who once held sway over twenty-five lesser sachems, had no successor in the grand sachemship. In 1762 Stiles added that perhaps twenty or thirty families of Pequots resided on the eleven hundred acres or so of poor land reserved to them in the northeastern part of Groton called Maushantuxet. A Groton resi- dent listed fifteen Pequot families living on this reservation in wig- wams in March 1762 and seven in frame houses.

In 1832 William T. Williams reported that about forty Pequots were still in existence, living on this reservation. They had Mo- hegan, Negro, and white blood, but remained a distinct tribe and re- tained their old hatred of the Mohegans. Williams saw most of the tribe together on one occasion. "They are more vicious, and not so decent or so good-looking as people as the Mohegans," he con- cluded. Nearly half of them had the surname Meazen. By that time, only about eighty of Ninigret's old Niantic branch still lived, mainly in Charlestown, Rhode Island, and only about seventy Mohegans, on good land in Montville, about three miles below Norwich Landing.

THE MASSACHUSETTS General Court reconvened at Newtown on August 3. This was the very day that Vane and Ley went down to their ship, which rode opposite Long Island in the bay. Vane's almost fanatical adherents escorted him to the dock; many of them accompanied him in the longboat to board the ship. The militia gave him several musket volleys and fired five cannons; the Castle fired five more as his ship slipped to sea. The hopes of the antinomian cause went with him, notwithstanding that for years afterward the antinomians counted on his messianic return. Winthrop, meanwhile, had not bothered to leave Court to join in the farewells.

Two days later Hooker hove in from Hartford, bringing the Connecticut chaplain Stone and the Massachusetts chaplain Wilson with him. They had come by water and stopped over at Providence with the Williamses. Hooker must also have brought his family or part of it, since his daughter Johanna married the widower Shepard at Newtown in early October. Hooker brought news from Providence of still other Pequots slain by Indians. That same August 5 Ludlow, Pynchon, and about twelve more foot travelers arrived in Boston with the scalp of Sassacus, of his brother, and of five other Pequot sachems, whom the Mohawks had done in with twenty of the grand sachem's best men. Mononoto escaped wounded. Winthrop estimates that by this time eight or nine hundred Pequots had been slain or taken.

When Stoughton got back to the fort at the Pequot mouth he named it Possession House and, from there, about midnight August 9, he wrote Winthrop of his track-down plans. He had been keenly interested in the country around Possession House, he said, but had become more interested in the country he had recently seen southwestward; "and probable 'tis the Dutch will seaze it if the English do not." Also, he added, it was too good for any but friends. On August 14, the eve of his intended night foray to Block Island, Stoughton reported that "we are informed of many Indians there; so we expect the toughest work we have yet met." But orders were already on the way for him to desist from further action. Miantonomy had been bringing Block Island to heel efficiently enough to make Stoughton's foray superfluous anyway.

Hooker met for several days with the clergy of the colony, effecting some reconciliation between Wilson and Cotton over Wilson's court speech in December. John Davenport preached a memorable lecture-day sermon on August 17 out of First Corinthians: "I exhort you brethren . . . that there be no division among you." All the churches observed a solemn fast on August 24, and on August 26 Stoughton and the soldiers came home. One man had died—of dysentery—and one had been incapacitated by asthma. Stoughton, on his way out, had left a sick soldier named Thomas Roberts at the Williams house, where Mrs. Williams finally got him on his feet by July 10 though he had lost his hearing.

In a victory atmosphere the great synod opened on August 30 at Newtown and chose Hooker and Bulkley moderators. Twenty-five ministers, plus nearly the same number of lay elders, plus the magistracy in a body, met for twenty-four days. When Wilson shouted, "You that are against these things [un-Scriptural enthusiasms and revelations] and that are for the spirit and the word together, hold up your hands!," a multitude of hands went up and the Boston laymen walked out. Wheelwright, however, stayed, silent, with Cotton.

On August 31 Williams passed on to Winthrop from the Narragansetts the hands of Wauphanck, slayer of Captain Stone; "no pleasing sight," says Williams. In June 1638 Williams notified Winthrop that Pametesick, one of the murderers of the three men in the clay-seeking shallop on the Connecticut, had been recognized in Uncas's retinue and should be apprehended. But by this time the hysteria had blown over, and the disposition of the sachems friendly to the English, including Miantonomy and Uncas, was to conceal such Pequots as were left. When or how Mononoto met his end the English never learned.

THE FIRST and most tedious task of the synod was to detach Cotton from the antinomian party. This took many teary speeches and exchanges of written arguments. At last Cotton made a sufficiently accommodating speech for the assembly to go ahead and denounce eighty-two antinomian errors together with nine "unsavory" or "unsafe" speeches. Cotton declined to sign the document, but did declare that he "disrelished all those Opinions and Expressions, as being some of them Heretical, some of them Blasphemous, some of them Erroneous, and all of them Incongruous."

On September 26, four days after the breakup of the synod, Winthrop and his singlemindedly anti-antinomian Assistants felt sufficiently buttressed to call an extra-legal purge election for the General Court scheduled to sit November 3. The late-October election in the towns sent twenty-one replacements and only twelve old deputies to the November showdown. Aside from Coddington and two other Boston antinomians, the new group was implacably, even fanatically, anti-antinomian.

Wheelwright went on preaching according to his lights at Mt. Wollaston as though the September synod and October election had never occurred; Mrs. Hutchinson brazenly kept up her "double-weekly" meetings at Boston as usual and still led walkouts when Wilson preached; the lay representatives of the Boston church who had withdrawn from the synod went about stirring up resentment against its proceedings; and—what may have bothered the magistrates most—the antinomians openly boasted that Vane would return with ample authority to set aside both synod and General Court in the cause of the covenant of grace. Many evidences, says Winthrop, "brake forth" of the antinomians' "discontented and turbulent spirits."

On October 17 "God himselfe was pleased to step in with his casting voice," as Welde puts it; though the event did not become public or even come to the attention of the magistrates for another five months: Mary Dyer, the comely, proper wife of a Boston milliner, gave birth to a stillborn monster, with Mrs. Hutchinson and a midwife, Mrs. Jane Hawkins, assisting. Both Mrs. Dyer and the midwife happened to be staunch followers of Mrs. Hutchinson; the midwife was also believed to be a witch. Mrs. Hutchinson asked Cotton what to do. He said to conceal the monster and keep quiet about it. So not until March, when a malicious rumor caused official inquiry, did this obvious providence of God against antinomianism make its awful impact on the colony. The Court had to go through with its work in November without the help of any divine intervention it knew of.

The General Court convened November 2. On the third, it banished Wheelwright and allowed him to the end of March to be gone. But he refused to promise to forego preaching, so the Court gave him only fourteen days to get out. The snow he found himself trudging through was a yard deep above the Merrimac and yet deeper farther north. He made it to Piscataqua and founded Exeter, New Hampshire, in April 1638. (When Massachusetts extended her jurisdiction over New Hampshire, the Wheelwrights and some others moved on up to Wells, Maine. Both he and Massachusetts moderated their earlier positions, and in May 1644, the Court repealed his sentence of banishment. He moved back down to New Hampshire in the spring of 1647 and took the pulpit at Hampton.)

Before the end of this November session, the General Court summoned all sixty-six signers of the March remonstrance in behalf of Wheelwright and his notorious sermon, and some other known abettors of his cause. About ten recanted and withdrew their names; five or six proved die-hard enough to be disfranchised, including Captain Underhill; and a total of fifty-eight of Boston plus another seventeen of five other towns were ordered to surrender their arms at Captain Robert Keayne's house within ten days, on a "just cause of suspition" (the order read) that these "opinionists . . . as other in Germany, in former times, may, upon some revelation, make some suddaine irruption upon those that differ from them in judgment." The outrage of the seventy-five proscriptees notwithstanding, "When they saw no remedy, they obeyed," Winthrop concludes.

It had been early in the session, on the sixth, that Winthrop wrote Margaret:

> Sweet Heart, I was unwillingly hindred from comminge to thee, nor am I like to see thee before the last daye of this weeke: therefore I shall want a band or 2 [collars] and cuffes. I pray thee also send me 6 or 7 leaues of Tobacco dried, and powdred. have care of thy selfe this colde weather, and speak to the folkes to keepe the goats well out of the Garden.

Thus he was able to preside at Mrs. Hutchinson's climactic trial of the seventh and eighth in clean cuffs and ruff, fortified with fresh filling for his pipe. Shepard's unheated little meetinghouse was jammed; Mrs. Hutchinson faced the robed magistrates and clergy from a front bench, irritable, sick, and occasionally wracked by pain from the early stages of her (at least) fifteenth pregnancy, which was going wrong.

She made herself as difficult as possible. The Court hardly got anywhere in proving she had broken the Fifth Commandment, which the magistrates interpreted as including magistrates among parents to be honored. At last six of the ministers gave testimony about a meeting they had had with her in which she had said: "The fear of man is a snare; why should I be afraid?" and had gone on to draw her familiar works-*versus*-grace distinction. Cotton wished at the time that she had not talked so frankly, though in Court he could not seem to recall anything damaging that she had said. When Dudley reminded her: "There have been six witnesses to prove this and yet you deny it," she replied: "I deny that these were the first words that were spoken." Next day, she insisted the ministers repeat their testimony under oath!

Late in that exasperating second day, she decisively undid herself in a long confession of her revelations, concluding with a revelation that God would deliver her out of the Court's hands and bring a curse on the judges, their posterity, and the whole state. Endecott, Dudley, and Peter in particular grew virulent toward Cotton for equivocating whether her revelation were the type condemned or approved in Scripture. But Cotton could not save Mrs. Hutchinson; Winthrop only barely rescued *him*. Coddington could not see what law of God or man she had broken, or why the clergy should feel so wronged to be told they preached an obsolete covenant of works. Dudley sighed, "We shall be all sick with fasting."

The Court sentenced Mrs. Hutchinson to banishment. On November 20 it committed her to the town of Roxbury in the home of the marshal there. It was a long, cold winter, and at the meeting-house on Sundays she had to listen to the "unsealed" clergymen Eliot and Welde by the hour and watch her sympathizers face excommunication.

She clung steadfastly to her "errors," as ministers who visited to help her repent found out to their consternation. Shepard, Welde, and Eliot compiled a list of sixteen of her heretical positions which they certified they could prove against her; so the magistrates gave license for her to stand trial before her own church at Boston on lecture day, March 15, 1638. She argued so well at this trial that the clergy hated to allow the public to hear her reasoning at length on such subjects as why she thought the soul, being light, could not live after the death of the body, though the spirit could. By late in the day, hardly the first two of the points in the indictment had been dealt with, but the congregation voted for Cotton to admonish her. In the course of his rhetoric, she interrupted to say, "*I did not hould any of thease Things before my Imprisonment.*" Shepard ringingly pointed out the lie in this statement (which Cotton had passed over after her interruption, saying he did not know she held any of these things till lately) before the meeting abruptly broke up at 6 P.M.

Mrs. Hutchinson went home with Cotton, to whose custody the Court had remanded her. He and Davenport, as the Court requested, worked on her the whole intervening week and succeeded in getting her to write retractions, or near retractions, of most of the opinions charged against her. This dejected her greatly, and she equivocated in reading them when her church trial resumed March 22. When people farther back could not hear her weaker-than-usual speaking, Cotton diplomatically rephrased her remarks. This helped sting Shepard to remind the congregation of her imposture. Dudley noted she did not look repentant. Peter and Richard Mather were among the visiting clergy who bore out Dudley and Shepard. Wilson launched a grand diatribe against her lying and her pride and railroaded the proceedings toward a vote of excommunication. When Eliot pointedly linked her lying and her profession to hold nothing but what Cotton did, Cotton at last abandoned her and lent his weight to excommunication—solely on her lie, not on doctrinal errors. Wilson wheeled victoriously upon the woman who had nearly cut him down. *"I doe cast yow out* & in the name of Christ *I doe deliver you up to Sathan. . . . I command yow* in the name of Christ Jesus & of this Church *as a Leper to withdraw your selfe owt of the Congregation."*

As she walked silently toward the door, Mary Dyer rose and accompanied her. A stranger in the assembly, says Winthrop, asked what young woman it was. The magistrates pricked up their ears when several unidentified whispers answered, "It was the woman which had the monster."

To Ann Hutchinson, who had predicted her persecution before she left England, this walk to the door "as a Leper" was a triumph. Her spirits revived, says Winthrop, "and she gloried in her sufferings, saying that it was the greatest happiness, next to Christ, that ever befell her." Indeed, counters Winthrop, it was a happy day for the *churches*.

1 2 : *Implications and Adaptations*

THE Pequot War had brought Massachusetts, Connecticut, and New Plymouth together in a common cause, often through Williams's Providence. The same August 31, 1637, that Williams sent up the hands of Wauphanck, the Bay magistrates appointed a day for an intercolonial meeting to agree on some articles of confederation. Although this confederacy did not materialize for a few more years, it did grow directly out of the cohesion induced by the war, together with the threat of antinomianism. The United Colonies, a powerful, supra-charter organization of the orthodox Congregationalist commonwealths—Massachusetts, Connecticut, New Plymouth, and New Haven—posed an American precedent of epochal significance.

The war came during the sudden expansion of New England to its approximate present boundaries. It can be viewed as an incident in that expansion, particularly of the founding of Connecticut; but it greatly accelerated further expansion. The very August 31 that Williams sent up the hands of Wauphanck, Theophilus Eaton and others of John Davenport's company went to look over Quinnipiack, where they soon founded New Haven Colony. Mason moved to Saybrook in 1638, Ludlow planted a new settlement at Fairfield in 1639; about sixty people had migrated to Stamford by 1642; Winthrop Jr. and Jonathan Brewster settled at Pequot, which officially acquired the name New London in 1658. Migration into the conquered Pequot domain, and imperialistically beyond, became a major trend of the times, simultaneous with a stream of Bay migrants to Maine, Rhode Island, New Plymouth, and New Netherland.

For Williams the war—together with his postwar trips to Hartford and Saybrook—integrated all his associations in America, cast his whole career in a new light, established him in a new role with sudden new value and prestige. The heightened experience of the war and its immediate aftermath marks a period of creative intensity which suddenly matured him. This is the period not only when he forged the first democracy and conscience-free commonwealth but systematically formulated (at first by exchanges of letters with Peter, Bulkley, Cotton, and others) his revolutionary position on complete separation of church and state and full religious liberty and personally left all institutionalized religion to strike out on his own as a Seeker of the lost Zion.

The war had unexpected side effects in many lives that changed the future in ways hard to measure. For instance, a Pequot servant orphan taught his language to John Eliot at Roxbury, whereupon Eliot started his mission at the Indian village of Nonantum, in the northwest part of present-day Newton and so launched his career as Apostle to the Indians. This work, among other things, brought a new relationship with our old friend Cutshamekin. It also brought Eliot into something of a jealous rivalry with Williams, who had long preceded him, with international recognition, as an apostle to the Indians.

Before the war was over, Miantonomy and Uncas were quarreling over the Pequot survivors and change of boundaries—a quarrel which assumed ever larger and, at last, tragic repercussions, as if the destruction of one whole people had not already been tragedy enough. The dispute over Pequot lands at the Connecticut–Rhode Island border which embroiled four colonies and at one time nearly ate up most of Williams's hard-won province was about to explode. It kept exploding for the balance of the century.

The Dutch-English rivalry, which flared twice into open war later in the century, clearly loomed already in the beginnings of the Pequot War and in the founding of Connecticut. The Connecticut-Massachusetts rivalry, which had had its origin in the power struggle within Massachusetts (or even within the Massachusetts Bay Company in England), persisted in the quibble over which colony had rashly started the war and which rescued the other. The king's revived intention to bring all New England directly under a royal governor tightened the Puritan anxiety already felt on other accounts and eventually split the Puritan solid front into opposing factions, within both Massachusetts and Connecticut.

The Pequot War realigned New England history—or marks a realignment—in which new problems, new issues, a new climate emerged. It catalyzed a critical cultural transition which proved to be a revolution. It started slavery in New England; it decisively set in motion the rapid extinction of Indians there; it abetted the repressive bigotry which crushed the antinomian party; it encouraged a coarse, opportunistic greed which began to run roughshod over former cherished principles and over anything in the carefully established existing order that interfered with private status or gain. "God Land," as Williams wrote Winthrop Jr. long later, had been displacing Winthrop Sr.'s model of Christian charity; "profit, praeferment, pleasure" was becoming the Trinity in New England "as in all the world beside." "We enjoy liberties of soule & body," he had written Winthrop Jr. earlier, "but it is licence we desire, except the Most Holy helpe vs."

Common soldiers freely discussed heretical doctrines in their camps, as their counterparts shortly did in the English civil war. It was during the Pequot War—near the time of Wheelwright's incendiary sermon—that Mary Winthrop Dudley complained that when she bade her maidservant do something, the maid bade her do it herself. Servants were running away, and not just Indian "servants." In 1642 Winthrop, Wilson, and Shepard took alarm at the sharp increase in fornication and rape, which Shepard speaks of as an "invndation . . . breaking in vpon us." Captain Underhill's adultery difficulties developed alongside his antinomian disgrace in the immediate postwar period, and war veterans had a conspicuous part in the rising rate of violent crime. One of the completely new problems that came with the war was the interminable series of bonuses and land grants to veterans.

The general change that the war signaled reflects also the rocket burst of immigration to New England up to 1640 and the revolutionary ferment in England, not to say throughout Western culture. Parliament revolted against the king about this same time and, before the first phase of the civil war was over, the common people were revolting against Parliament. New England felt a deep involvement in this transoceanic upheaval.

The Pequot War further reflects the transition from scarcity to a semblance of sufficiency in New England. Or, more precisely, the war saw those measures initiated which, within just a few years, resulted in a solid economic security. Since November 1633 New England had suffered scarcity of food at the same time that the scarcity of workmen raised wages of carpenters and laborers excessively— from the point of view of those paying for their services. The leaders of society complained at the idleness and drink of wage earners who did not need to work steadily to live better than before. Hugh Peter preached at Boston and Salem on November 26, 1635, calling for the formation of a joint-stock enterprise for fishing in the public interest as the only probable means to free people from the "oppression" the seamen and merchants held them under by their high rates. He here referred principally to the English monopolists of the Newfoundland-banks fisheries and of fishing equipment, which they sold to Massachusetts at a profit of 100 per cent and up. A month before Peter's arrival in America, the General Court had put old Dudley in charge of a committee to establish a fishing trade, but inertia and the difficulties of acquiring equipment retarded the scheme until the vigor of Peter shot it in the arm.

The public stock enabled a sufficient accumulation of supplies to break the Newfoundlanders' grip, and the General Court went on to establish a fishing plantation at Cape Ann (later called Gloucester), exempting settlers of all public charges for seven years, and a similar plantation at Nantasket (later Hull) in 1641. Winthrop records the substantial victory of these efforts in the haul of 1640–41 which sent about 300,000 dry fish to market, mainly the West-Indies market. As everyone knows, this cod-fishing industry became the basis of the Bay's economic empire of the not very distant future.

In the course of collecting provisions to send to Saybrook sometime in the war period, Peter wailed: "I am sorry for the short provisions in the Bay; it is so all over. Help Lord!" In April 1636 the *Charity* of Dartmouth reached Nantasket in a storm with thirty-nine hogsheads of meal, twenty-five of peas, and lesser quantities of malt, prunes, and *aqua vitae*, in spite of having let Piscataqua buy up all it wanted earlier. Peter made a deal by which he relieved the skipper of the entire remaining cargo at half the usual prices and then distributed it among the towns as emergency relief. Only with the greatest difficulty did Connecticut and the Bay provision their expeditionaries in the war, and then not very well.

At the conclusion of the war Connecticut found herself in extremity. Such corn as could be had cost as much as twelve shillings a bushel. The commissioners sent Mason, William Wadsworth, and

Deacon Stebbins "to try what Providence would afford." They eventually, despite the discouragement of some English whom Mason does not identify, got all the way up to the pleasant village of Pocomtuck (later Deerfield). There they found so much corn at reasonable rates that the Indians brought fifty laden canoes down to Hartford and Windsor in a majestic procession. When the Connecticut General Court made Mason major-general of the colony and had Hooker deliver the staff of office into his hand, it would have been hard to say which service, the military or the economic, filled them with greater gratitude.

While Mason, by the way, moved to Saybrook, Stoughton went back to England to a lieutenant-colonelcy for Cromwell; Patrick and Underhill saw service against Indians for the Dutch in New Netherland. Gardener grew old at Saybrook. In 1657 he hosted a twentieth-anniversary reunion there with Hurlbut, Chapman, and Mason, which inspired him to write up his old notes on the war in 1660. King Philip's War, which broke out forty years after the outbreak of the Pequot War and as an inexorable sequel, reawakened much interest in the latter and put it in a different perspective.

Shepard observed that the Pequots and antinomians rose and fell together. (It was the next day after the August 31 that Williams sent up the hands of Wauphanck, we have seen, that the antinomian-condemning synod convened at Newtown.) Shepard might have added that the threat of famine rose and fell with them.

So, in a deep sense, did the idea of the holy commonwealth. The Pequot War in retrospect could be viewed as a watershed over which the solemn objectives of Zion and the burden of sadness that had largely occasioned them, gave way to land grabbing, exploitation, and the buoyant, rapacious spirit that came of physical struggle and of conquering the wilderness, privation, and Pequots. At the end of the war, the Puritans' relation to the earth, as they vaguely realized, had somewhat changed, and with it, Heaven had undergone subtle and irreversible changes as well.

1 3 : *The Antinomian Aftermath*

THE Court had ordered Ann Hutchinson to be gone from the colony by the last of March, 1638. Just before she left Boston for her Mt. Wollaston farm, one of the elders asked her about Mary Dyer's monster, which everyone had now heard about and assumed must be a divine sign requiring interpretation. Mrs. Hutchinson confirmed the rumor and further told the elder that she meant to have the phenomenon chronicled but concealed the truth on Cotton's advice.

Cotton, when Winthrop called him to account, admitted he had advised concealment, one of his reasons being that if it had been his own case he should have desired concealment. The gravity of the matter moved Winthrop to consult the other magistrates and the other three elders of the Boston church, and in April the monster was dug up. Winthrop gives a morbidly detailed description of it in his *Journal*, in his published account of the antinomian court trials, and in a signed affidavit which found its way to Archbishop Laud; he further officially notified Hooker, Bradford, and others of the clinical facts, and furnished them yet again to Robert Browne, an agent of the Suffolk gentleman, Sir Symonds D'Ewes (Browne passed them on to D'Ewes in his report of September 1639). The official, not to say ceremonious disclosure of the monster had a decisive effect in convincing lingering waverers in the Bay that the hand of God had been directed against antinomianism.

Mrs. Hutchinson meanwhile, on March 28, had taken a boat to Mt. Wollaston, intimating her intention of going from there by water with her sister and family to join Wheelwright at Piscataqua. She seems to have been torn between living under Wheelwright's ministry or under the guardianship of her husband—though she might have expected that her husband would follow if she decided for Piscataqua. Suddenly she set forth with others of her family and party on the long walk (via the route east rather than west past the Blue Hills) to Portsmouth, Rhode Island, where her husband, a son or two, Coddington, Dr. John Clark, *et al.*, were building. She tarried awhile with the Williamses at Providence, badly needing rest and her husband needing more time to make ready for her.

Williams reported to Winthrop April 16 that

> Mrs. Hutchinson (with whome and others of them I haue had much discourse) makes her Apologie for her Concealment of the monster, that she did nothing in it without Mr. Cottons advice, though I cannot belieue that he subscribes to her Applications of the Parts of it. The Lord mercifully redeeme them, and all of vs from all our delusions and pitie the desolations of Zion and the Stones thereof.

> I find their longings great after Mr. Vane, although they think he can not return this year: the eyes of some are so earnestly fixed upon him that Mrs. Hutchinson professeth if he come not to New, she must to Old England.

> I haue endeauored by many arguments to beat off their desires of Mr. Vane as G.G. [Governor-General] and the chief are satisfied unless he come so for his life, but I haue endeauored to discouer the snare in that also.

So Williams verifies that the monster still weighed on Mrs. Hutchinson's mind and that she still looked to Vane as the champion who would avenge her cause. Williams also discloses that he thought her unrealistic. He never agreed with her doctrines—he even saw through her exploitation of Cotton. But he treated her with his usual compassion and, by and large, had a good impression of her. She undoubtedly deepened his own appreciation of the need for toleration ("The Lord mercifully redeeme . . . all of vs from all our delusions . . .") no matter how intolerant she may have sounded. She may have helped him see a new significance in his own banishment, which we know he was wrestling to interpret in writing at this time.

Mrs. Hutchinson proceeded to Portsmouth, where she fell deathly sick. Dr. Clark fortunately was on hand to tend her. Six weeks after her arrival she gave birth to an unformed fetus consisting of about thirty large and small lumps, as Clark reported to Winthrop at the latter's insistence. Cotton, receiving an earlier, amateurish report from Mr. Hutchinson, preached a sermon in very bad taste on a lecture day, to the effect that the "monster" consisted only of man's seed without any alteration or mixture from the woman and therefore might signify her error in denying inherent righteousness and in claiming there was nothing of ours in faith and love. By the next lecture day, when Clark's letter had punctured that theory, Cotton had the grace to acknowledge its untenability in his sermon; and he forbore to substitute any other oracular reading of God's meaning in His recent "providence."

On April 12 the churches of Massachusetts kept a general fast, on the Court's advice, for fear of the coming of a governor-general, for prayers that many friends on their way from England would arrive safely, "and for establishment of peace and truth amongst us," says Winthrop, acknowledging that antinomianism yet raged. It had been a severe winter, and the spring continued unusually cold, with a heavy snowfall as late as April 23 (May 4 New Style).

On the crisp following day, April 24, Governor Winthrop and Deputy-Governor Dudley went over to Concord—an appropriate name for the occasion—and each chose a thousand acres in keeping with a grant of the Court. Winthrop yielded Dudley first choice. His daughter Mary and Dudley's son Samuel having recently joined in wedlock, they named a couple of large stones on the creek boundary "the Two Brothers," says Winthrop, "in remembrance that they were brothers by their children's marriage."

The Court of elections convened May 3. Shepard enjoined the deputies to maintain the privilege to the death of keeping government in the hands of church members, so that brambles—"the fickle minds of a heady multitude"—would never rule over trees. The Court quickly reelected Winthrop governor. The same night, he came down with a "sharp fever," which brought him near death. It took him a month to recover. This illness climaxed the depressed mood he had remained in all year despite his great triumph of 1637 in returning to power and putting down the antinomian insurrection. In January 1638, midway between Mrs. Hutchinson's court trial and her church trial, he had turned fifty and, on that occasion, written a soul-searching memoir reappraising his life. It revealingly concludes:

> The Doctrine of free justification lately taught here, took mee in as drowsy a condition, as I had been in (to my remembrance) these twenty yeares, and brought me as low (in my owne apprehension) as if the whole work had been to begin anew. But when the voice of peace came, I knew it to bee the same that I had been acquainted with before, though it did not speak so loud nor in that measure of joy that I had felt sometimes.

The cost of damping the antinomian conflagration—in bitterness, repressiveness, and the loss of gifted citizens who withdrew voluntarily or involuntarily or could or would not enter at all—left the commonwealth under a pall of emotional depression and self-doubt, culturally stifled, permanently scarred. Bay Puritanism went on in its old forms, but the victorious participants were most aware of anybody that it was not the same and could never be again. The supposed zenith of the Puritan establishment as memorialized in the Cambridge Platform of 1648 (the ultimate official declaration of the united church-state system and anti-antinomian doctrine) came during a simultaneous recognition of the continuing decay of religion itself in the Bay. Change was the real issue in 1637. In suppressing antinomianism, the Bay version of orthodoxy was resisting change and intensifying bigotry. The powerful effort which went into this resistance did retard the rate of change of some things for some time. Yet the effort proved so taxing that it left Puritanism in Massachusetts inwardly spent. It could not spring back with its previous resilience. This fact in itself marks an important change as well as an incapacity to cope with any similar-scaled assault on the old order in the future—much less with a constant, subsurface corrosion of the order on a comparable scale. Worse for the perpetuity of the old order, it rendered itself unreceptive to the creative vitality of the times and so less able to combat change than if it had incorporated some innovations—in addition to those it found itself incorporating in spite of itself. Not until the Great Awakening toward the middle of the next century did Bay Puritanism regain that potent impetus which had spawned transoceanic colonies and overthrown a king; but the rejuvenation of the 1740's coincided with Puritanism's final decisive transmutation which neutralized, shifted, or negated the generative aims of the movement. The very triumph of orthodoxy over antinomianism, which appeared to reverse the prevailing direction of the West in the Bay, only gave the Bay a reputation for repressiveness that in turn intensified the pressure of the type which antinomianism had first brought to bear upon the Bay in an organized way. Winthrop, depressed and ailing, knew at heart that the vanquishing of the antinomians had been a Pyrrhic victory.

Following Winthrop's re-election, the May Court of 1638 officially changed the name of Newtown to Cambridge, where the college was getting underway. Shepard's village got the honor of the

site partly because it had proved safer for orthodox Congregationalism. At this same May Court an ominous letter was read from the
clerk of the Council in England ordering the Bay to send back its
charter by the first ship. The Court refused but could find no way
to relieve a permanent anxiety about the colony's future.

That spring and summer, especially April and August, 1638, saw a
large-scale clearing-out of rigid Separatists to Providence and antinomians to Aquidneck, whereby, as Winthrop notes, those places
began to be well peopled. He also notes that twenty ships came over
to Massachusetts that summer, bringing at least three thousand persons; so new settlements sprang up within the Bay. Political and
religious composure returned.

Because Cotton finally turned against Mrs. Hutchinson, it by no
means follows that he reversed his antinomian stand on justification.
Rather than relinquish it, he thought seriously of joining Davenport
at New Haven. Winthrop and others, however, persuaded him that
this degree of doctrinal disagreement could be indulged without
jeopardy to the holy experiment.

Still, any way one looked at the convulsion which had fissured
that experiment irreparably, Cotton had been suspiciously intimate
with the discredited conspirators and had played out the whole
crisis too coolly, as though to stay on top whichever party won. Did
he share the antinomians' fantasy that Vane would return as the
king's personal governor-general? The full emotional impact of the
crisis and his equivocal role in it did not hit him until after the
lapse of a surprisingly long interval. He echoed Winthrop that he
had been caught asleep. If so, he finally waked up and went through
something of the inner wrenching that others on both sides had
gone through a year and a half or so before. It was in his fast-day
sermon of January 13, 1639, that he finally broke down and, to the
trickle of hot tears, regretted his sloth and credulity while many and
dangerous errors spread in the church. He retraced the whole
process by which these errors, framed in words so near the "truths"
he had preached, deceived him—the more so, he said, in that the de-
ceivers usually denied to him what they were saying to others. He
now, in this sermon (according to Winthrop's summary of it)
formally acknowledged that those gone to Aquidneck who had been
seducers of others, had been justly banished. Those who had merely
been misled (they would be most of his listeners, and he surely
wished to be thought of as having been somewhat misled himself)

should be borne withal, he said. The congregation seemed to sympathize with him in the painful choice of loyalties circumstances had forced upon him and to accept this belated "apology" at face value. His place in their esteem, by every indication that survives, suffered no impairment.

The January 1639 fast day had been called by the governor and Council on the motion of the clergy, because of the spread of small-pox and other epidemics, "also, the apparent decay of the power of religion, and the general declining of professors [of Christianity]," notes Winthrop. In bidding farewell to Captain Underhill in May 1642, Winthrop told him that a great scourge of God hung over the heads of this people and land, "for God is wroth with the Countri," Underhill recalled the words in his own spelling eighteen years later, "and will otter his sore desplesure agaynst it; but whether I may life to see it I queschon. . . ."

Mrs. Hutchinson's future physician and Williams's future fellow-agent to England, John Clark, arrived in Boston just as the anti-nomian trials commenced in General Court.

I thought it not strange [Clark recalled in 1652] to see men differ about matters of Heaven, for I expect no less upon Earth. But to see that they were not able to bear each with other in their different understandings and consciences, as in those utmost parts of the World to live peaceably together, whereupon I moved the latter, for as much as the land was before us and wide enough . . . to turn aside to the right hand, or to the left: The motion was readily accepted, and I was requested with some others to seek out a place.

The "others" included William Hutchinson and one or more of his sons, who therefore were abroad when Ann came to trial in New-town.

They thought to go north to escape the heat of summer but then to go south to escape the cold of winter and, while their vessel struggled with the shoals off Cape Cod, they crossed by land with Long Island or Delaware Bay in mind; "so to a town called *Providence* we came, which was begun by one M. *Roger Williams* . . . by whom we were courteously and lovingly received, and with whom we advised about our design." Williams readily suggested two places in that vicinity: Sowams and Aquidneck. The visitors' vessel not yet arrived, Williams escorted Clark and two others on a land trip to Plymouth, where the magistrates, says Clark, "very lovingly gave us a meeting." They told Clark that Sowams was the flower of the garden of their patent but cheerfully urged Aquid-neck. Williams then prevailed on the Narragansett sachems to grant Clark, Coddington, Hutchinson, and their fifteen associates the right to settle Aquidneck (the island of Rhode Island), which they for-mally proceeded to do in March 1638, at Portsmouth, choosing the handsome ex-treasurer Coddington sole magistrate and enunciating the principle of separation of church and state.

Coddington, it gradually became apparent, interpreted his office as a feudal barony and alienated the majority of the community, including the Hutchinsons. But the further developments in Rhode Island and in the tragic life of Mrs. Hutchinson are stories for an-other time.

14 : *The Double Journey*

O N an unseasonably cold rainy Monday, September 16, 1638, Williams set out on the hundred-mile walk for Hartford through the rolling, swampy wilderness of jungle-thick, crimson-tinged scrub and saplings, leading the giant Miantonomy, Miantonomy's wife and children, many minor sachems, and a guard of more than 150 warriors, also Williams's neighbor Richard Scot and a well-bred young arrival of the past year in Providence, Edward Cope, to finish some business about Pequot survivors and settle a peace between the Narragansetts and Mohegans.

The expedition camped three nights en route in the woods. Half-way to Hartford it met some Narragansetts returning from Connecticut who complained that Pequots and Mohegans had set upon and robbed them. Some Wunnashowatuckoogs, subjects of Miantonomy, brought more ominous news—that two days before, about 660 Pequots, Mohegans, and confederates had robbed them, spoiled about twenty-three fields of corn, roughed up four Narragansett men in the party, and now lay in wait to prevent the Hartford parley. The Wunnashowatuckoogs heard several of the ambush planners say they meant to boil Miantonomy in the kettle.

Williams's inquiries satisfied him that these reports from the west were true. Scot and Cope advised turning back; Williams concurred, but with the intention of re-embarking from Narragansett Bay by water. If they could get up the Connecticut in their canoes, they might circumvent the ambush and deal with the ambushers through the higher authority of Uncas and of the government of Connecticut, which could effectively pressure Uncas. But Miantonomy and his council decided that not a man should turn back; all should die first. Which may be less a measure of Miantonomy's undoubted courage than of his hatred for Uncas and contempt for inland tribes.

Miantonomy set up a stricter watch by night and deployed forty or fifty sannups on either side of the path during marches by day, with an extra guard in dangerous places for himself and family and sub-sachems. These aristocrats kept the path, while Williams led the procession, Scot and Cope immediately behind him.

Miantonomy, it so happened, had waited to begin this trip until Monday, instead of Saturday as originally planned, because Williams would not travel on Sunday. They therefore passed the appointed site of ambush two days later than the time previously given out by Miantonomy. Also, a rumor of great numbers of English in company with the Narragansetts, instead of the actual three, frightened the ambushers away; "so that we came safe to Connecticut," says Williams.

The party probably ferried across the Connecticut to the main landing, which flanked the center of Hartford, and crossed Little Meadow to the Windsor-Wethersfield road, which ran roughly parallel to the river. A half-block left, a short block right, and they defiled into the central square, or Meeting House Yard, where Haynes and the other magistrates probably performed a ceremonial greeting with musketeer escort, if they had not done so at the landing. (The Connecticut men still acknowledged Winthrop Jr. as governor notwithstanding that he had long since abandoned his office and made no move to renew his lapsed commission. Haynes, though only a commissioner in title—commissioned, with seven others, by the Massachusetts General Court in 1635—seems to have assumed *de facto* gubernatorial leadership—which likely bore on Ludlow's impatience to move again. In 1639 the freemen of the three towns elected Haynes first governor of Connecticut under the locally drawn Fundamental Orders.)

Even though Miantonomy was two days late, Uncas had not yet arrived. Instead, he sent messengers to say he was lame and could not come. Haynes said it was a lame excuse and sent more peremptorily for him. Williams never could understand why the Connecticut people kept trusting Uncas and distrusting Miantonomy instead of vice versa.

Most of the Narragansett sannups evidently roamed the countryside deer hunting. Williams undoubtedly accompanied Haynes on down the Windsor-to-Wethersfield road a couple of blocks, where

Haynes's great frame house occupied the corner overlooking Little River, which intersected the Connecticut to form Little Meadow. Turning right on the River Bank Highway alongside Little River, Williams would have come to Hooker's big house on the lot adjoining Haynes's, then, on across Meeting House Alley, to the co-minister Stone's and, next to his the elder's, William Goodwin's. Turning the corner to the right at the Road-from-the-Palisade-to-Centinel-Hill, he would next have passed (on his right) the house of the magistrate John Steele, one of the vanguard settlers of Hartford, and next that of Clement Chaplin, then come again to the Meeting House Yard at its west edge. Edward Hopkins lived catter-cornered southwestward across Little River from Haynes.

Having come to Hartford on an official mission of state, Williams probably lodged with the principal magistrate (and wealthiest citizen). This, in fact, was the occasion Williams referred to many years later when Haynes "said vnto me, in his owne howse at Hartford" that he would then have to confess that God had meant Rhode Island to be a refuge for minority consciences and that he and Hooker were under a cloud with the Bay, "as you have bene." It must have proved a most satisfactory reunion with the man who, as governor of Massachusetts, had pronounced Williams's sentence of banishment three years before.

Mason must have been on hand; he had been corresponding with Williams about the meeting beforehand. And Williams's renewed friendship with his acquaintances from olden days in England—Hooker and Stone—would have sealed the memorableness of this Hartford sojourn; even if Scot baited Hooker about his high tone toward Scot's sister-in-law Ann Hutchinson.

Uncas at last showed up sometime in the course of the day, Thursday. Haynes then charged him with the recent outrages against the subjects of Canonicus and Miantonomy. One of the Mohegans replied that they had numbered only a hundred men, not 660. Uncas admitted he had been with them, though he did not see all they did; he thought his men only roasted corn! So charges and countercharges flew. The Narragansett delegation had no witnesses on hand to testify about the numbers and the spoiling, which meant the conference could get no further on that matter that day. Haynes and Williams, with others, finally induced the towering Miantonomy and the towering Uncas to shake hands. Miantonomy invited Uncas and all his company to dine with him on venison some of the Narragansetts had bagged. The magistrates joined in urging Uncas, but Uncas adamantly to the last declined. The deliberations all doubtless took place, as had similar negotiations at Hartford in the spring, in the primitive meetinghouse which the town a couple of years later turned over to Hooker for a barn.

In a private conference there Miantonomy gave in the names of Pequot sachems and slayers of Englishmen he and Canonicus knew still to be living—one on Long Island, three at Mohegan, one at Niantic, and one at either Pequot or Mohegan. The magistrates insisted that these be put to death, that the rest be divided among the Mohegans and Narragansetts, and the Pequot tribal name abolished. Miantonomy also knew of ten or eleven other Pequots, the remainder of nearly seventy who had subjected themselves to the Narragansetts but had since slipped back to Mohegan and Pequot; he had brought along the only two or three who remained in his jurisdiction.

Uncas in turn said he did not know the names of those in his jurisdiction, vaguely recalling forty on Long Island, that some other sachems of this area had some, and he himself but twenty. Thomas Stanton, who lived on around the bend of Little River from the leading men of Hartford, on Mill Road, testified that Uncas dealt falsely; others substantiated that Uncas had fetched thirty or forty Pequots from Long Island at one time. Uncas then admitted he had thirty but said he could not give the names. The magistrates gave him ten days to bring in the correct number and names and requested Williams to send to Niantic to get the names of the Pequots there to transmit to Connecticut.

The parley issued in the signing of a formal peace between the Mohegans and Narragansetts on Saturday, though Williams left with a large number of the Narragansetts on Friday—for Plymouth, where his presence had been requested in the trial of four Englishmen for the murder of an Indian. To avoid traveling Sunday, he left Hartford in time to make Plymouth by late Saturday afternoon.

From the hillside overlooking the half-moon bay, Williams's incredulous old friends likely took their one-time preacher, approaching at the head of a host of Indian warriors, as making a kind of triumphal re-entry into his former home village. Bradford himself undoubtedly received him. If Brewster, Alden, Winslow, Standish, Prence, and other distinguished acquaintances who now lived in nearby villages were not on hand to greet him as yet, they would have shown up to a man at the hilltop church services the next day and at the court that convened in the same room the day after that. This Plymouth reunion could hardly have been less satisfactory for Williams than the one at Hartford.

Even the trial turned out to be a big success. It concerned the murder of an Indian messenger, Penowonyanquis, about twelve miles from Providence sometime in early August of that year (1638). The messenger had just carried beads and three beaver skins somewhere eastward on behalf of Canonicus's son and was returning with his reward of five fathom of wampum and three wool coats when four white men intercepted him where the path passed near a swamp in the woods. The leader, Arthur Peach of Plymouth, "a lustie and a desperate yonge man," according to Bradford, but "of good parentage and fair conditioned," according to Winthrop, was a shiftless Pequot War veteran who had recently got a maid with child. He called to the messenger to "drink" tobacco with him and, when the messenger had the pipe in his mouth, ran him through the leg and belly in one thrust. Peach missed with a second thrust; another bandit missed and ran his sword into the ground. The wounded messenger had just enough opportunity to duck into the swamp and fall. When his pursuers sped by him, he dashed deeper into the swamp, and they at length gave up their search.

Toward nightfall he struggled back to the path and lay waiting for help. Three Narragansetts presently came across his groaning form and rushed an old Indian to Williams, who rushed to the spot. Faint as the dying man was, he told Williams part of the story and said he had told the details to the Indians who had discovered him. Next day, they got him to Providence, but he had lost too much blood and apparently also had incurred peritonitis. By Indian messenger and other information Williams learned that the culprits were heading for Aquidneck. He sent to the pioneer colonists there, who arrested three of them; the fourth escaped back to Piscataqua by pinnace. On Winthrop's advice, Williams sent the prisoners to Plymouth, where the General Court indicted them September 4.

Now, at their trial late this same month, the three defendants confessed, and Bradford ordered them hanged in the presence of Williams's Narragansett companions.

The Pilgrim magistrates also had a further request of Williams's services: to investigate a murder of a Plymouth man by two Narragansetts five years before between Plymouth and Sowams. Williams immediately started work on the case when he got back to Providence. Thus he had become simultaneously engaged in official business on behalf of four colonies.

Hardly had he pulled into Providence when he reported to Winthrop: "I am newly returned from a double journey to Connecticut and Plymouth." He mentions that recently arrived Englishmen had told some Indians of a great sachem (governor-general) whose ships would soon land, to whom all the sachems in the land should be as nothing. That was the big news among the Indians. Winthrop would not likely have found less disturbing Williams's mentioning that Vane, now in England, had written Coddington and other substantial men to move from Boston as speedily as they might to Aquidneck, fearing some evil to be ripening in Boston.

Which brings Williams back to his basic theme: "The most holy and mighty One blast all mischievous buds and blossoms, and prepare us for tears in the valley of tears, help you and us to trample on the dunghill of this present world, and to set affections and cast anchor above these heavens and earth, which are reserved for burning."

[238]

Bibliography

PRIMARY

Acts of the Commissioners of the United Colonies of New England, 2 vols., in David Pulsifer, ed. *Records of the Colony of New Plymouth,* IX–X (Boston 1859).

ADAMS, CHARLES FRANCIS JR., ed. *Antinomianism in the Colony of Massachusetts-Bay, 1636–1638* (Boston 1894).

AINSWORTH, HENRY. *The Book of Psalmes* (Amsterdam 1612).

———. *Counterpoyson* ([London?] 1608).

AMES, WILLIAM. *English Pvritanisme* (London 1640).

———. *The Marrow of Sacred Divinity* (London 1642).

——— and JOHN ROBINSON. *Letters that Passed betwixt M. Ames and M. Robinson touching the Bitterness of the Separation* (1611), in Ashton, *Works of Robinson,* III.

BAILLIE, ROBERT. *Anabaptism, the Trve Fovntaine of Independency, Brownisme, etc.* (London 1647).

———. *A Dissvasive from the Errours of the Time* (London 1645).

BISHOPE, GEORGE. *New England Judged* (London 1661).

BOLTON, CHARLES K., ed. *Portraits of the Founders* (Boston 1919).

BRACKENBURY, RICHARD. Deposition (Jan. 20, 1681). *Essex Inst. Hist. Colls.,* I (1859).

BRADFORD, WILLIAM. *A Dialogue, or the Sume of a Conference between Som Younge Men borne in New England and Sundery Ancient Men that came out of Holland and Old England . . . 1648,* in *Plymouth Church Records 1620–1859,* I. Col. Soc. Mass. *Pubs.,* XXII (1920).

———. *A Dialogue or Third Conference* (1652), ed. Charles Deane. Mass. Hist. Soc. *Procs.* (1870).

———. *Letter Book.* 1 Mass. Hist. Soc. *Colls.,* III (1810).

———. Letter to Merchant Adventurers countersigned by Allerton (Sept. 8, 1623), in R. G. Marsden. "Documents." *Am. Hist. Rev.,* VIII (Jan. 1903).

———. Letters to Winthrop. *Winthrop Papers,* IV & 4 Mass. Hist. Soc. *Colls.,* VI.

———. Narrative of first year (1620–21), in *Mourt's Relation,* ed. Henry M. Dexter (Boston 1865).

———. *Of Plimmoth Plantation,* facsimile edition (London 1896); Worthington C. Ford, ed. *History of Plymouth Plantation 1620–1647,* 2 vols. (Boston: Mass. Hist. Soc.-Houghton Mifflin 1912); William T. Davis, ed. *Bradford's History of Plymouth Plantation,* Orig. Narrs. Early Am. Hist. (N.Y.: Scribner's 1908); Samuel Eliot Morison, ed. *Of Plymouth Plantation* (N.Y.: Knopf 1952); Charles Deane, ed. *History of Plymouth Plantation.* 4 Mass. Hist. Soc. *Colls.,* III (1856).

BRADSTREET, ANN. *Meditations Divine and Morall* (1664). Ms. booklet in Houghton Library.

———. *Several Poems* (1678), in John H. Ellis, ed. *Works* (N.Y.: Smith 1932; reprint of 1867 edition).

BROWN, JAMES. Memorandum on the First Settling of Providence (sometime between 1675 & 1732). Ms. in R.I. Hist. Soc.

BROWNE, EDMUND. Letter and Report to D'Ewes (Sept. 17, 1639). Col. Soc. Mass. *Pubs.,* VII (1905).

BROWNE, ROBERT. *A "New Years Guift"* (Dec. 31, 1588), ed. Champlin Burrage (London 1904)

———. *A Treatise of Reformation without Tarying for Anie* (Middleburg 1582), ed. T. G. Crippen (London 1903).

———. *A Trve and Short Declaration* (Middelburg 1583?).

BURGESS, WALTER H. Documents on Sturton-en-le-Steeple, in *John Robinson* (London: Wms & Norgate 1920), appendix.

BURRAGE, CHAMPLIN. *The Early English Dissenters in the Light of Recent Research (1550–1641),* 2 vols. (Cambridge, Eng.: Cambridge U. 1912). [Vol. I gives extensive extracts from the period, and Vol. II is a collection of source materials.]

———, ed. *John Pory's Lost Description of Plymouth Colony* (Boston & N.Y.: Houghton Mifflin 1918).

CALVIN, JOHN. "The Catechism of the Church of Geneva that is a Plan for Instructing Children in the Doctrine of Christ," in *Theological Treatises,* tr. J. K. S. Reid (London: SCM 1954).

———. *Institutes of the Christian Religion,* tr. John Allen, 7th Am. edition, rev. Benjamin B. Warfield, 2 vols. (Philadelphia: Presb. Bd. of Ch. Ed. 1936).

———. *Letters,* ed. Jules Bonnet, tr. David Constable, 2 vols. (Edinburgh 1855).

———. *Sermons . . . vpon the Epistle of Saincte Paule to the Galatians* (London 1574).

———. *Sermons . . . vpon the X. Commandements of the Lawe,* tr. John Harmar (London 1581).

———. *Two and Twentie Sermons . . . [on] the Hundredth and Nineteenth Psalme,* tr. Thomas Stocker (London 1580).

CARTWRIGHT, THOMAS. *A Treatise of Christian Religion or The Whole Bodie and Substance of Divinitie,* 2nd ed. (London 1616).

CHAPIN, HOWARD M., ed. *Documentary History of Rhode Island,* 2 vols. (Providence: Preston & Rounds 1916, 1919).

CLAP, ROGER. *Memoirs,* ed. Sydney Strong (N.Y. n.d.); also in Alexander Young, ed. *Chronicles of the First Planters of the Colony of Massachusetts Bay* (Boston 1846).

CLAP, SAMUEL. *Verses upon the Death of our Honourable Gouernour John Endicott* (1665), Col. Soc. Mass. *Pubs.*, VIII (Dec. 1903).

CLARK, JOHN. *Ill Newes from New-England* (London 1652).

CODDINGTON, WILLIAM. *A Demonstration of True Love unto You the Rulers of the Colony of the Massachusetts* (London 1674).

———. Letters to Winthrop and Winthrop Jr., in 4 Mass. Hist. Soc. *Colls.*, VI–VII; *N. Eng. Hist. & Gen. Reg.*, IV (1850); *Hutchinson Papers*, I; *Winthrop Papers*, IV–V. To Fox (June 25, 1677), in George Fox and John Burnyeat. *A New-England-Fire-Brand Quenched* (London 1678 & 1679), II. Deposition (1677), in 2 Mass. Hist. Soc. *Colls.*, VII.

COTTON, JOHN. *An Abstract or the Lawes of Nevv England, as They are now Established* (London 1655). 3 Mass. Hist. Soc. *Colls.*, VIII.

———. *The Bloudy Tenent, Washed, and Made White in the Bloude of the Lambe* [and appended to it:] *A Reply to Mr. Williams his Examination* (London 1647).

———. *A Brief Exposition of the Whole Book of Canticles, or Song of Solomon* (London 1642).

———. *Christ the Fountaine of Life: or, Sundry Choice Sermons on Part of the Fift Chapter of the First Epistle of St. John* (London 1651).

———. *A Conference Mr. John Cotton held at Boston with the Elders of New-England* [presented by Francis Cornwell] (London 1646).

———. *The Controversie concerning Liberty of Conscience in Matters of Religion* [answers to the "prisoner in Newgate"] (London 1646).

———. *The Covenant of Gods Free Grace* (London 1645).

———. *An Exposition upon the Thirteenth Chapter of the Revelation* (London 1656).

———. *Gods Mercie Mixed with His Ivstice* (London 1641).

———. *Gods Promise to His Plantations* (London 1630). *Old South Leaflets* No. 53.

———. *Gospel Conversion* (London 1646).

———. *The Keyes of the Kingdom of Heaven* (London 1644).

———. *A Letter of Mr. John Cottons . . . to Mr. Williams* (London 1643).

———. Letter to Francis Hutchinson (Aug. 12, 1638). 2 Mass. Hist. Soc. *Colls.*, X. To Cromwell (July 28, 1651). *Hutchinson Papers*, I. In Reply to Sir Richard Saltonstall (n.d., c. 1651). *Hutchinson Papers*, II. Letter of Resignation to Bishop of Lincoln (May 7, 1633), in Young. *Chronicles of the First Planters*.

———. *A Modest and Cleare Answer to Mr. Balls Discourse of Set Formes of Prayer* (London 1642).

———. *Of the Holinesse of Church-Members* (London 1650). [Declining of Presbyterian invitations to return: preface.]

———. *The Powring ovt of the Seven Vials: or an Exposition, of the 16 Chapter the Revelation, with an Application of it to Our Times* (London 1642).

———. *A Practical Commentary, or an Exposition . . . upon the First Epistle Generall of John* (London 1656).

———. Reply to Hooker on Justification, Assurance, and Grace. Ms. in Colonial Office of Public Record Office, London (read Oct. 7, 1637 by Arch. Laud). Microfilm, Library of Congress, British Museum, Reel No. 4.

———. *Some Treasures Fetched out of Rubbish: or, Three Short but Seasonable Treatises (found in a Heap of Scattered Papers) . . . concerning the Imposition and Use of Significant Ceremonies in the Worship of God* (London 1660).

———. *The Way of the Churches of Christ in New-England* (London 1644).

———. *The Way of the Congregational Churches Cleared* (London 1648) [bound with and following Hooker's *Survey*. Cotton's poem on the deceased Hooker appears after the preface to Hooker's book.]

CONANT, ROGER. Petition to the General Court (May 1671), in Young. *Chronicles of the First Planters.*

CRADOCK, MATHEW. Letter to Endecott (Feb. 16, 1629). 2 Mass. Hist. Soc. *Colls.*, VIII (1826) and *Records of Massachusetts*, I.

CUSHMAN, ROBERT. Letters, in Bradford. *Of Plimmoth Plantation* and *Letter Book.*

———. *Reasons and Considerations touching the Lawfulness of Removing out of England into the Parts of America* (1622), in *Mourt's Relation.*

———. *A Sermon Preached at Plimmoth in Nevv-England December 9, 1621. In an Assemblie of his Maiesties Faithfull Subiects, there Inhabiting. Wherein is Shewed the Danger of Selfe-Loue, and the Sweetnesse of True Friendship* (London 1622).

DANKERS, JASPER and PETER SLUYTER. *Journal of a Voyage to New York and a Tour of the Several of the American Colonies*, tr. & ed. Henry C. Murphy. *Memoirs* of the L.I. Hist. Soc., I (Brooklyn 1867).

DAVENPORT, JOHN. *A Discourse about Civil Government* (Cambridge, Mass. 1663).

DAVENPORT, RICHARD. Letter to Peter (c. July 17, 1637). 4 Mass. Hist. Soc. *Colls.*, I, & *Winthrop Papers*, III.

DE VRIES, DAVID PIETERSZOON. *Short Historical and Journal-Notes of Various Voyages . . . 1633–43* (Amsterdam 1655), tr. H. C. Murphy, rev. A. C. Crowell & J. F. Jameson, in Jameson, ed. *Narratives of New Netherland 1609–1654.* Orig. Narrs. Early Am. Hist. (N.Y.: Scribner's 1909).

DEXTER, HENRY M., ed. *Mourt's Relation* (London 1622), reprint (Boston 1865).

DOW, GEORGE FRANCIS, ed. *Two Centuries of Travel in Essex County . . . 1605–1799* (Topsfield, Mass.: Topsfield Hist. Soc. 1921).

DUDLEY, MARY WINTHROP. Letter to Margaret Winthrop (winter 1636/37). 5 Mass. Hist. Soc. *Colls.*, I, & *Winthrop Papers*, III.

DUDLEY, THOMAS. Letter to Lady Bridget, Countess of Lincoln (Mar. 12, 1631). Mass. Hist. Soc. *Colls.*, VIII (1802).

EDWARDS, THOMAS. *Gangraena* (London 1646).

EEKHOF, A., ed. *Three Unknown Documents concerning the Pilgrim Fathers in Holland* (The Hague: Nijhoff 1920).

ELIOT, JOHN. *The Day-Breaking, if not the Sun-Rising of the Gospel with the Indians in New-England* (London 1647). 3 Mass. Hist. Soc. *Colls.*, IV (1834).

——. *A Late and Further Manifestation of the Progress of the Gospel amongst Indians in Nevv-England* (London 1655). 3 Mass. Hist. Soc. *Colls.*, IV.

——. Letter describing New England (May 1650). Mass. Hist. Soc. *Procs.*, II (Mar. 1885). Letters to Winthrop (1631, 1636, 1639, 1640, 1644). *Hutchinson Papers*, I, 4 Mass. Hist. Soc. *Colls.*, VI, & *Winthrop Papers*, III–IV. To Boyle (1670, 1677–88). 1 Mass. Hist. Soc. *Colls.*, III. To Shepard, Whitfield, *et al. Tracts relating to the Attempts to Convert to Christianity the Indians of New England.* 3 Mass. Hist. Soc. *Colls.*, IV (1834).

—— and JONATHAN MAYHEW. *Tears of Repentance* (London 1653). 3 Mass. Hist. Soc. *Colls.*, IV.

ENDECOTT, JOHN. *The Humble Petition and Address of the General Court sitting at Boston in New-England, unto the High and Mighty Prince Charles the Second. . . . Feb. 11, 1660* (Boston 1660).

——. Letters to Winthrop (1631, 1636, 1639, 1640, 1644) and to Winthrop Jr. (1646, 1651). *Hutchinson Papers*, I, 4 Mass. Hist. Soc. *Colls.*, VI, & *Winthrop Papers*, III–V.

Examination of Mrs. Ann Hutchinson at the Court of Newtown, in Thomas Hutchinson. *History of the Colony and Province of Massachusetts-Bay,* ed. Lawrence Shaw Mayo, 3 vols. (Cambridge: Harvard U. 1936), II, appendix II.

Facsimiles of Signatures and Seals. 4 Mass. Hist. Soc. *Colls.*, VI, VII, appendices.

FENNER, HOWLONG HARRIS. Deposition (1708). R.I. Hist. Soc. *Pubs.*, IV, & *Harris Papers.*

FIRMIN, GILES. *Separation Examined* (London 1652).

Forms of Government agreed to by the First Settlers on the Island of Rhode Island (Mar. 7, 1638) and Introduction to Code of Laws (1647). 2 Mass. Hist. Soc. *Colls.*, VII.

FULLER, SAMUELL. Letter to Bradford (Aug. 2, 1630), in Bradford. *Letter Book.*

——. Will (July 30, 1633), abstract. *N. Eng. Hist. & Gen. Reg.*, IV (1850).

GARDENER, LION. *Relation of the Pequot Warres* (1660). 3 Mass. Hist. Soc. *Colls.*, III.

GORGES, SIR FERDINANDO. *A Briefe Narration of the Originall Undertakings of the Advancement of Plantations into the Parts of America* (London 1658), in *America Painted to the Life* (London 1659).

——. *Briefe Relation* (1622), Correspondence, etc., in James Phinney

Baxter, ed. *Sir Ferdinando Gorges and his Province of Maine*, 3 vols. (Boston 1890).

GORTON, SAMUELL. *Simplicities Defence against Seven-Headed Policy* (London 1646). *Force Tracts*, IV, No. 6 (Wash., D.C. 1846).

GROOME, SAMUEL. *A Glass for the People of New-England* (1676). *Mag. of Hist.*, XXXVII, No. 3, Extra No. 147 (1929).

HARRIS, WILLIAM. *Harris Papers*, ed. Clarence S. Brigham. R.I. Hist. Soc. *Colls.*, X (1902).

——. Testimony to Dudley's Justice. R.I. Hist. Soc. *Procs.* (1893).

HIGGINSON, FRANCIS. *Journal of his Voyage to New England*, in Stewart Mitchell, ed. *The Founding of Massachusetts* (Boston: Mass. Hist. Soc. 1930).

——. Letter to his Friends at Leicester (1629). *Hutchinson Papers*, I.

——. *New-Englands Plantation.* 1 Mass. Hist. Soc. *Colls.*, I; Mitchell, ed. *The Founding of Massachusetts;* and Dow, ed. *Two Centuries of Travel in Essex County.*

HOOKER, THOMAS. Abstracts of Two Sermons from the Short-Hand Notes of Henry Wolcott, of Windsor (Hartford, May 31, 1638). Conn. Hist. Soc. *Colls.*, I (1860).

——. *The Danger of Desertion: or a Farvvell Sermon* (London 1641).

——. Letters to Winthrop (May, Aug. 1637; c. Dec. 1638). 4 Mass. Hist. Soc. *Colls.*, VI, *Winthrop Papers*, III, IV, & Conn. Hist. Soc. *Colls.*, I.

——. *The Poore Doubting Christian Drawne unto Christ* (London 1629).

——. *The Sovles Exaltation* (London 1638).

——. *The Sovles Hvmiliation*, 3rd ed. (London 1640).

——. *The Sovles Ingrafting into Christ* (London 1637).

——. *The Sovles Preparation for Christ* (London 1632).

——. *The Sovles Vocation or Effectval Calling to Christ* (London 1638).

——. *A Survey of the Summe of Church-Discipline* (London 1648).

HOWES, EDWARD. Letter to Winthrop Jr. (Mar. 21, 1638). *Winthrop Papers*, IV.

HUBBARD, WILLIAM. *The General History of New England . . . till the Year 1680* (Boston 1682). 2 Mass. Hist. Soc. *Colls.*, V.

——. *A Narrative of the Troubles with the Indians in New-England. . . . To which is added a Discourse about the Warre with the Pequods* (Boston 1677).

HULL, JOHN. *Diary.* Am. Antiq. Soc. *Trans.* & *Colls.*, III.

HUMFREY, JOHN. Letters to I. Johnson and Winthrop (1630). 4 Mass. Hist. Soc. *Colls.*, VI; to Winthrop (Sept. 1646). *Winthrop Papers*, V.

Hutchinson Papers, The, 2 vols. (Albany: Prince Soc. 1865).

JOHNSON, EDWARD. *Wonder-Working Providence of Sions Saviour in New-England 1628–1651* (London 1654), ed. J. Franklin Jameson. Orig. Narrs. Early Am. Hist. (N.Y.: Scribner's 1910); also: ed. William Frederick Poole (Andover 1867).

JOHNSON, ISAAC. Letter to Downinge (July 8, 1629); to Winthrop (Dec. 17, 1629); and Will (Apr. 20, 1627). 4 Mass. Hist. Soc. *Colls.*, VI, & *Winthrop Papers*, II.

JOSSELYN, JOHN. *An Account of Two Voyages to New-England* (1638, 1663) (London 1675; Boston 1865).

KEAYNE, ROBERT. Notebook, Extract, in Adams. *Antinomianism in the Colony of Massachusetts-Bay.*

——, recorder. *Report of the Trial of Mrs. Anne Hutchinson before the Church in Boston, Mar. 1638.* Mass. Hist. Soc. *Procs.* (Oct. 1888) [from a copy by Ezra Stiles 1771].

LECHFORD, THOMAS. *Plain Dealing: or Nevves from New-England* (London 1642). 3 Mass. Hist. Soc. *Colls.*, III.

LUDLOWE, GEORGE. Letter to Winthrop (c. 1637), with note appended by Williams. *Winthrop Papers*, III.

MARTIN, SIR WILLIAM. Letter to Winthrop (Mar. 29, 1636). *Hutchinson Papers*, I.

MASON, JOHN. *A Brief History of the Pequot War*, ed. Thomas Prince (Boston 1736). 2 Mass. Hist. Soc. *Colls.*, VIII.

MATHER, COTTON. *Magnalia Christi Americana* (London 1702); also: reprint (Hartford 1820), 2 vols.

——. "Serious Thoughts in Dying Times," in *Death Made Easie & Happy* (London 1701).

——. *The Wonders of the Invisible World* (Boston 1693; reprint London 1862).

—— and INCREASE. Introduction to John Quick. *The Young Mans Claim* (Boston 1700).

MATHER, ELEAZAR. *A Serious Exhortation to the Present and Succeeding Generations in New-England* (Cambridge, Mass. 1672).

MATHER, INCREASE. *Autobiography.* Ms. transcription by A. P. Marvin of orig. ms. in Am. Antiq. Soc.

——. *A Brief Relation of the State of New England, from the Beginning of that Plantation to this Present Year, 1689* (London 1689).

——. *A Discourse concerning the Danger of Apostacy* [1677] (Boston 1685).

——. *An Earnest Exhortation to the Inhabitants of New-England* (Boston 1676).

——. *An Essay for the Recording of Illustrious Providences* (Boston 1684); reprint (London 1856) as *Remarkable Providences.*

——. *Ichabod. Or, a Discourse, shewing what Cause there is to Fear that the Glory of the Lord, is Departing from New-England* (Boston 1702).

——. *A Narrative of the Miseries of New-England, by Reason of an Arbitrary Government Erected there* (London[?] 1688).

——. *A Relation of the Troubles which have Hapned in New-England, by Reason of the Indians there . . . 1614 to . . . 1675* (Boston 1677).

——. *Renewal of Covenant the Great Duty Incumbent on Decaying or Distressed Churches* (Boston 1677).

MAVERICK, SAMUEL. *A Briefe Discription of New England and the Severall Townes therein* [1660] (Boston 1885).
———. Letter to Winthrop (Mar. 11, 1641). *Winthrop Papers*, IV.
MAYHEW, JONATHAN. *A Discourse concerning Unlimited Submission and Non-Resistance to the Higher Powers* (Boston 1750).
MEGAPOLENSIS, JOHANNES, JR. *A Short Account of the Mohawk Indians* (1644), tr. J. F. Jameson. *Narratives of New Netherland.*
MICHAËLIUS, JONAS. Letter of Aug. 11, 1628, tr. J. F. Jameson. *Narratives of New Netherland.*
MORRELL, WILLIAM. *Poem on New-England.* 1 Mass. Hist. Soc. *Colls.*, I (1792).
MORTON, NATHANIEL. *New England's Memorial* (1669), 5th ed., ed. John Davis (Boston 1826); also: 6th ed. (Boston 1855).
MORTON, THOMAS. *The New English Canaan* (Amsterdam[?] 1637); also: ed. Charles Francis Adams, Jr. (Boston 1883).
Mourt's Relation. See Dexter.
Narragansett Country, Documents on. R.I. *Recs.*, III; 1 Mass. Hist. Soc. *Colls.*, V; 5 Mass. Hist. Soc. *Colls.*, IX; R.I. Hist. Soc. *Pubs.*, VII (1899) & VIII (1900); & *Harris Papers.*
Narrative concerning the Settlement of New England (anon.) to Secretary Coke (1630). Mass. Hist. Soc. *Procs.*, IV (1862).
NORTON, JOHN. *Abel Being Dead yet Speaketh* (London 1658).
———. *Memoir of John Cotton* (1658), ed. Enoch Pond (Boston 1834).
O'CALLAGHAN, E. B. and B. FERNOW, eds. *Documents relative to the Colonial History of the State of New York*, II (Albany 1858) & XIV (1883).
PAGITT, EPHRAIM. *Heresiography*, 3rd ed. (London 1646).
PETER, HUGH. *Artikells and Couenant* (Rotterdam 1633), in Burrage. *Early English Dissenters*, I.
———. *A Dying Fathers Legacy to an Onely Child* (London 1661).
———. Letters to Winthrop. *Winthrop Papers*, IV & V; to Winthrop Jr. (1636), III & V.
PLOOIJ, D. and J. RENDEL HARRIS, eds. *Leyden Documents relating to the Pilgrim Fathers* (Leyden: Brill 1920).
Plymouth Church Records 1620–1859, I. Col. Soc. Mass. *Pubs.*, XXII (1920).
POPE, CHARLES H., ed. *The Plymouth Scrap Book: the Oldest Documents Extant in Plymouth Archives* (Boston: Goodspeed 1918).
PRATT, PHINEHAS. *A Declaration of the Affairs of the English People that First Inhabited New England* (1662), ed. Richard Frothingham Jr. 4 Mass. Hist. Soc. *Colls.*, IV (1858).
PRENCE, THOMAS. Letter to Williams (c. 1670) [copy in Winslow Papers], 1 Mass. Hist. Soc. *Colls.*, VI.
PRINCE, THOMAS. Ms. Note (c. 1760) appended to ms. of Shepard. *Autobiography.* Photostat in Widener Library.
PURCHAS, SAMUEL. *Pvrchas his Pilgrimage*, 3rd ed. (London 1617); also: *Pvrchas his Pilgrimes*, 4 vols. (London 1625).

PYNCHON, WILLLAM. *The Meritorious Price of Our Redemption* (London 1650). Photostat (Boston: Cong. Library 1931).

RASIERES, ISAACK DE. Letter to Blommaert (c. 1628), tr. J. F. Jameson, in *Narratives of New Netherland.*

Records of Charlestown, The Early, in Young. *Chronicles of the First Planters.*

Records of the Colony of Rhode Island and Providence Plantations, 10 vols. (Providence 1856–65), esp. I: 1636–1663 (1856).

Records of the First Church, Boston. Ms. in Mass. Hist. Soc.

Records of the Governor and Company of the Massachusetts Bay in New England, ed. Nathaniel B. Shurtleff, 5 vols. (Boston 1853).

Records of Plymouth Church. See Plymouth.

Records of Salem Church. See White, D. A.

Records of Salem, Town, 1634–1659, ed. W. P. Upham. 2 Essex Inst. *Hist. Colls.,* I (1869).

Records of the Town of Plymouth, ed. W. T. Davis, 3 vols. (Plymouth 1889–1902).

Records of the Town of Portsmouth, The Early, ed. Clarence S. Brigham (Providence 1901).

Records of the Town of Providence, The Early, 21 vols. (Providence 1892–95). Includes Providence Town Papers, vols. XV & XVII.

ROBINSON, HENRY. *Liberty of Conscience: or the Sole Means to Obtaine Peace and Truth* (London 1643/44), in William Haller, ed. *Tracts on Liberty in the Puritan Revolution 1638–1647,* 3 vols. (N.Y.: Columbia U. 1933), III.

ROBINSON, JOHN. *A Letter of Advice to the Planters of New England,* in *Mourt's Relation.*

——. Letters to Carver, Bradford, Brewster, and from Robinson and Brewster to Sir Edwin Sandys (Dec. 15, 1517). Bradford. *Of Plimmoth Plantation & Letter Book;* 4 Mass. Hist. Soc. *Colls.,* I (1852); & Aston, ed. *Works,* III, appendix 2.

——. *A Manvmission to a Manvduction* (1615). 4 Mass. Hist. Soc. *Colls.,* I.

——. *Observations Divine and Morall, for the Furthering of Knoledg, and Vertue* (n.p. 1625).

——. *Works,* ed. Robert Ashton, 3 vols. (Boston 1851).

—— and WILLIAM BREWSTER. *Seven Artikles,* in Edward Arber, ed. *The Story of the Pilgrim Fathers . . . as Told by Themselves & Their Contemporaries* (London 1897); also in Ford, ed. *Bradford's History;* etc.

SCOT, KATHERINE. Letter to Winthrop Jr. (June 17, 1658). 5 Mass. Hist. Soc. *Colls.,* I.

SCOT, WILLIAM. Letter to Fox (June 1677), in Fox and Burnyeat. *A New-England-Fire-Brand Quenched,* II.

SCOTTOW, JOSHUA. *A Narrative of the Planting of the Massachusetts Colony anno 1628* (Boston 1694). 4 Mass. Hist. Soc. *Colls.,* IV (1858).

SHEPARD, THOMAS. *Autobiography.* (ms. c. 1649). Photostat in Widener

Library. Also: printed in Col. Soc. Mass. *Pubs.*, XXVII & in Young. *Chronicles of the First Planters.*

——. *The Clear Sun-Shine of the Gospel Breaking Forth upon the Indians in New-England* (London 1648). 3 Mass. Hist. Soc. *Colls.*, IV (1834).

——. Election Sermon (May 3, 1638). *N. E. Hist. & Gen. Reg.*, XXIV (1870).

——. Letter to Winthrop (c. Dec. 1636). *Winthrop Papers*, III.

——. *The Parable of the Ten Virgins Opened & Applied* (London 1660).

——. *The Sincere Convert* (London 1672).

——. *Theses Sabbaticae* (London 1654).

——. *Three Valuable Pieces . . . and a Private Diary; containing Meditations and Experiences never before Published* (Boston 1747).

SMITH, CAPTAIN JOHN. *Advertisements for the Unexperienced Planters of New England, or Any Where* (London 1631).

——. *The Generall Historie of Virginia, New-England, and the Summer Isles* (London 1624).

——. *New Englands Trials* (London 1620), ed. Charles Deane (Cambridge, Mass. 1873).

SMYTH, JOHN. *The Differences of the Churches of the Seperation* (London 1608).

——. *Works*, ed. W. T. Whitley, 2 vols. (Cambridge, Eng.: Cambridge U. 1915).

STILES, EZRA. *Memoirs of the Pequots* (c. 1755, 1762, 1783). 1 Mass. Hist. Soc. *Colls.*, X.

STOUGHTON, ISRAEL. Letter to John Stoughton (1635 [undated]). Mass. Hist. Soc. *Procs.*, LVIII (June 1925).

TWICHELL, JOSEPH H., ed. *Some Old Puritan Love-Letters* (N.Y. 1893).

UNDERHILL, JOHN. *Nevves from America . . . containing, a Trve Relation of their War-like Proceedings these Two Yeares Last Past* (London 1638). 3 Mass. Hist. Soc. *Colls.*, VI (1836).

URQUHART, THOMAS. Statement on Williams from *Logopandecteision* (London 1653). R.I. Hist. Soc. *Pubs.*, new ser., XIV (1900).

VANE, HENRY. *A Brief Answer to a Certain Declaration.* . . . (1637). *Hutchinson Papers*, I.

VICARS, JOHN. *The Schismatick Sifted or, the Picture of Independents, Freshly and Fairly Washt-over Again* (London 1646).

VINCENT, PHILIP. *A Trve Relation of the Late Battell Fought in New-England, between the English and the Pequet Salvages* (London 1638). 3 Mass. Hist. Soc. *Colls.*, VI.

WARD, NATHANIEL. Letter to Winthrop Jr. (Dec. 24, 1635). 4 Mass. Hist. Soc. *Colls.*, VII & *Winthrop Papers*, III.

——. *The Simple Cobbler of Aggavvamm in America*, 4th ed. (London 1647); reprint (Salem 1906).

WELDE, THOMAS. Preface to Winthrop. *A Short Story of the Rise, Reign, and Ruine of the Antinomians* (London 1644).

WHEELWRIGHT, JOHN. Letter to Winthrop (Apr. 1, 1643). 5 Mass. Hist. Soc. *Colls.*, I.

——. *A Sermon Preached at Boston . . . vpon a Fast Day the XVJth of January [sic]. 1636[/7].* Mass. Hist. Soc. *Procs.*, IX (Aug. 1866).

WHEELWRIGHT, JOHN JR. *Mercurius Americanus* (London 1645).

WHITE, DANIEL APPLETON, comp. *New England Congregationalism . . . illustrated by the Foundation and Early Records of the First Church in Salem* (Salem 1861).

WHITE, JOHN. *The Hvmble Reqvest* (1630), facsimile (N.Y.: N.E. Soc. in City of N.Y. 1912).

——. Letter to Winthrop (c. 1637). *Winthrop Papers*, III.

——. *Planters Plea* (1630), facsimile, ed. Marshall H. Saville. Sandy Bar Hist. Soc. & Mus. *Pubs.*, I (Rockport 1930). Also in Young. *Chronicles of the First Planters.*

WHITING, SAMUEL. *Concerning the Life of the Famous Mr. Cotton*, in Young. *Chronicles of the First Planters.*

WIGGIN, THOMAS. Letter to Secretary Coke (Nov. 19, 1632), in James Savage. "Gleanings for New England History." 3 Mass. Hist. Soc. *Colls.*, VIII.

WILLIAMS, DANIEL. Letter to Town of Providence (Aug. 24, 1710), in John Bartlett, ed. *Letters of Roger Williams.*

WILLIAMS, ROGER. *An Answer to a Letter sent from Mr. Coddington . . . to Governor Leveret* (Boston, between 1677 & 1680) (Providence: Soc. Col. Wars in R.I. 1946); also in R.I. Hist. Soc. *Procs.* (1875–76).

——. *An Answer to a Scandalous Paper* (Aug. 25, 1658) (Providence: R. Wms. Press 1945).

——. *The Blovdy Tenent, of Persecution, for Cause of Conscience, Discussed, in a Conference betweene Trvth and Peace* (London 1644).

——. *The Bloody Tenent Yet More Bloody: by Mr. Cottons Endevour to Wash it White in the Blood of the Lambe* (London 1652).

——. *Christenings Make Not Christians, or a Briefe Discourse concerning that Name Heathen, commonly given to the Indians. As also concerning that Great Point of their Conversion* (London 1645), ed. Henry M. Dexter. *R.I. Hist. Tracts* No. 14 (1881).

——. *The Examiner Defended* (London 1652).

——. *Experiments of Spiritual Life & Health, and their Preservatives* (London Apr. 1652), reprint (Providence 1863).

——. *The Fourth Paper Presented by Major Butler, etc.* (London 1652), ed. Clarence S. Brigham (Providence: Club for Col. Reprints 1903).

——. *George Fox Digg'd Out of his Burrovves* (Boston 1676).

——. *The Hireling Ministry None of Christs, or a Discourse touching the Propagating the Gospel of Christ Jesus* (London Apr. 1652).

——. *A Key into the Language of America: or, an Help to the Language of the Natives of that Part of America, called New-England* (London 1643).

——. *Letters and Papers 1624–1682* [photostats], comp. Howard M. Chapin (Boston: Mass. Hist. Soc. 1924).

———. *Letters,* ed. John R. Bartlett. *Narr. Club Pubs.,* VI (Providence 1874). [Invaluable as this collection is, it misses a number of items, gives a few incompletely, and often proves less precisely accurate than its sources; wherefore the inadvisability of relying wholly upon it.] Letters to Lady Barrington (Apr., May 1629): *N.E. Hist. & Gen. Reg.* (for 1889), XLIII. Henry M. Dexter, ed. *Some Letters Written by Roger Williams. R.I. Hist. Tracts.* No. 14 (1881). Clarence S. Brigham, ed. *Ten Letters of Roger Williams, 1654–1678.* R.I. Hist. Soc. *Pubs.* (Oct. 1900). More letters: R.I. Hist. Soc. *Procs.* (1877–78; 1883–84); R.I. Hist. Soc. *Colls.,* I (1792) & (Apr. 1928); Protest (Dec. 8, 1680), in *Early Recs. of Town of Providence;* to Clark (undated): *R.I. History* (Oct. 1944); 2 Mass. Hist. Soc. *Colls.,* VIII, 3 Mass. Hist. Soc. *Colls.,* I & IX, 4 Mass. Hist. Soc. *Colls.,* V & VI, 5 Mass. Hist. Soc. *Colls.,* I; *Winthrop Papers,* III–V; Mass. Hist. Soc. *Procs.,* III (Mar. 1858), 2 Mass. Hist. Soc. *Procs.,* III (Mar. 1887); to Commissioners of United Colonies (Oct. 5, 1654) & to Leveret (Oct. 11, 1675), in *Acts of the Commissioners of the United Colonies,* II. Earliest source of many letters: Isaac Backus. *History of New England with Particular Reference to the Denomination of Christians called Baptists,* 2 vols. (Boston 1777) & James D. Knowles. *Memoir of Roger Williams* (Boston 1834).

———. *Queries of Highest Consideration* (London 1664). *Narr. Club Pubs.,* II.

WILLISON, GEORGE F., ed. *The Pilgrim Reader* (Garden City: Doubleday 1953).

WINSLOW, EDWARD. Correspondence with Commissioners of United Colonies (Apr., Sept. 1651). *Acts of the Commissioners,* I.

———. *The Danger of Tolerating Levellers in a Civill State* (London 1649).

———. *Good Newes from New-England* (London 1624). Also in Arber. *Story of the Pilgrim Fathers* & in Alexander Young, ed. *Chronicles of the Pilgrim Fathers . . . 1602 to 1625,* 2nd ed. (Boston 1844). Cf. also: 1 Mass. Hist. Soc. *Colls.,* VIII.

———. *Hypocrisie Unmasked* (London 1646), ed. Howard M. Chapin (Providence: Club for Col. Reprints 1916).

———. *A Journey to Packanokik;* Letter "to a Friend" (Dec. 11, 1621); & *A Letter Setting Forth a Brief and True Declaration of the Worth of these Plantations,* in *Mourt's Relation.*

———. Letters to Winthrop. 4 Mass. Hist. Soc. *Colls.,* VI; *Winthrop Papers,* III & V (Aug. 2, 1644); *N.E. Hist. & Gen. Reg.,* XXIX (1875).

———. *New-Englands Salamander* (London 1647).

WINTHROP, JOHN. *Christian Experience* (Jan. 1638); Notebook *Experiencia;* etc.: *Winthrop Papers,* I. *General Observations for the Plantation of New-England* (c. Aug. 1629); *A Modell of Christian Charity* (spring 1630); etc.: *Winthrop Papers,* II. *Reasons to Proue a Necessitye of Reformation from the Corruptions of Antechrist*

(c. Mar. 1631); etc.: *Winthrop Papers*, III. *Discourse on Arbitrary Government* (July 1644); etc.: *Winthrop Papers*, IV.

WINTHROP, JOHN. *A Declaration of Former Passages and Proceedings betwixt the English and the Narrowgansets* (Boston 1645). *Photostat Americana*, 2nd ser. (Boston: Mass. Hist. Soc. 1936). Also in *Acts of the Commissioners*, I.

——. *Defence of an Order of Court made in . . . 1637; Liberty and Weale Public Reconciled* (1637); & *A Reply to an Answer made to a Declaration. . . .* (1637): *Hutchinson Papers*, I. *Defense of the Negative Vote* (June 1643): *Hutchinson Papers*, I & *Winthrop Papers*, IV.

——. Diary, Correspondence, etc. liberally reproduced in Robert C. Winthrop. *Life and Letters of John Winthrop*, 2nd ed., 2 vols. (Boston 1869). Correspondence with Margaret, in Twichell, ed. *Some Old Puritan Love-Letters*. Letters to D'Ewes (1633-36). Col. Soc. Mass. *Pubs.*, VII. Letters to Bradford, in Bradford. *Of Plimmoth Plantation*. Abstract of letters to Hooker, in *Journal*, II, addenda.

——. Journal: *First Manuscript Volume. 1630-1636* [photostat] (Boston: Mass. Hist. Soc. 1932); "First Year of Winthrop's Journal," in Mitchell, ed. *The Founding of Massachusetts* & in *Winthrop Papers*, II & Mass. Hist. Soc. *Procs.*, LXII; James Savage, ed. *The History of New England from 1630 to 1649. by John Winthrop*, new ed., 2 vols. (Boston 1853); & James K. Hosmer, ed. *Winthrop's Journal*, 2 vols. Orig. Narrs. Early Am. Hist. (N.Y.: Scribner's 1908).

——. *A Monstrous Birth, Brought Forth att Boston in New England October 1637.* [affidavit]. Colonial Office of Public Record Office, London; microfilm, Library of Congress, British Museum, Reel 4.

——. *A Short Story of the Rise, Reign, and Ruine of the Antinomians, Familists & Libertines, that Infected the Churches of Nevv-England* (London 1644).

WINTHROP, JOHN, JR. Diary (Nov. 11-Dec. 5, 1646). *Winthrop Papers*, V & 2 Mass. Hist. Soc. *Procs.* (Oct. 1892).

——. Letters to his Father. *Winthrop Papers*, II-V. Letters to Williams (Nov. 10, 1650) in Bartlett, ed. *Letters of Williams*; (Feb. 6, 1664) & (Jan. 6, 1675): 4 Mass. Hist. Soc. *Colls.*, VI.

Winthrop Papers, The. 5 vols. to date (Boston: Mass. Hist. Soc. 1929-47).

WISE, JOHN. *Churches Quarrel Espoused*, 2nd ed. (Boston 1715).

——. *A Vindication of the Government of New-England Churches* (Boston 1717).

WOOD, WILLIAM. *Nevv-Englands Prospect* (London 1639). Also: 1624 ed. (Boston: Prince Soc. 1865).

WOODBERYE, HUMPHRY and WILLIAM DIXY. Depositions (Feb. 16, 1681), in John Wingate Thornton. *The Landing at Cape Anne* (Boston 1854).

SECONDARY

"Account of the First Century Lecture, held at Salem 6 Aug. 1729" (anon. public ms.). 1 Mass. Hist. Soc. *Colls.*, IV.

ADAMS, CHARLES FRANCIS, JR. "Old Planters about Boston Harbor." Mass. Hist. Soc. *Procs.* (June 1878).

———. *Three Episodes of Massachusetts History*, 2 vols. (Boston & N.Y. 1892).

ADAMS, HERBERT B. "Allotments of Land in Salem, to Men, Women, and Maids." Essex Inst. *Hist. Colls.*, XIX (1882).

———. "The Fisher-Plantation at Cape Anne." *Ibid.*

———. "Origin of Salem Plantation." *Ibid.*

ADAMS, JAMES TRUSLOW. *The Founding of New England*, 2 vols. (Boston: Little, Brown 1921).

AMORY, THOMAS COFFIN. *William Blaxton 1595–1675*. Bostonian Soc. *Pubs.*, I (1886).

ANDREWS, CHARLES McLEAN. *The Colonial Period of American History*, 4 vols. (New Haven: Yale 1934–38).

ARNOLD, SAMUEL GREEN. *History of the State of Rhode Island and Providence Plantations*, 2 vols. (N.Y. 1859–60).

ASHTON, ROBERT. "Memoir of John Robinson," in *The Works of Robinson*, 3 vols. (Boston 1851) & in 4 Mass. Hist. Soc. *Colls.*, I.

AUGUR, HELEN. *An American Jezebel* (N.Y.: Brentano's 1930).

AUSTIN, JOHN OSBORNE. *The Genealogical Dictionary of Rhode Island* (Albany 1887).

BACKUS, ISAAC. *History of New England with Particular Reference to the Denomination of Christians called Baptists*, 2 vols. (Boston 1777).

BACON, LEONARD and JOHN DAVIS. "Memoir of Isaac Allerton." 3 Mass. Hist. Soc. *Colls.*, VII (1838).

BAINTON, ROLAND H. "The Struggle for Religious Liberty." *Church Hist.*, X (June 1941).

———. *The Travail of Religious Liberty* (Philadelphia: Westminster 1951).

BANKS, CHARLES EDWARD. *The English Ancestry and Homes of the Pilgrim Fathers* (N.Y.: Grafton 1929).

———. *The Planters of the Commonwealth . . . 1620–1640* (Boston: Houghton Mifflin 1930).

———. "William Bradford and the Pilgrim Quarter in London." Mass. Hist. Soc. *Procs.*, LXI (Dec. 1927).

———. *The Winthrop Fleet of 1630* (Boston: Houghton Mifflin 1930).

BATTIS, EMERY. *Saints and Sectaries: Anne Hutchinson and the Antinomian Controversy . . . .* (Chapel Hill: U. of N.C. 1962).

BAXTER, JAMES PHINNEY. "Memoir," in *Sir Ferdinando Gorges and his Province of Maine*, 3 vols. (Boston 1890), I.

BELKNAP, JEREMY. *The History of New Hampshire*, 3 vols. (Boston 1792).

BOLTON, CHARLES KNOWLES. *The Real Founders of New England* (Boston: Faxon 1929).

BOLTON, REGINALD PELHAM. *A Woman Misunderstood* (N.Y.: Bolton 1931).

BOWEN, CATHERINE DRINKER. *Francis Bacon: the Temper of a Man* (Boston & Toronto: Little, Brown 1963).

———. *The Lion and the Throne: the Life and Times of Sir Edward Coke (1552-1634)* (Boston & Toronto: Little, Brown 1956).

BRADBURY, FRANK E. "Laws and Courts of the Massachusetts Bay Colony." Bostonian Soc. *Pubs.*, X (1913).

BRADSTREET, HOWARD. *The Story of the War with the Pequots Re-Told.* Conn. Tercent. Commiss., Com. on Hist. *Pubs.*, V (New Haven: Yale U. 1933).

BRIDENBAUGH, CARL. *Cities in the Wilderness* (N.Y.: Ronald 1938).

BROCKUNIER, SAMUEL HUGH. *The Irrepressible Democrat: Roger Williams* (N.Y.: Ronald 1940).

BROOKS, DEXTER M. *Of Plymouth Plantation* (Plymouth: Leyden 1949).

BROWN, ROBERT E. "Democracy in Colonial Massachusetts." *N. Eng. Quarterly*, XXV (Sept. 1952).

BURGESS, WALTER H. *John Robinson* (London: Wms. & Norgate 1920).

BURRAGE, CHAMPLIN. *The Early English Dissenters in the Light of Recent Research (1550-1641)*, 2 vols. (Cambridge, Eng.: Cambridge U. 1912).

———. *New Facts concerning John Robinson* (Oxford: Oxford U. 1910).

BURRAGE, HENRY S. *Gorges and the Grant of the Province of Maine 1622* (Portland[?] 1923).

CALAMANDREI, MAURO. "Neglected Aspects of Roger Williams' Thought." *Church Hist.*, XXI (Sept. 1952).

CALDER, ISABEL M. "John Cotton and the New Haven Colony." *N. Eng. Quarterly*, III (1930).

CALLENDER, JOHN. *An Historical Discourse on the Civil and Religious Affairs of the Colony of Rhode-Island*, ed. Romeo Elton. R.I. Hist. Soc. *Colls.*, IV (1838).

CAULFIELD, ERNEST. *The Pursuit of a Pestilence* [influenza]. Am. Antiq. Soc. *Procs.*, LX.

———. *Some Common Diseases of Colonial Children.* Col. Soc. Mass. *Pubs.*, XXXV (1942; printed 1951).

CHAMBERLAIN, MELLEN. *A Documentary History of Chelsea, including the Boston Precincts of Winnisimmet, Rumney Marsh, and Pullen Point 1624-1824*, 2 vols. (Boston: Mass. Hist. Soc. 1908).

———. "Governor Winthrop's Estate." 2 Mass. Hist. Soc. *Procs.*, VII (Dec. 1891).

———. "Samuel Maverick's Palisade House of 1630." Mass. Hist. Soc. *Procs.* (Jan. 1885).

CHANDLER, PELEG W. *American Criminal Trials*, 2 vols. (Boston 1841).

CHANNING, EDWARD. *A History of the United States,* I (N.Y.: Macmillan 1905).

CHAPIN, HOWARD M. *Roger Williams and the King's Colors* (Providence: Soc. Col. Wars R.I. 1928).

———. *The Trading Post of Roger Williams* (Providence: Soc. Col. Wars R.I. 1934).

CHAUNCY, CHARLES. *Seasonable Thoughts on the State of Religion in New-England* (Boston 1743).

COTTON, JOHN. "An Account of the Church of Christ in Plymouth (1760)." 1 Mass. Hist. Soc. *Colls.,* IV.

Cotton's House in Boston, Notes on. 3 Mass. Hist. Soc. *Colls.,* V.

COVEY, CYCLONE. *A Cyclical Return to the Timeless Three-Clock Revolution* (Stillwater: Okla. State U. 1966).

———. *The American Pilgrimage: the Roots of American History, Religion and Culture* (N.Y.: Collier Books 1961).

———. "Did Puritanism or the Frontier Cause the Decline of Colonial Music?" *Journ. of Research in Mus. Ed.* (summer 1958).

———. "Puritan Morals," in Vergilius Ferm, ed. *Encyclopedia of Morals* (N.Y.: Philos. Library 1956).

CURTIS, EDITH. *Anne Hutchinson* (Cambridge, Mass.: Washburn & Thomas 1930).

CUTTER, WILLIAM RICHARD, ed. *Historic Homes and Places . . . of Middlesex County* (N.Y.: Lewis 1908).

DAVIS, ANDREW MCFARLAND. "A Few Words about the Writings of Thomas Shepard." Cambridge Hist. Soc. *Procs.,* III (1909).

DAVIS, SAMUEL. "Notes on Plymouth, Massachusetts." 2 Mass. Hist. Soc. *Colls.,* III (1815).

DE FOREST, L. EFFINGHAM and ANNE LAWRENCE. *Captain John Underhill: Gentleman Soldier of Fortune* (N.Y.: De Forest 1934).

DEMING, DOROTHY. *The Settlement of the Connecticut Towns,* ed. C. M. Andrews, *Conn. Tercent. Commiss., Com. on Hist. Pubs.,* VI.

———. *Settlement of Litchfield. Op. cit.,* VII.

DEXTER, HENRY MARTYN. *As to Roger Williams* (Boston 1876).

———. "Elder Brewster's Library." Mass. Hist. Soc. *Procs.* (Oct. 1889).

———. "English Exiles in Amsterdam, 1597–1625." Mass. Hist. Soc., *Procs.* (June 1890).

——— and MORTON. *The England and Holland of the Pilgrims* (Boston & N.Y.: Houghton Mifflin 1905).

DEXTER, MORTON. "Alleged Facts as to the Pilgrims." Mass. Hist. Soc. *Procs.* (June 1895).

———. *The Story of the Pilgrims* (Boston & Chicago 1894).

Dictionary of American Biography.

Dictionary of National [British] *Biography.*

DIMAN, J. LEWIS. Introduction to Williams. *George Fox Digg'd Out of his Burrovves. Nar. Club Pubs.,* V (Providence 1872).

DORR, HENRY C. *The Narragansetts.* R.I. Hist. Soc. *Colls.,* VII (1885).

———. *The Planting and Growth of Providence. R.I. Hist. Tracts* No. 15 (1882).

DORR, HENRY C. *The Proprietors of Providence, and their Controversies with the Freeholders.* R.I. Hist. Soc. *Colls.,* IX (1897).

DOW, GEORGE FRANCIS. *Domestic Life in New England in the Seventeenth Century* (Topsfield 1925).

———. *Every Day Life in the Massachusetts Bay Colony* (Boston: Soc. for Preserv. of N.E. Antiqs. 1935).

DOYLE, JOHN ANDREW. *The English in America: the Puritan Colonies,* 2 vols. (London 1887).

DRAKE, SAMUEL G. *The Book of the Indians of North America* (Boston 1835).

———. *The History and Antiquities of the City of Boston . . . 1630 to . . . 1670* (Boston 1854).

———. "Notes on the Indian Wars in New England." *N.E. Hist. & Gen. Reg.,* XV.

DUNN, RICHARD S. "John Winthrop, Jr., Connecticut Expansionist: the Failure of his Designs on Long Island, 1633–1671." *N.E. Quarterly,* XXIX (Mar. 1956).

———. "John Winthrop, Jr., and the Narragansett Country." *Wm. & Mary Quarterly* 3, XIII (Jan. 1956).

EARLE, ALICE MORSE. *Customs and Fashions in Old New England* (N.Y. 1893; reprint: Scribner's 1914).

EEKHOF, A. and EDGAR F. ROMIG. *John Robinson* (The Hague: Nijhoff 1928).

EGGLESTON, EDWARD. *The Transit of Civilization from England to America in the Seventeenth Century* (N.Y.: Appleton 1914).

ELIOT, JOHN. *The Settlement of the First Churches in Massachusetts.* 1 Mass. Hist. Soc. *Colls.,* I (1804).

EMERSON, EVERETT H. "Calvin and Covenant Theology," *Church Hist.,* XXV (June 1956).

———. *John Cotton* (N.Y.: Twayne 1965).

EMERSON, RALPH WALDO. "The Transcendentalist," in *Miscellanies* (Boston 1856).

ENDECOTT, CHARLES M. *Memoir of John Endecott* (Salem 1847).

FELTON, E. C. "Samuel Skelton, M.A." *N.E. Hist. & Gen. Reg.,* LIII (1899).

FENN, WILLIAM WALLACE. "John Robinson's Farewell Address." *Harvard Theol. Rev.,* XIII (July 1920).

FESSENDEN, G. M. "A Genealogy of the Bradford Family." *N.E. Hist. & Gen. Reg.,* IV (1850).

FOSTER, THEODORE. "Materials for a History of Rhode Island," in *Early Attempts at Rhode Island History,* ed. William E. Foster. R.I. Hist. Soc. *Colls.,* VII (1885).

FRENCH, ALLEN. *Charles I and the Puritan Upheaval* (Boston: Houghton Mifflin 1955).

GRAY, F. C. "Remarks on the Early Laws of Massachusetts Bay." 3 Mass. Hist. Soc. *Colls.,* VIII.

GREENLAW, LUCY HALL. "Early Generations of the Brewster Family." *N.E. Hist. & Gen. Reg.,* LIII (1899).

GRIFFIS, WILLIAM ELLIOT. *The Pilgrims in their Three Homes* (Boston & N.Y. 1898).

HALLER, WILLIAM JR. *The Puritan Frontier* (N.Y.: Columbia U. 1951).
———. *The Rise of Puritanism* (N.Y.: Columbia U. 1938).

HARASZTI, ZOLTÁN. *The Enigma of the Bay Psalm Book* (Chicago: U. of Chicago 1956).

HAWTHORNE, NATHANIEL. "Mrs. Hutchinson," in *Fanshawe and Other Pieces* (Boston 1876).

HAZARD, PAUL. *The European Mind: the Critical Years*, tr. J. Lewis May (New Haven: Yale U. 1953).

HEDGES, JAMES B. *The Browns of Providence Plantations: Colonial Years* (Cambridge: Harvard U. 1952).

HERRICK, CYRIL ALLYN. "The Early New-Englanders, What did they Read?" *Library* (Jan. 1918).

HILL, CHRISTOPHER. *Puritanism and Revolution: Studies in Interpretation of the English Revolution of the 17th Century* (London: Secker & Warburg 1958).

HIRSCH, ELIZABETH FEIST. "John Cotton and Roger Williams; their Controversy concerning Religious Liberty." *Church Hist.*, X (Mar. 1941).

HOADLEY, CHARLES J. *The Warwick Patent* (Hartford 1902).

HODGES, ALMON D. JR. "Notes concerning Roger Williams." *N.E. Hist. & Gen. Reg.*, LIII (1899).

HOMER, JONATHAN. "Description and History of Newtown, in the County of Middlesex." 1 Mass. Hist. Soc. *Colls.*, V.

HOPKINS, STEPHEN. *An Historical Account of the Planting and Growth of Providence*, ed. William E. Foster. R.I. Hist. Soc. *Colls.*, VII (1885).

HOSMER, JAMES KENDALL. *The Life of Young Sir Henry Vane* (Boston & N.Y. 1888).

HOWLAND, JOHN ANDREWS. "The Date of Passing the Sentence of Banishment on Roger Williams." R.I. Hist. Soc. *Procs.* (1886–87).

HUBBARD, ELBERT. *Little Journeys to the Homes of Reformers: Anne Hutchinson* (N.Y. 1907).

HUFELAND, O. "Anne Hutchinson's Refuge in the Wilderness." Westchester Co. Hist. Soc. *Pubs.*, VII (1929).

HUNTER, JOSEPH. Biographical Notice of Philip Vincent. 4 Mass. Hist. Soc. *Colls.*, I.
———. "Collections concerning the Early History of the Founders of New Plymouth." 4 Mass. Hist. Soc. *Colls.*, I (1852).

HUTCHINSON, THOMAS. *History of the Colony and Province of Massachusetts-Bay*, ed. Lawrence Shaw Mayo, 3 vols. (Cambridge: Harvard U. 1936).

JOHNSON, EDGAR A. J. "Economic Ideas of John Winthrop." *N.E. Quarterly*, III (Apr. 1930).

JONES, EMMA C. BREWSTER, ed. *The Brewster Genealogy 1566–1907*, 2 vols. (N.Y.: Grafton 1908).

JORDAN, W. K. *The Development of Religious Toleration in England,* 4 vols. (Cambridge: Harvard U. 1932–40).

KNAPPEN, MARSHALL M. *Tudor Puritanism: a Chapter in the History of Idealism* (Chicago: U. of Chicago 1939).

KNOWLES, JAMES D. *Memoir of Roger Williams* (Boston 1834).

M'CLURE, DAVID. "Settlement and Antiquities of the Town of Windsor, Connecticut" (1797). 1 Mass. Hist. Soc. *Colls.,* V.

MANIERRE, WILLIAM REID. *Cotton Mather and the Plain Style* (doctoral diss. U. of Mich. 1958).

MASSON, DAVID. *The Life of John Milton,* new ed., 7 vols. (London 1896).

MATTHEWS, ALBERT. "Note on the Indian Sagamore Samoset." Col. Soc. Mass. *Pubs.,* VI (1899, printed 1904).

MAYO, LAWRENCE SHAW. *John Endecott* (Cambridge: Harvard U. 1936).

———. *The Winthrop Family in America* (Boston: Mass. Hist. Soc. 1948).

MECKLIN, JOHN M. *The Story of American Dissent* (N.Y.: Harcourt Brace 1934).

MILLER, PERRY. *The Marrow of Puritan Divinity.* Col. Soc. Mass. *Pubs.,* XXXII (Feb. 1935).

———. *The New England Mind: the Seventeenth Century* (Cambridge: Harvard U. 1939).

———. *Orthodoxy in Massachusetts 1630–1650* (Cambridge: Harvard U. 1933).

———. Introduction to *Roger Williams: his Contribution to the American Tradition* (Indianapolis & N.Y.: Bobbs-Merrill 1953).

———. "Thomas Hooker and the Democracy of Early Connecticut." *N.E. Quarterly,* IV (Oct. 1931).

MORGAN, EDMUND S. *The Puritan Dilemma: the Story of John Winthrop* (Boston: Little, Brown 1958).

MORISON, SAMUEL ELIOT. *Builders of the Bay Colony* (Boston & N.Y.: Houghton Mifflin 1930).

———. "The Course of the *Arbella* from Cape Sable to Salem." Col. Soc. Mass. *Trans.,* XXVII (1932).

———. "Did William Bradford Leave Leyden before the Pilgrims?" Mass. Hist. Soc. *Procs.,* LXI (Nov. 1927).

———. *Harvard College in the Seventeenth Century,* 2 vols. (Cambridge: Harvard U. 1936).

———. *The Puritan Pronaos* (N.Y.: NYU 1936).

———. Review of R. V. Coleman. *Roger Ludlow in Chancery* (Westport 1934). *N.E. Quarterly,* VII.

NEAL, DANIEL. *The History of New-England,* 2nd ed., 2 vols. (London 1747).

OSGOOD, HERBERT L. *The American Colonies in the Seventeenth Century,* 3 vols. (N.Y.: Macmillan 1904).

PAINE, GEORGE T. *A Denial of the Charges of Forgery in connection with the Sachems' Deed to Roger Williams* (Providence 1896).

PALFREY, JOHN GORHAM. *History of New England,* 5 vols. (Boston 1858–90).

PARKS, HENRY BAMFORD. "John Cotton and Roger Williams Debate Toleration 1644–1652." *N.E. Quarterly*, IV (Oct. 1931).

PATTEN, E. B., comp. *Isaac Allerton* (Minneapolis: Imperial 1908).

PEARSON, A. F. SCOTT. *Thomas Cartwright and Elizabethan Puritanism 1535–1603* (Cambridge, Eng.: Cambridge U. 1925).

PEW, WILLIAM ANDREWS. *The Right Honorable the Lady Arbella and her Friends* (Salem: Newcomb & Gauss 1930[?]).

PHIPPEN, GEORGE D. "The 'Old Planters' of Salem, who were Settled here before the Arrival of Governor Endecott, in 1628." *Essex Inst. Hist. Colls.*, I.

PLOOIJ, D. *The Pilgrim Fathers from a Dutch Point of View* (N.Y.: NYU 1932).

POTTER, ELISHA R. *The Early History of Narragansett*. R.I. Hist. Soc. *Colls.*, III (1835).

POTTER, GEORGE R. "Roger Williams and John Milton." R.I. Hist. Soc. *Colls.*, XIII (Oct. 1920).

POWICKS, FREDERICK JAMES. "John Robinson and the Beginnings of the Pilgrim Movement." *Harvard Theol. Rev.*, XIII.

PRESTON, RICHARD ARTHUR. *Gorges of Plymouth Fort* (Toronto: U. of Toronto 1953).

PRINCE, THOMAS. *A Chronological History of New England, in the Form of Annals* (Boston 1736, 1755), 5 vols. in 1 (Edinburgh 1887).

RANTOUL, ROBERT. "Beverly" (1835). 3 Mass. Hist. Soc. *Colls.*, VII.

Reference Guide to Salem, 1630, A: Forest River Park, rev. ed. (Salem: Bd. of Park Comms. 1935).

R.I. Hist. Soc. *Colls.*, VIII (1900) & XI (Oct. 1918): Identification of Williams's Wife.

ROBINSON, GEORGE W. *John Winthrop as Attorney* (Cambridge, Mass. 1930).

ROSE-TROUP, FRANCES. "John Humfry." *Essex Inst. Hist. Colls.*, LXV (1929).

——. *John White, the Patriarch of Dorchester* (N.Y. & London: Putnam's 1930).

——. *Roger Conant and the Early Settlements on the North Shore of Massachusetts* (n.p.: Conant family 1926).

ROSSITER, CLINTON L. *Seedtime of the Republic: the Origin of the American Tradition of Political Liberty* (N.Y.: Harcourt 1953).

——. "Thomas Hooker." *N.E. Quarterly*, XXV (Dec. 1952).

RUGG, WINNIFRED KING. *Unafraid: a Life of Anne Hutchinson* (Boston & N.Y.: Houghton Mifflin 1930).

RUTMAN, DARRETT B. *Winthrop's Boston: a Portrait of a Puritain Town, 1630–1649* (Chapel Hill: U. of N.C. 1965).

SABINE, GEORGE H. *A History of Political Theory* (N.Y.: Holt 1937).

SAVELLE, MAX. *The Foundations of American Civilization: a History of Colonial America* (N.Y.: Holt 1942).

SCHNEIDER, HERBERT WALLACE. *The Puritan Mind* (N.Y.: Holt 1930).

SHELLEY, HENRY CHARLES. *John Underhill: Captain of New England and*

New Netherland (N.Y.: N.Y. Gen. & Bibl. Soc. 1932); also (N.Y. & London: Appleton 1932).

Shipton, Clifford K. *Roger Conant* (Cambridge: Harvard U. 1944).

Shurtleff, Harold R. *The Log Cabin Myth: a Study of the Early Dwellings of the English Colonists in North America,* ed. Samuel Eliot Morison (Cambridge: Harvard U. 1939).

Simpson, Alan. "How Democratic was Roger Williams?" *Wm & Mary Quarterly,* 3, XIII (Jan. 1956).

———. *Puritanism in Old & New England* (Chicago: U. of Chicago 1955).

Smith, Bradford. *Bradford of Plymouth* (Philadelphia & N.Y.: Lippincott 1951).

Staples, William R. *Annals of the Town of Providence.* R.I. Hist. Soc. *Colls.,* V (1843).

Stead, George Albert. "Roger Williams and the Massachusetts-Bay." *N.E. Quarterly,* VII (June 1934).

Stearns, Raymond Phineas. *The Strenuous Puritan: Hugh Peter 1598–1660* (Urbana: U. of Ill. 1954).

Sterry-Cooper, William. *Edward Winslow* (Birmingham, Eng.: Reliance 1953).

Sylvester, Herbert Milton. *Indian Wars of New England,* 3 vols. (Cleveland 1910).

Taylor, Henry Osborn. *Thought and Expression in the Sixteenth Century,* 2nd rev. ed., 2 vols. (N.Y.: Macmillan 1920).

Thornton, John Wingate. *The Landing at Cape Anne* (Boston 1854).

Trinterud, Leonard J. "The Origins of Puritanism." *Church Hist.,* XX (Mar. 1951).

Trumbull, Benjamin. *A Compendium of the Indian Wars in New England* (1767), ed. Frederick B. Hartranft (Hartford: Michell 1926).

Turner, Henry E. *Settlers of Aquidneck and Liberty of Conscience* (Newport 1880).

———. *William Coddington in Rhode Island Colonial Affairs.* R.I. Hist. *Tracts* No. 4 (1878).

Tuttle, Julius H. "Writings of Rev. John Cotton," in *Bibliographical Essays: a Tribute to Wilberforce Eames* (Cambridge: Harvard U. 1924).

Upham, William P., ed. "An Account of the Dwelling-Houses of Francis Higginson, Samuel Skelton, Roger Williams, and Hugh Peters." Essex Inst. *Hist. Colls.,* VIII (1868).

Usher, Roland G. *The Pilgrims and their History* (N.Y.: Macmillan 1918).

Vinton, John Adams. "The Antinomian Controversy of 1637." *Cong. Quarterly* (1873).

Walker, George Leon. *History of the First Church in Hartford, 1633–1883* (Hartford 1884).

Warren, Winslow. "The Pilgrims in Holland and America." Col. Soc. Mass. *Pubs.,* XVIII. (Dec. 1915).

WATERS, THOMAS FRANKLIN. *A Sketch of the Life of John Winthrop the Younger* (Cambridge: Ipswich Hist. Soc. *Pubs.*, VII 1899).

WEBBER, C. H. and W. S. NEVINS. *Old Naumkeag* (Salem 1877).

WEDGWOOD, C. V. *The Great Rebellion: the King's Peace 1637–1641* (N.Y.: Macmillan 1956).

————. *The Great Rebellion: the King's War 1641–1647* (London: Collins 1958).

WILLIAMS, WILLIAM T. "Notes on Lion Gardener" (July 1832). 3 Mass. Hist. Soc. *Colls.*, III.

WILLISON, GEORGE F. *Saints and Strangers* (N.Y.: Reynal & Hitchcock 1945).

WINSLOW, OLA ELIZABETH. *Master Roger Williams: a Biography* (N.Y.: Macmillan 1957).

WINSOR, JUSTIN. "Books and Autographs of Elder William Brewster." Mass. Hist. Soc. *Procs.* (Mar. 1887).

————. *The Memorial History of Boston . . . 1630–1880*, 4 vols. (Boston 1880).

————, ed. *Narrative and Critical History of America*, 8 vols. (Boston & N.Y. 1884–88).

WINTHROP, ROBERT C. *Life and Letters of John Winthrop*, 2nd ed., 2 vols. (Boston 1869).

WOLKINS, GEORGE G. *Edward Winslow (O.V. 1606–11)*, *King's Scholar and Printer*. Am. Antiq. Soc. *Procs.*, LX (1950).

WROTH, LAWRENCE E. *Roger Williams*. Brown U. Papers, XIV (Providence: Brown U. 1937).

ZIFF, LARZER. *The Career of John Cotton: Puritanism and the American Experience* (Princeton: Princeton U. 1962).

Index